ENJOY THE JOURNEY —

EVEN KEEL:

LIFE ON THE STREETS OF ROCK & ROLL

BY

RON KEEL

WWM

WILD WEST MEDIA PRODUCTIONS

Wild West Media Productions
284C East Lake Mead Parkway, #310
Henderson, Nevada 89015

First Edition: January 2014

Front & Back Cover Photography: Mark Weiss – www.markweiss.com

www.RonKeel.com

Photo: Mark Weiss

If all I had to show for all the years and all I've done
Were the people that I've called my friends,
And the songs that I have sung

If the sum of all my days could be measured by the mile
I'd be a wealthy man and say,
It was all worthwhile

Night after night – year after year
Pouring my heart out hoping someone will hear
Doing what I was born to do
I gave it all to you

Well I can still see Mama's tears
When I left home to hit the road
Left a trail of broken hearts everywhere I go

Keeping nothing for myself,
And not much more for those I love
I'll leave behind some music
And hope that'll be enough

Day after day – time after time
Pouring my heart out in rhythm and rhyme
Doing what I was born to do
I gave it all to you

"Hello Mr. Ron Keel, I am glad to have the opportunity to first of all THANK YOU for all the great kickass rock/metal music that got me through some rough times while I was in the service, as well as making the good times much much better. You lived the life through the wild, glorious L.A. 1980's metal scene and I hope one day you write a book."
Fred Collins – Corporal, United States Marine Corp

"Met you a life time ago in a rural Pennsylvania bar gig ...anyway glad to still see you still rockin'. You should write a book. No matter what...you were and I'm sure you still are a hell of a nice down to earth person!"
Carla Horoszy – Scranton, PA

"My brother Chris was a big fan of yours. As a kid, I used to break into his room and steal his records, that's how I got turned on to your music. He was a firefighter killed in the World Trade Center on 9/11."
Dave Pickford – New York City

1 - DOES ANYBODY BELIEVE (7)
2 - THE COWBOY ROAD (29)
3 - WILD FOREVER (42)
4 - LIVE (52)
5 - I NEVER TOLD YOU (69)
6 - GIMME THAT (84)
7 - SPEED DEMON (95)
8 - AMERICAN METAL (106)
9 - COLD DAY IN HELL (116)
10 - QUIT WHILE YOU'RE AHEAD (131)
11 - GUITAR SOLO (144)
12 - MY BAD (158)
13 - LAY DOWN THE LAW (169)
14 - THE RIGHT TO ROCK (178)
15 - NO PAIN NO GAIN (190)
16 - THE FINAL FRONTIER (210)
17 - DRIFT AWAY (228)
18 - DIE FIGHTING (242)
19 - STREET OF BROKEN DREAMS (256)
20 - MY HORSE IS A HARLEY (261)
21 - TO HELL & BACK (273)
22 - SINGERS, HOOKERS & THIEVES (281)
23 - THE SHOW MUST GO ON (292)
24 - WHEN LOVE GOES DOWN (304)
25 - BROTHERS IN BLOOD (317)

INTRODUCTION

On January 28th, 2014, I released my first full solo album, "Metal Cowboy." Still driven to create but free from the restrictions of a world gone mad I tapped into the same emotional well from which I have drawn inspiration for everything from "Cold Day In Hell" to "My Horse Is A Harley."

My 2004 acoustic album "Alone At Last" is a personal favorite, but the acoustic nature of that project makes it a novelty, a side view if you will, and not a complete representation of who I am. That's what I tried to accomplish with "Metal Cowboy" – it's not a KEEL album, and it's certainly not a country album. It's a metal cowboy album, and it's Ron Keel to the core. In this music you can hear my western heart beating, my metal voice screaming, and the sound of an iron horse thundering down the streets of rock & roll.

Yes, I've changed. I never lost the rebellious teenager who was driven to scream about sex, drugs, and rock & roll, but I also became a grown man, compelled to sing about real life, love, heartache, joy and pain. I'll always love the sound of a solid drum groove and a badass guitar riff echoing off the walls of an arena, but there's also a sweet sound that happens when a fine-tuned acoustic guitar bounces off the walls of high desert canyon.

I know there's more behind me now than in front of me. The toughest part about this deal was putting on the brakes long enough to take the time to turn around and reflect upon the last half-century and write it down. While still at the peak of health, there is nonetheless a lot of tread worn off my tires and the man who quickly and effortlessly vaulted from one side of the stage to the other now exists only in these pages and on the old video recordings. The pains of a life lived fully are there in the knees, and in the hands that have made love to guitars for so long they now have trouble opening the ketchup bottle.

Now that this book is finished, I realize there's a lot I left out, either because of context or quantity constraints. Steeler, Keel, The Country Years, and IronHorse each really deserve books of their own. I definitely have enough stories left over for a sequel at some point. Many people that are very close to me only received the briefest of mentions, and for that I apologize – I could have written an entire book about my life and love with Renée; the times Aaron Fischer and I, or Jon Rich and I, or Mark Workman and I, have shared could fill their own volumes respectively. Some dear friends – Shannon Champion comes to mind – are a huge part of my story even though our friendships may not have received mention. I could – and just might – write a book about my amazing experiences in the tribute/impersonator industry. And I ended up writing extensive sections about singing – and songwriting – that I left out because I realized they would make solid foundations for books of their own, so perhaps my work as an author is not yet done.

I feel so lucky to have enjoyed the incredible array of experiences life has given me. The overwhelming feelings of success and failure, not only in music but in life and love; to have been given the chance to touch people's lives with my music and to be touched in return. I am even thankful for the broken heart because in its wake I found true love where otherwise I might not have been able to recognize or understand it.

There are no framed posters or albums on the walls of my home studio/office. No photos of me with famous people, no copies of the Billboard charts, any memorabilia or reminders of the glory days gone by. Other than my favorite guitars, the only things hanging up in there are two paintings, one by my daughter Kelly and the other by my wife Renée, and a framed document that I wrote that contains a personal and spiritual list of passions and daily goals. I'm a guy who's always looking around the next bend in the trail, focusing on the peak of the next mountain I'm gonna climb, not someone who spends a lot of time looking back at where I've been.

I invite you to take this journey with me, one page at a time.

This is a story about a working class kid who became a rock star – an outcast and misfit that grew up trying to figure out the same shit as everybody else: who the hell am I, what's life all about and what am I gonna do with mine, and how do I survive in this crazy world.

I was an honor student, and a high school dropout. I've been homeless and I've lived in mansions and five star hotels. From hitchhiking to sports cars, from Madison Square Garden to the Buffalo Chip Saloon, from the mean streets of downtown Los Angeles to the backroads of the Wild West and back again, I've had a lot of dreams – and nightmares – come true.

I've been married and divorced several times, I'm a father and a grandfather, I've made a fortune and pissed it away and made it back. I've climbed mountains, sailed the sea, and traveled the world, slept with psychos and centerfolds, gone from heavy metal hero to honky tonk has-been – and back again. As a musician and singer, I've participated in roughly fifty album projects so far; I've been a rock star and a country singer, as well as a songwriter, a radio and TV show host, a TV and film actor, a celebrity impersonator/tribute artist, a record producer, manager, video director, sound engineer, production manager, a roadie, a Las Vegas show producer and entertainment director, a counselor at Rock & Roll Fantasy Camp, I was Lynyrd Skynyrd's T-shirt guy, and now I'm an author. At the core of it all, I'm an entertainer. And whether in my songs, on stage or backstage, in interviews and meetings, around a campfire or at a bar with a shot of whiskey in my hand, one thing is constant: I'm a storyteller.

One of my childhood ambitions was to be an author, but the story you're about to read was one I never thought I'd write. When I was ten years old, you could find me in the sanctuary of my crowded bedroom bouncing back and forth from the typewriter to the drum set, banging out a couple of chapters of cheesy sci-fi adventures, and then banging out Top 40 tunes. The drums won out; the inner struggle between literary aspirations and hormones lasted only as long as it took me to realize that *if I joined a band, girls would like me*.

And I thoroughly enjoyed it, girls. But now, it's finally time to write that book...

I'll try to get you to Hollywood as quickly as possible, because I know you want to hear about that, but you gotta grow up with me a little bit first. And I realize most people (except my ex-wives and my kids) want the wild side, so I've dug up as much dirt as I care to admit to and provide enough sex and drugs to satisfy those appetites. Yes kids, I use the words "pussy" and "cocaine" more than a few times. But I must confess up front there are no interventions, no visits to rehab, no overdoses or car crashes (well, maybe just one car crash). While I've got my demons and addictions, they have never overpowered my obligation to my craft, and despite some of what's been said and written about me, my focus has always remained on the task at hand – the music, the songs, the shows, the recordings, the business, the journey. These things woven together make up the true tapestry of who and what I am, and all the stuff that goes with it – the fame and glory, the adulation and excess – have always been secondary to the thrill of creating and expressing myself. No drug can match the highs I've experienced writing a timeless song or delivering an unforgettable show, executing a master vocal in a recording session, building something out of nothing, transforming a dream into a reality. For me, no drug is that powerful.

So, welcome to "Life on the Streets of Rock & Roll." I intend to treat this as if we were sitting at the aforementioned bar or around the campfire, and just tell some stories. I'll throw in some songs for emphasis; and we'll let some other folks have their say every now and then.

I thank everyone who allowed us to interview them for this book, and all the fans and journalists that permitted their messages to be included, even those who slammed me with derogatory comments. Special thanks to Derric Miller for the interviews with my sister Sherleen and my music teacher George B. Schmitt. I feel that the perspectives of others are important components of my story, because in my business you are what people think of you, and after this life you are what people remember about you.

If you're a fan who's followed and hopefully enjoyed the twists and turns of my career, or even if you've never heard of me, the goal of this narrative is to entertain you. When it's over, I don't expect you to like me or understand me – I just want us both to enjoy the ride.

Now that it's done, I realize that it was almost as much fun reliving it as it was living through it.

So grab a beer and relax while I talk the rock and rock the talk...

1

DOES ANYBODY BELIEVE

There was a time
When friends were more than people that you knew
There was a place
Where we could do what we were born to do
There was a way that we could be what we were meant to be
Love was alive, and so were we

There's no use keeping score in a game that never ends
Is it all worth dying for, if you never really lived?

Does anybody believe in anything anymore
Can you see inside your dreams
And wish for something more
Is there anything we want that's still worth fighting for
Does anybody believe?

("Does Anybody Believe" – lyrics by RK 2008 – from the KEEL album "Streets Of Rock & Roll" released 2010)

8

KEEL 2010 –photo: Alex Solca

"Thanks for all the music when I was growing up. You have been & still are the soundtrack for my life."
Thomas P. DuBay, Denver, Colorado

"Ron Keel is a musical piece of shit. Never has one guy done so much with so little."
Anonymous internet message board post

APRIL 26, 2014
KEEL 30th ANNIVERSARY SHOW – M3 FESTIVAL, BALTIMORE MARYLAND

There is no feeling in the world quite like it. Standing feet shoulder width apart, chest out, head back. Your left hand in a white-knuckle grip around the microphone, your right hand in a white-knuckle grip halfway down the microphone stand. As the song begins, a storm of emotions wells up inside you – you fight thoughts of all else and focus on the reason you're here. The reason for damn near everything else you've done your entire life, the purpose to which your dedication has danced on the edge of obsession since your earliest childhood memories.

It's time to sing.

Your heart is pounding as your stomach muscles tighten and your mouth opens. Your entire body tenses with a magnetic force that emanates from the very depths of your soul. Your feelings walk a tightrope between utter fear and invincible confidence as the first notes of the song's vocal escape your throat. The initial lines establish your tone and level, and halfway through the first verse you are where you were born to be. You are home, within the song.

The song is "Come Hell Or High Water," the opening song of the KEEL 30th Anniversary Show. On stage where I belong, at the Merriweather Post Pavilion in Baltimore, with some of my best friends playing music together again, and I feel the emotional click-click-click of life's roller coaster climbing the lift hill again as I embark on the last ride.

I had one hell of a good run with my rock band KEEL from 1985 to 1989 – three albums on the charts, several semi-hit singles and videos, world tours which included shows with icons such as Bon Jovi, Motley Crue, Aerosmith, Van Halen and more, before going our separate ways.

I've always compared KEEL (wherever KEEL appears in all caps, I'm referring to the band) to a tornado; it could have laid waste to your house and left your neighbor's home untouched. Some people never heard of us; to others, we were one of their favorite bands, our music a special part of their lives and our concerts unforgettable memories from a unique place in time.

I have a collection of cloth banners that were made by fans, brought to the concerts, and either thrown onto the stage or gifted to us afterward. Many of them are incredibly intricate works of art, with the band's signature logo and full color renderings of me and the guys, sometimes including Gene Simmons as well. Many fans considered Gene, who produced our first two major label albums, the sixth member of KEEL. Some of these banners were really huge – I can imagine these kids explaining to their Moms where the bed sheets went – and most are emblazoned with phrases such as "KEEL ROCKS!" and "YOU GOT IT – THE RIGHT TO ROCK!" Some even have the logo cut out of leopard skin fabric and painstakingly sewn onto the cloth.

At times in my life, I've hung these banners proudly in my home studio for inspiration, and the walls of our rehearsal rooms have been decorated with these priceless trophies. Yes, I consider them trophies – and this isn't a nostalgic reflection. I felt the same way about those banners when the paint was still wet and the sheets still white and clean – they meant as much to me then as they do now, every bit as important as any praise or award.

Because you see, once upon a time, I was one of those kids. I would play air guitar in front of the mirror, I would stand in line overnight to get a concert ticket, I would fight my way to the front row and thrust my fist in the air, screaming at the top of my lungs and singing along with every song. I loved KISS, Aerosmith, Van Halen, AC/DC, Judas Priest, Scorpions. Their music was the soundtrack of my teens. But damned if I would have *ever* made a banner for any of them...so maybe I like to think my band and our music meant that much to some of the KEEL fans (we call them KEELaholics) that crafted those priceless banners.

In the 20 years between KEEL gigs, four of the members of the classic lineup (myself, guitarists Marc Ferrari and Bryan Jay, and drummer Dwain Miller) remained friends, some of us working together on music or business, even jamming with each other upon occasion. For most of the 90's, a reunion was the last thing on our minds and not even a remote possibility as we each carved our own path through life and pursued other passions, interests, jobs and careers. In 1998 we got back together, albeit only in the studio, to finish and/or polish some unreleased music which became the "KEEL VI: Back In Action" album. At the time, there was some talk of doing some shows, and even a couple of financially lucrative possibilities, but it would be another eleven years before we hit the stage together again.

In 2007 an event called Rocklahoma almost single-handedly resurrected the genre by bringing together several days' worth of the bands that shaped the rock culture of the 80's. Similar events followed suit, and we felt the pull of that old familiar urge to get back out there on the big stage, in front of the big crowds, and deliver our music the way it was meant to be. 2009 would mark our 25th Anniversary as a band; our debut 1984 album "Lay Down The Law" had just been re-released to an enthusiastic response, "The Right To Rock" album was being recognized in the media for its place in history, and a prominent booking agent promised us that if we did pull the trigger on the reunion, he would be able to secure a select number of bookings for KEEL at some of these major festivals. Marc Ferrari had recently come out to Las Vegas and sat in with my band on a little mini-KEEL set and it felt great, Bryan Jay and I were writing some songs together for TV and films. It felt like if we didn't turn the ignition over now, the car would be forever stuck in the garage. So on November 18th, 2008, the announcement was made public that KEEL was officially back in business.

In the years that followed, we put an exclamation point on everything we'd ever accomplished – we wrote, recorded and released our best album ever ("Streets Of Rock & Roll"), played some of the biggest rock festivals in the U.S. (including Rocklahoma & M3), did our first-ever headline tour of Europe, and triumphantly returned to rock Hollywood where it all started.

Halfway through the opening song of the show I take my first deep breath almost two minutes in, and I look out into the crowd, smiling and pumping my fist in the air. It feels good, it sounds good, and I turn my back to the audience and lock eyes with the guys in the band. We nod to each other and launch into the guitar solo together.

This is what it's like being in a band.

Clan mentality is a primal instinct that has been a genetic necessity for our survival since the dawn of time; strength in numbers, being part of a group, a sense of belonging to a collective. A rock band is like a tribal hunting party, a sports team, an outlaw gang, a military task force and a corporate conglomerate all rolled into one. Being in a good rock band feels like being on the Super Bowl champion football team, like winning the gunfight at the O.K. Corral, like whipping the snot out of the dickheads at school who made fun of you because you had long hair and a pierced ear.

I've always been a loner. My only sibling is my sister Sherleen, a decade of difference between us; by the time I was three years old, she was a teenager, and when I was eight she went off to college, leaving me to become the only child in the Keel household. During those first eight years of my life Sherleen had a profound influence on me and the man I would become. Two pivotal moments come to mind, and both occurred in Atlanta, Georgia, when I was two and three years old.

The first was February 19th, 1964. My sister was super keyed up, as were most teenage girls in America on that evening. Just before 8:00 PM we took our places on the living room floor in front of the old black and white TV. I'm not sure if Sherleen forced me to watch or if I was just caught up in her excitement. A few moments later, everything changed, the course of my life altered, my destiny determined as if molten steel had been poured into a forge and then hardened. The host of the TV show – some guy named Ed Sullivan – said "Ladies and Gentlemen, The Beatles," and the whole world erupted into deafening applause and then I heard rock & roll coming from the tiny 2-inch television speaker. Four guys playing and singing and rocking out. I was only two years old, but I remember it like it was yesterday. I stared wide-eyed at that screen and decided right then and there what

I was going to do with my life: I was going to play and sing rock & roll music on TV.

"I remember the first time I saw Ron's band KEEL perform, all the girls were screaming over him, and I though shit, I changed his diaper. I was very proud of him, it was just kind of like watching when the Beatles came out and all the girls were going crazy, but this time, you know, it was my little brother. So it was kind of like a paradox."
Sherleen Clivner - Sister

It couldn't have been long after seeing the Fab Four on TV (this occurred in the same house in Atlanta, and we never stayed in the same place very long) that the second incident took place. Since the appearance of The Beatles on the Ed Sullivan show, I had been obsessed with my sister's record player – a "turntable" upon which spun black vinyl discs called "records" and from which emanated glorious rock & roll music. She was amassing a collection of 7-inch 45 rpm singles which contained the hits of the day, and occasionally she would have friends over to listen to them together. *Girl* friends.

I openly admit to being enamored with the females of our species at a very early age. Somewhere in an old box of family pictures there's a sequence of photographs of me, not long after mastering the skill of walking upright, chasing the little neighbor girl all over the front yard until she would give me a kiss. And at the tender age of three, I already had my priorities in order, so when my sister had her GIRL friends over to listen to ROCK & ROLL records, you can imagine where little brother was: as close as I could possibly get. I remember the scratching of the needle on the vinyl disc and the giddiness with which they listened to "Love Potion #9" by The Searchers, and another light bulb went off over my head – GIRLS liked ROCK & ROLL too.

Our parents, Roy and Lucille, grew up in a hard time, Southerners during the Great Depression, offspring of sharecroppers, farm folk sleeping on dirt floors and picking cotton all day. They knew little about the challenges of raising a son in the 70's, so I was pretty much left to my own devices unless I stepped out of line. A lone wolf cub, who would grow to be the leader of the pack.

I had my chores, mostly yard work which I developed an intense distaste for (I apparently did not inherit my grandparents' skill for working the land) and going to the construction site with my Dad on weekends where he instilled in me a strong work ethic which has remained a cornerstone of my character. Be the first to arrive – if you get to work on time, you're already late – be the last to leave, take pride in your work, enjoy what you do while busting your ass to do it. Never back down from a challenge.

Mom and Dad were country folks. Their upbringing, their way of life, their mannerisms, their accents and their music. The songs of Johnny Cash, Merle Haggard, Hank Williams Sr. and George Jones competed with my sister's music on the family's stereophonic record player. These songs, many of which were about hard times and heartache, were polar opposites of the rock & roll songs which bristled with rebellion and young love (and sex). As a child, I identified more with the upbeat sound and wild promises of rock & roll – I had not yet been to jail, never been cheated on, never lost my job, never been a homeless drifter, never been drunk, and never had my ass kicked, so the inspiration behind country music was lost on me.

In years to come, I would experience all those things, and that genre's gritty honesty about the cold hard facts of life would resonate deeply within me.

I spread my legs and lean way back, the body of the guitar nestled in my crotch and the headstock thrusting upward as if it were my cock. Power chords in overdrive blast through the speakers and bounce back off the sky into my ears and into my very soul, connecting everything. It feels so good in my hands.

I have no idea why my Dad took me to my first guitar lesson when I was six years old. I loved music and I'd been on a collision course with it since seeing The Beatles on TV, but my practical application of this passion had been limited to pretending the furniture was a drum set, or imagining the hairbrush was a microphone. Beating on things while screaming came naturally to me – pressing the flesh of my tiny fingers onto a set of six steel wires did not.

So either Roy was just being a cool parent, or more likely, he could drop me off at the guitar lesson and then spend the better part of the hour at the bar down the street. Unfortunately, probably for both of us, that was my first and last guitar lesson.

He rented me a jumbo Gibson acoustic guitar that was bigger than I was, drove me to a local music studio, and pushed me into a little soundproof room with the instructor, an old guy with crazy white hair like Einstein. Once I was seated with the massive instrument on my skinny lap, Einstein opened up a book of sheet music on a stand, an intimidating array of lines and dots and symbols which made absolutely no sense to me. He demanded that I painfully force my tender young fingertips onto the unforgiving strings while he pounded out time on the music stand with a wooden baton and yelled at me. It was one of the longest hours of my life.

That first experience with the six-string did nothing to diminish my passion for music, but for the next couple of years it was back to singing into the hairbrush.

I was born a nomad, with the road in my blood. It was a combination of genetics and environment – my grandparents on both sides were immigrants from Germany and Ireland, and throughout my early childhood my father would relocate our family often as he went from one construction job to another. Roy was a mason, a setter of tile, and a master of his trade who, like me, had a hard time with authority, whether it was the boss man or the lawman. He was always moving, either because the job was finished or he was tired of taking shit from whoever he was working for, and he was fearless and confident in his ability to make a living with his own two hands wherever he was. My sister and I remember our Mom coming into our room and shaking us while we slept, saying "Wake up – we're moving." She'd literally wrap us in our blankets and guide us outside, where Dad would have the car waiting with a U-Haul trailer hooked up to it. I was born in Savannah, Georgia, and six months later we were in Atlanta; I remember going to kindergarten in Punta Gorda, Florida, first grade in Charleston, South Carolina, and part of second grade back in Savannah before my Dad got a job in Pennsylvania that moved us to a tiny town called Fort Loudon and kept us there until I finished third grade the following year. He was contracted to lay the miles of 4"x4" ceramic tile which line the walls of numerous tunnels through the Tuscarora mountain range, and in later years I would drive through those tunnels on a tour bus and take pride in the fact that in his small way, my father really helped build this country. In fact, I see his work everywhere – in the tiled bathrooms of Holiday Inns across the nation, in the custom upscale homes in Scottsdale, Arizona, and in those miles of tunnels in the Appalachian Mountains.

Once my Mom took my sister and I to a park nearby that marks the birthplace of James Buchanan, the 15th President of the United States. The spot where he was born in a cabin is now marked by a 300-ton rock pyramid 31 feet tall, which is surrounded by an iron spiked fence. To an eight year old kid, a 31-foot stone pyramid was a mountain I just had to climb and I could not resist the urge to conquer it, so while no one was looking I made an attempt to climb that fence in order to scale the pyramid.

I first put one foot on the bottom hinge of the gate, and then pulled myself up with both hands. Somehow I slipped, and suddenly found myself impaled on the fence, a vicious iron spike embedded deep into my throat right above my larynx. I was literally hanging there with that spike in my throat until my Mom rushed to lift me off the fence. Blood was everywhere, she and my sister panicked and got to me into the car and to the nearest emergency room which seemed like quite some distance, even with my mother driving like a bat out of hell and me in the backseat holding my hand over the bleeding gash in my throat.

All kids have accidents which scare the hell out of them and their families, it's part of growing up. I have always thought it interesting that my most traumatic childhood injury involved my throat, which was pierced by an iron spike just a fraction of an inch away from my vocal chords, and I remember laying there on the hospital bed while the doctors stitched me up and tried to console my mother.

"He's going to be just fine, Mrs. Keel," one of them said. "There's no significant damage, but his voice may be affected. There's no way to know until the wound heals."

The horizontal scar on my throat remains a constant reminder of that day. I sometimes joke about having my vocal chords surgically enhanced, but the truth is I came real close to never singing a note because of that 'accident.'

We lived in a trailer park in Fort Loudon, until the trailer burned down on Thanksgiving. It was the first time I lost every physical possession I had, but not the last. Surprisingly, a few important pieces of family memorabilia, such as photographs, survived and I have them still; in later years, I would find out why. My father had deliberately set the fire to collect the insurance money, and had done it with some type of delayed method to insure that we were in Georgia visiting family for the holiday when it occurred. I remember arriving at my Aunt Annie's house in Savannah after six hundred miles on the road, and her breaking the news to us that our neighbors had called to say the trailer burned. Mom broke down sobbing, so maybe she had no clue that the blaze had been set intentionally.

That year my sister went off to college, leaving me, at eight years old, to become the only kid at home. There have been times in our lives when Sherleen and I have been close, and there have been periods when we have been distant, even estranged; we're closer now than ever, but when she went off to college I felt like I was losing my best friend. Even though a little brother can be a pain in the ass to a teenage girl, she had shared a love of music with me, and her departure created a void in my cultural development right between The Monkees and Creedence Clearwater Revival that I have never recovered from...

In 1969 Phoenix, Arizona, was the fastest growing metropolitan area in the United States, and the ensuing boom in the construction industry dictated the Valley Of The Sun become the next home for the Keel family. I screamed and cried when Dad told me we were moving yet again, and although now I know what it feels like to tell your kids something they don't want to hear, Phoenix became what I have always considered my first true home. Arizona is where I got my first kiss and my first ass-kicking; where I learned to play music and where I learned to drive. It's where I had my first band and my first paying gig, my first girlfriend and my first day job. Where I drank my first beer and where I wrote my first song. But it all started with the ass-kicking.

Our little rented apartment was in a bad neighborhood, and consequently a very rough school district and although I went to school on the first day of fourth grade with the excitement and anticipation of making new friends, I came home bloody and bruised from a welcome-to-the-neighborhood beating administered by about a dozen classmates who felt that was the appropriate greeting for a new white kid in their school. They all gathered around me at recess and invited me to accompany them to the farthest corner of the schoolyard, and I became the focus of their "let's kick the white boy's ass" game. The next thing I knew, my Mom was taking me to karate lessons.

I was not healthy as a child. My parents were both heavy smokers, and indulged in some very questionable dietary habits. Country food – a lot of deep-fried fat, white bread and white sugar. And that was just what I could stomach – on our dinner table could always be found such questionable items as "beef tripe" (cow stomach), "chitlins" (pig intestines), "cracklins" (little rock hard chunks of fried pig skin), and so on.

Between my sister and me, Roy and Lucille had two children die at birth. My mother smoked two packs a day while carrying me. When she was six months pregnant with me, the doctors told her they couldn't find a heartbeat, that her unborn child was dead in the womb, and that they were going to remove it. The only reason I'm here today is she didn't trust doctors any more than I do, and decided to carry the pregnancy to term. There followed a long list of doctors during my first decade of life, as sickness and poor health plagued my formative years.

I grew up in a toxic cloud of cigarette smoke and I know it had some adverse effects on me. While I was spared from the asthma that Sherleen has suffered from most of her life, I went from one ailment to the next, from respiratory disorders to excruciating ear infections, a never-ending cycle of colds and flu. I was extremely skinny and weak, the last one to ever get picked for any sporting or athletic activity, and two things that saved me right around this time were the Arizona climate and a tonsillectomy. The desert air suited me, and the removal of my tonsils & adenoids at the age of 10 (the only surgery I've ever had, I might add) improved my overall health dramatically. I was still a geek, but I was a healthier geek.

In the early 70's, the Wild West was still very much alive in Arizona. Many of today's thoroughfares were dirt roads back then, and where subdivisions and Wal-Marts now stand were once desert fields filled with cactus and rattlesnakes. When Roy moved us into a house at 35th Avenue & Thomas, you could go bow hunting for rabbits in the fields out back – now it's an apartment complex. And Superstition Mountain, the sacred home of the Apache Thunder God, lay at the end of a long dirt road which is now Highway 60; the bleak landscape dotted with an occasional trailer instead of the communities and shopping malls that now mark the trail to what was then the most formidable wilderness in North America. That road between Phoenix and Apache Junction has become somewhat of a pilgrimage for me through the years, from the first treks to the Superstition Wilderness in Dad's Jeep to my high school hitchhiking trips to see my girlfriend Maria, to playing country music in the local Apache Junction bars and driving the Apache Trail to gig at the tourist trap/ghost town Tortilla Flat in the 90's, and now returning whenever I get the chance to visit the Mountain and pay my respects to one of my favorite places on earth. In those days, before satellite imaging and before the foothills were dotted with golf courses and custom homes, the Superstition Wilderness was still a place of danger and mystery, where countless treasure seekers died or disappeared searching for the Lost Dutchman's Gold Mine. A place where you didn't dare go without a loaded gun and a full canteen, over 100,000 acres of the most desolate and unforgiving terrain on the planet.

My father was in his element in the Arizona desert, he was drawn to that wilderness when we moved there, and our camping trips together were frequent and fraught with adventure. There was no road too rough, no river too wild, and no obstacle too formidable for his spirit. He taught me to conquer fear on the side of a mountain both on foot and in four wheel drive, and on April 12th, 1972, when I was just 11 years old, we climbed together to the very top of Superstition Mountain on the Eastern side from Peralta Trailhead. I remember the date because I kept a journal all that day, taking notes whenever we took a break. He carried nothing but a .45 caliber pistol and a backpack full of iced-down Schlitz beer, and I struggled to keep up with him, often rounding a crest in the cliffs to see him sitting on a rock with a beer in one hand and a cigarette in the other, waiting for me to catch up. He taught me a couple of valuable lessons that day; at one point, our self-imposed path (we followed no trail) required that we scrabble over a cone-shaped rock overhanging a cliff with a 500-foot drop, and after he fearlessly traversed it, he just looked back at me and "Come on." One slip and I would have been gone, but rather than show my fear I followed him and realized then and there that he trusted me and believed in my ability to overcome whatever obstacles lay ahead. And he also taught me that day that the journey is more important than the destination – although we did indeed reach the summit of Superstition Mountain that afternoon after an eight hour hike, the experiences along the way were what really mattered.

My Dad's real first name was Rynia. I believe that his mother, my grandmother, intended to name him Reiner and did not know the correct spelling, and probably mispronounced it as well. He was literally born in a dirt-floored cabin in the Georgia woods, thus there was no birth certificate. He was never really even sure exactly how old he was, but claimed to remember Charles Lindbergh's historic solo flight from New York to Paris, which occurred in 1927, but then again he also said he was reincarnated from a passenger on the Titanic.

Growing up with a name like Rynia, in the tough Depression-era south, must have been similar to the classic Cash song "A Boy Named Sue." Combine that with the unforgiving lifestyle of sharecroppers who eked out a living picking cotton, and my old man grew up tough as nails and strong as a bear. And despite having only a sixth-grade education, he was extremely intelligent with a gift for mathematical matters and mechanics.

He didn't always do the right thing or make the right decision, he was often hanging out at a bar with fellow drunks instead of hanging out with me, and he would come home from those bars with a surly and sometimes violent disposition. He didn't quite know what to do with kids, his dirt poor upbringing hadn't prepared him for the challenges of parenting, and real communication wasn't easy for him. He never once could bring himself to say "I love you." But he was a larger-than-life type of character, who commanded respect and attention. He was the hardest working person I've ever known, and he partied hard to match. He could fight, he could shoot, he could fix any mechanical problem with a coat hanger and a tin can, he created masterpieces with tile and mortar, he could drive a truck up a vertical cliff face, and he loved his music. In his younger years he had played guitar, and professed to have once jammed with the likes of Hank Williams Sr., Ernest Tubb, and Marty Robbins, but his rough trade had swollen his fingers and turned his hands into leather. Every now and then he would pick up a guitar and bang out a few chords with those big meaty paws of his, but the ability to finger a clear open chord and let it ring had been replaced by his formidable skill with a hawk and trowel.

He was always referred to as "Roy," except on rare occasions when my Mom would call him by his real name, usually in exasperation. When she did, she used the originally intended pronunciation "Reiner." On his business cards and in the phone book listings, he was always "R. L. Keel." For someone so resourceful and creative, the best he could do when I was born was pass on the ridiculous misspelled mispronounced name Rynia. And just like he never used it, neither did I, except on the first day of class or my first day in a new school, when during roll call the teacher would butcher my name, I'd raise my hand, and everybody would laugh.

Playing with some neighbor children shortly after we moved into the house on 35th Drive, one kid asked me my name, and when I told him Rynia, he said "I'm just going to call you Ron." And it stuck, becoming legally changed to Ronnie Lee Keel in 1986 when I got my second passport, prior to my first tours abroad to Europe and Japan.

In addition to the really weird name, I was the tallest skinniest clumsiest nerd in Madrid Elementary School in the early 70's. My Mom shopped for my clothes, and her tastes couldn't have been further from what was cool at the time. I topped off my look with a ridiculous short haircut and goofy glasses, thus assuring me that I wouldn't be bothered by any of the girls in school or strike up any friendships with the athletes in my class.

I remember getting in a lot of fights for no good reason. I was a verbal and physical punching bag for my peers, and a lot of times bullies just wanted to fight me because I was the tallest guy in school and I think it made them feel bigger to take me on. Thanks to my long reach and my height, it was hard to land a solid punch on me, and I'd had enough karate lessons by that time to be able to hold my own with most of them. I remember one time my parents had to foot the doctor's bill for a classmate whose jaw I had broken, even though he had started the fight, and after he could talk again he showed up at our doorstep and apologized.

All I really wanted to do was hit a real drum with a real stick. On a visit south of the border to Nogales, I had begged my parents to buy me a set of souvenir bongos, and I would sit and bang on them with my hands to every song on the radio, TV, or record player. This was around the time when I got my first transistor AM radio, and that was a big deal at the time. It was a small handheld model about the size of a cigarette pack, with two dials on it – one turned it on and controlled the volume, and the other controlled the frequency, and I would put it under my pillow and listen to music until the batteries died. That Christmas (1972), I got my first RECORDING DEVICE – a cassette player with a built-in AM-FM radio player. I could use the external microphone to record myself singing along with the radio. On New Year's Eve, my parents went to a party and left me home alone, and from six PM to midnight I taped the "Top 100 Songs Of The Year" on my new recorder as Casey Kasem counted them down. There was some great rock & roll on the radio that night – Alice Cooper's "School's Out," The Hollies' "Long Cool Woman," "Day After Day" by Badfinger, "Bang A Gong" by T-Rex, Argent's "Hold Your Head Up" (which we would eventually cover in KEEL), "Layla" – and I still remember screaming in disappointment at midnight when the #1 song of the year was "The First Time Ever I Saw Your Face" by Roberta Flack. I did, however, thoroughly enjoy the epic "American Pie" by Don McLean, which clocked in at #3.

So I couldn't believe it when I heard that my school was starting a band class. I was hungry to learn the magic language of the notes on the page, so I was really excited when the new music teacher, George Schmitt, came to visit my fourth grade class.

Now over forty years later, he's still my mentor and one of my best friends, almost like a second father to me.

He went to each student's desk and asked them if they'd like to participate in the new school band. Most kids will say yes when asked this, because children have a natural love of music and band class sounds like a lot more fun than math or English. When someone would say yes to him, George would ask them what instrument they wanted to play, and then instruct them to open their mouths, hold out their hands, and stretch out their arms. Certain types of lips and teeth are better suited to instruments like saxophone or trumpet. When my turn came, I told him I was going to be a drummer.

"All the boys want to play drums," he said. "Already got too many drummers. Stretch out your arms." Well, you already know I was the tallest kid with the longest arms in class, so when I extended them in front of me, I was mortified by his response: *"You're going to make a great trombone player."*

No amount of pleading with him could change his mind. He didn't understand that I had been carrying this burning desire ever since watching Ringo and The Beatles on the Ed Sullivan show seven years before, that this was my plan, my goal, my one dream. I was devastated - I was already a geek, all I needed to complete that image was to be seen toting a trombone back and forth to school.

My parents knew how badly I wanted to play drums and how bummed out I was by my first encounter with Mr. Schmitt, to the extent that my Mom went to the school to meet with him and ask him to reconsider. He needed a certain amount of each instrument to build a proper band, and couldn't have ten drummers and no trombone players - my take was the fewer trombones in any band, the better. I didn't care about any of that; I was looking down the road at my own rock star dream, and God damnit I was going to play the drums.

So when band class started that fall, I think there were seven drummers. And you can bet your ass that I was one of them.

I bought a lot of gear at Arizona Music through the years, but my first time in the store was to rent a snare drum for band class. While I was excited to have a real Ludwig snare drum in my possession, I was eagerly anticipating my first time behind a drum set. That rented snare drum was a means to an end. The school supplied all the other stuff - a big bass drum, cymbals, and a five-piece drum kit - but each of the student drummers had to rent or buy their own snare drum. At any rate, it was a step in the right direction, and a helluva lot cooler than my bongos.

George was, and still is, an amazing music teacher. A lifelong musician, he could play any horn and was an expert drummer, and had worked his ass off to earn a master's degree in music from Indiana University. He was great with the kids, and his passion for music was infectious - at least it was for me. You gotta understand how difficult it is to take forty ten-year-old children who know basically nothing about music or musical instruments, put them in a room together with piles of sheet music in front of them, and within a matter of weeks we were playing SONGS. He was great at making the boring and mundane fundamentals fun - quarter notes, whole notes, and half notes, tuning, timing, and tone, they all fascinated me and I couldn't wait for each class to start.

Before we could play the drum set, we had to learn the basics and prove ourselves on the individual drums. The coolest guys got to play the snare drum, the tall kid with the long arms had to start on the big bass drum, one mallet on either side, and the real losers bashed a couple of cymbals together now and then. I paid my dues on all of them, and I had a natural talent and a hunger to learn. Of course one of the first things every drummer needs to learn is how to twirl their sticks, but I never could master the conventional twirl so I came up with my own unique version by using my thumb to swing the stick forward around my middle finger in circles; it's a pretty cool twirl if I do say so myself, and one which few have ever been able to duplicate. I remember doing it one day in music class a thousand times straight, without dropping the stick, while the others kept count.

Apparently not everyone shared my enthusiasm about band class, because kids started to drop out when they realized that this was work. Those that didn't practice at home or apply themselves in class fell in the ranks, and consequently got discouraged and quit. Those that practiced and excelled became the leaders of their sections and received the honor of being "first chair." We started out with seven drummers and I think we ended up with three, and I'll give you three guesses as to who was "first chair."

The big kids in the seventh and eighth grade classes got to play the whole drum set. I just looked at it with longing and wonder, waiting for my chance. It didn't take long; one day after school some of the older students were hanging out in the band room fooling around, making noise and showing off, and once the drum throne was vacant I seized the opportunity. Right foot on the bass drum pedal, boom. Left foot on the hi-hat pedal, chick chick. Left stick hits snare drum, whap, hit the cymbal with the right stick while simultaneously stomping the bass drum, crash/boom. Within moments I was playing my first beat, kick-snare-kick-kick-snare, quarter notes on the hi hat, and it felt natural, it was easy, it was liberating, it was exhilarating, and the girls immediately thought I was COOL. This was the m oment I'd been waiting for since I first saw Ringo and The Beatles on TV all those years ago – I was playing the DRUMS.

My skills progressed beyond my grade level while most of the other drummers in class bailed out. My first concert was at Alhambra Elementary School on Grand Avenue, in the big auditorium that looks like the Alamo (when I went back to Phoenix for the KEEL Reunion rehearsals, it was still there – we had to drive right by it – but the rest of the school is gone). To me, it was like Madison Square Garden, full of hundreds of family and friends that made up our audience, and all the best players from around the district assembled for the concert. I was thrilled to be on that stage, playing music with my school band. We played a lot of Chicago, Stevie Wonder, stuff that had horn parts, and a song Mr. Schmitt had found for us called "The Big Rock" that had a drum solo for me. I just loved everything about it and playing on stage seemed to satisfy an addiction that I had been born with, a feeling so strong it has remained one of the most intense passions I have ever experienced.

It wasn't long after that we did another concert outside at my school, a smaller event, but I've always had a saying: "There are no small shows." There was the kiddie band (I was still in the fifth grade), we were like the opening act for the seventh and eighth grade band, but I was the only drummer that showed up – all the seventh and eighth grade drummers were MIA. My Mom and Dad were in the audience, and before the show started Mr. Schmitt came to over to me. "You're all I've got," he said. "None of the other drummers are going to be here. Go play those drums." And I played the whole show, the only drummer that day, and I felt like Superman; I'd proven something to myself, my family, and my teacher, and that's powerful stuff, man.

That's when George and I started getting really close. He could tell I was serious, and I think it justified all the crap that he went through, the low teacher's pay and the backtalk from kids who didn't give a shit that were just taking band class to get out of doing real school work. He knew I had the fire, he knew I was a player, that I had it in my heart, in my blood, in my soul. So instead of going easy on me and giving me preferential treatment, he drove me harder. I remember one day in class, I was playing drums and showing off and overplaying, all tom tom fills and no groove and he stopped the entire band cold. He got a mean look in his eyes, and he stormed back to the drum set and leaned over the toms into my face and tore me a new asshole. "That's not music!" he shouted. "You're all over town, there's no backbeat, there's no feel, you gotta quit showing off and play for the song, man!" I was mortified at the time, but it was probably the most effective lesson I ever learned in school – that the SONG must always come first.

"One day I got a call from Ron's parents. They said, Mr. Schmitt, you gotta come over here and talk to him – he says he wants to be a professional musician. So I came over and said look, you're a good kid, you study hard, you get good grades, wouldn't you like to be a doctor, a lawyer, why do you want to be a musician, it's a really ruthless business. He was crying, banging on stuff, yelling "I want to be a musician!" And I went and told his parents, 'You've got a musician on your hands, you better let him do it.'"
George Schmitt – Music Teacher

2

THE COWBOY ROAD

Well I could've been a banker – a lawyer or a thief
But I chose to play this old guitar, and sing what I believe
Could have stayed in school – played by the rules
But that ain't how I roll
I took a left turn at the crossroads
And went down the cowboy road

We've all got a choice to make – a chance we've gotta take
I'll ride the road less traveled
I might bend but I won't break
I know what I believe in, and I'm right where I belong
Rolling on – just one more song
Going down the cowboy road

It ain't paved and it ain't pretty
It gets rough and it gets dirty
It's a hundred miles to hell and back
But man you know it's worth it
When you get to where you're going and you know
You've been down the cowboy road

("The Cowboy Road" – lyrics by RK 2013 – from the Ron Keel album "Metal Cowboy" released 2014)

"Ron...it has been 20+ years since your music rocked and changed my world...Thank You...your effort, skill and devotion still keeps my desire to pass it down to my children....Man....thanks a million times over for staying true to what you do.....and you do it well....nothin' but love from Denver dude!"
Mike O – Denver, CO

"Bands like KEEL killed rock, that's why kids listen to hip-hop today."
1967apple – YouTube comment

At thirteen, my rock & roll revolution was in high gear. I was no longer a child, I was a TEENAGER and I felt I was entitled to all that goes along with that status.

I had already been playing in bands for a couple of years. It was only natural to move the afterschool jam over to my house, and on any given evening my parents and our neighbors were subjected to a brutal cacophony of loud out-of-tune renditions of whatever we were trying to play at the time. After showing such promise in the school band under Mr. Schmitt's tutelage, my very own drum set showed up under the Christmas tree – a red sparkle 3-piece kit which my folks had purchased from a mail-order catalog for the sum of $79.00, which I beat the shit out of for hours every day.

The local department store had a rack in the music section which contained the Top 30 Singles each week on vinyl 45 rpm records. I think they were like seventy-five cents each, and between helping my Dad on construction jobs, my paper route, and a meager allowance I scraped up the money to buy all 30 of them one week. On a shelf in my bedroom beside my drums I kept the record player and I would put on headphones and play along with those songs. Each week I would go back to the store and buy any new songs which had cracked the Top 30, thus keeping my collection current. Every day I'd come home from school, breeze through my homework and then it was time for my real education to begin. On those old record players, you could just set a stack of 45's on the spindle and when one would finish, the next would drop, and when they were all done I flipped them over and played along to the B-sides. I sang along as I played, rigging a fake mic on a fake boom stand. I'd shut my eyes and sing and play, and sometimes when I opened my eyes I'd see my Mom standing there holding the door to my room open, just watching me. I'd stop playing and take off the headphones, and she'd say "Dinner's ready." I'd eat real quickly and then get back to practicing. I honestly don't know how Mom and Dad put up with it every day, for hours at a time, but they never once asked me stop as long as my homework and my chores were done.

They either realized I was serious, or perhaps they thought getting me a better sounding drum set would be more pleasant to their own ears, because they invested $500.00 in a nice red Ludwig drum set with real cymbals instead of the cracked and bent aluminum trash can lids that had passed for cymbals on the mail-order kit. It damn sure sounded better but it was louder and I played it even longer every day so I guess Mom and Dad got their money's worth.

I loved comic books as a kid. It was a quarter mile walk down a dirt alley to get to the local convenience store, and a quarter of a dollar to buy a comic there. I didn't go for the superheroes – my favorites were Tarzan and Batman, wild and dark protagonists who used their instincts, strength, talents and resources to overcome their enemies. I amassed quite a collection in the early 70's, keeping them in plastic, organized alphabetically. Then I sold them all for $500.00 to buy my first P.A. system; it was very much a coming-of-age moment for me, trading my childhood for my future.

In the sixth and seventh grades, I learned to play the valved horns, both treble clef instruments like trumpet, coronet, and French horn as well as the bass clef horns such as tuba and baritone. Of course I kept on drumming, and earned first chair on just about every instrument I played. I never did learn how to play trombone.

My first musical road trip was during the summer between eighth grade and high school. Mr. Schmitt rounded up the top music students from our school district and we took a bus to San Diego, where we spent a week at Band Camp. It was awesome, staying in a dorm with the other guys in the band and playing music all day. After rehearsals, when most kids would hit the beach, I stayed behind in the music room to jam with the big boys – we usually had a keyboard player, bass and guitar, a few horn players, everybody would take turns singing, and we'd rock out. There were always a few girls hanging around for inspiration. We had an oriental kid who not only played guitar really well but he had *long hair* which I thought was cool; one day after we had wrapped it up, he sat down with an acoustic guitar and played "Stairway To Heaven" and the young girls absolutely melted at his feet, totally forgetting about the epic drum solo I had just bashed out.

That was all it took – I forgot all about that first painful experience with the guitar at the age of six, and made up my mind that I was going to play "Stairway To Heaven."

Years before, Sherleen had gotten an acoustic guitar as a Christmas gift which she never took an interest in. It was packed in a closet without strings, and the first thing I did when I got home from Band Camp was buy a set of nylon strings and a Mel Bay "Learn To Play Guitar" book. The nylon strings allowed me to learn without the pain of the unforgiving steel wires digging into my fingertips, and the book had instructions on how to tune it by ear. I already knew how to read sheet music from learning the trumpet, so it was a matter of memorizing where all those notes were on the various strings and frets of that guitar. That first day, I couldn't put it down; I skimmed through the basics, learning "Aura Lee" (the original melody which became Elvis' "Love Me Tender") and "Twinkle Twinkle Little Star" and quickly realized that I did not have the patience for that shit.

So I closed that "Learn To Play Guitar" book forever and put "Led Zeppelin IV" on the turntable, placing the needle on "Stairway To Heaven," and began to sound out Jimmy Page's legendary intro one note at a time. As soon as I figured out how to put my index finger over the three highest strings on the fifth fret and pick down from highest to lowest (the first three notes of "Stairway") I knew I was going to be able to play guitar. And within eight hours of stringing that cheap old flat top guitar I was playing my own bastardized version of the song's intro – it wasn't correct, but you could tell what song it was.

The next day, I went back to the store and bought my first songbook, a huge collection of The Beatles' classic hits, and continued my self-training. The next step was chords, and the book had little diagrams on the sheet music to tell you where to put your fingers. The problem was, it didn't tell you which finger to put where, so I figured out what worked best for me and even now I play some of the major open chords wrong, most notably "E" major and "D" major. Or maybe I'm right, and everybody else plays them wrong...

In my life I've learned and forgotten thousands of songs, but not the first song in that book, "Across The Universe" from the "Let It Be" album. It was in alphabetical order, and I plowed through them one at a time then moved on to songbooks full of Eagles tunes and various other "Hits Of The 70's" collections.

I got slammed upside the head that summer with a fistful of hard rock, as network television began to bring the concerts into America's living rooms late at night. I had heard a band called KISS when a friend turned me on to an unmarked cassette recording – at that time, I was unaware of their makeup and theatrics, but I was drawn to the primal power of the music – and was blown away when they brought that music to life in bloody flaming glory on my TV set on "Don Kirshner's Rock Concert." I would never have believed that ten years later, KISS bassist Gene Simmons would be sitting beside me in a recording studio producing my major label debut album.

My first taste of Aerosmith was that same summer when they crushed "Train Kept A Rollin'" on "Midnight Special." Twelve years hence, I would be the opening act for their "Done With Mirrors" tour finale in New England at Sullivan Stadium. And heavy metal was born for me in the form of Black Sabbath's blistering live broadcast of "Paranoid" – a decade later I would, for a brief moment in time, be the lead singer in that band.

I loved this loud, wild side of rock & roll which included these bands and others like Alice Cooper, Foghat, Grand Funk Railroad, and Bachman-Turner Overdrive. It didn't totally satisfy my musical hunger, but became an important staple of my diet. I was still maintaining my collection of those Top 30 45 rpm singles, and one look at the Top 100 songs of 1975 can tell you exactly what other musical influences affected me that year. The singer in me loved acoustic-driven music like the Eagles and Jim Croce, the drummer in me enjoyed the aggressive backbeats of funk and Motown, but the guitar player within me had definitely fallen in love with the power chords of hard rock. On a personal level I was exploring the dark side, slipping away to the field out back with one of Dad's beers and one of Mom's cigarettes, and it wasn't long before I added smoking pot to my list of vices. I had been a Boy Scout throughout these younger days, and while I loved the outdoor lore and woodcraft, Scouting also got us out of the house where we could sneak cigarettes to the Scout meetings in our socks and smoke pot at camp.

In a society that doesn't really have a true rite of passage, the transition to high school was a big deal for my generation. We were one step closer to getting laid and driving, and we had some measure of independence. That fall, becoming a freshman at West High School in Phoenix opened up a new world of possibilities for me; sure, there were Math, English and History classes, but my combination of intelligence and talent for cheating allowed me to concentrate on more important subjects like the West High School Marching Band, the Orchestra, and the Stage Band as well as a personal favorite, Journalism Class, where I got to write for the school newspaper.

The first part of the year, in preparation for football season, the Marching Band had to arrive an hour before school started for rehearsal. Because I was a freshman, and because I was big and tall, I was given the task of carrying the huge bass drum on my chest, suspended by a shoulder harness, marching around the field in full uniform in the Arizona heat while pounding the mallets into the sides of that drum. Once I passed out from heatstroke, sending myself and the drum to the turf. I didn't mind the Marching Band, I was playing *music* in a *band* and *girls* were watching, plus I had the challenge of the orchestra class which focused on the classical masterpieces, and also the stage band, where I could play the entire drum kit and work with electric instruments like guitar, bass, and keyboards.

The only music class I was turned down for was the "Choir" or "Chorus" as they called it; the instructors determined that my singing voice had no redeeming qualities and suggested instead that I take a Woodshop class and learn to work with my hands.

I openly admit that during this time in my life, and for years to come, I was not a good singer. I confess to having no natural talent or singing ability – what I have I got from hard work, determination, trial and error, and learning a skill much as a mechanic learns to repair an engine, or a carpenter learns to drive a nail. For a decade, even after the Steeler album was acclaimed as a cultural milestone, I was a rock star in search of his voice. I would cringe upon listening to myself recorded, and my real friends were kind enough to be blunt in their criticisms and inform me that I was a nice guy, a good drummer, but I would *never* be able to sing.

Despite my critics, of which I was one, it didn't take me long before I had my first actual rock & roll band together, IMPACT, with some guys from school. I was the drummer and lead singer, Gary Bullock on bass, Mike Nesbitt on guitar. We had a couple of oriental guitar players, Rodney Ito then Peter Kwong (neither was the kid from band class that had so inspired me with his version of "Stairway To Heaven). A buddy who worked on the school newspaper had access to a printing press (that's how shit got printed back then), and he made me a little stack of my first business cards, black ink on white paper: IMPACT – A Rock N Roll Band – Ron Keel and my phone number. My first legit gig was a backyard pool party; the opening song was "Proud Mary." We started playing weekends at the local amusement park, a place called Legend City, kind of like a Wild West version of Disneyland. They had several outdoor stages throughout the park, and you had to work your way up to the privilege of playing the main stage by paying your dues on the Green Stage, which wasn't a stage at all but a grass mound so unlevel that my drums wouldn't stand up straight and our guitar amps kept falling over.

I'd been teaching myself to play guitar for about eight months, learning cover songs and starting to write my own songs. One night at the Legend City gig a drummer friend from the school band showed up in the crowd, and I invited him up to sit in on the kit. I grabbed Peter's axe and went out front on guitar and vocals for the first time, and experiencing that freedom was like being struck by lightning – a rock & roll frontman was born in that instant and I knew where I belonged. To this day I still play drums and love that primal fulfillment that you can only get behind a drum set, but from that moment on I was home – center stage.

In my sophomore year at West High School, I cultivated my role as a misfit and outcast. After football season, I began walking the two miles to school rather than ride the bus with the other kids in my neighborhood, transforming myself along the way by untucking my shirt, taking off my nerd glasses, and pulling my hair from behind my ears and messing it up. Upon arriving at school, my first stop was usually the Smoking Area where the other misfits would hang out, and I started making friends with some of the older guys there who smoked cigarettes and pot.

Determined to be a guitar hero, I formed my next band – NOVA - with a couple of guys I met in the Smoking Area – a black bassist named Irvin Archer and a drummer named Jim Shaw. We took over the Legend City gig, the music got heavier and the clothes got cooler – I was wearing all black and tying scarves to my guitar, Irvin played an SG bass and wore hippie clothes. I made us a sparkly logo on the front of the kick drum, and we played our first real paying gigs at high school dances and parties.

In school, when the teachers thought I was so diligently taking notes and working on my assignments, I was really writing lyrics.

Irvin quit to play with the neighborhood guitar monster who was Jimi Hendrix junior, and I was devastated. It was the first time somebody ever quit my band. Not long after that, he went ice skating, fell down on the ice, and somebody skated over his left hand and he never played bass again. A girl I knew told me about a professional band called Blue Steel that needed a drummer immediately for a string of gigs at the Arizona State Fair – their drummer had quit without notice and they were in a bind, and although I was more into guitar by then I couldn't pass up the opportunity. They hired me without an audition. We never even rehearsed – they just came by the house one afternoon and picked up me and my drum kit and hauled my ass down to the fairgrounds.

I was so green. It was my first time on a real concert stage, and I'd never had a crew. We pulled up behind the stage, and crew guys started unloading my drums, and I said "Hold on, where are you taking my drums?" They put them on the riser and I adjusted them into place. Then they started putting microphones on my drums, and I asked why they were doing that, and they said "So the audience can hear them." I informed them that I played really loud and didn't need microphones, but they insisted. And then they put two wedge-shaped speakers on the floor on either side of me, and I asked what those were. They called them "monitors" and said they would enable me to hear the other instruments and voices. I thought that was pretty cool.

The lead singer was a wiry and fit man named Jeremy Cloude, who exuded confidence and charisma. He gave me no instructions and no song list, he just turned around and said "Watch me," and I did. He would snap his fingers to give me the tempo, and use hand signals to guide me into the tunes and in and out of the breaks, very much like Elvis directed his band. Jeremy was a primary influence on my 'frontman persona', the way he moved like a spider on stage and controlled both the audience and the band with his stage moves. The keyboardist was Paul Bruce, the brother of Alice Cooper guitarist Michael Bruce; after that first string of State Fair gigs we supposedly had a record deal with Capitol and I was shopping for a Trans Am before I had a driver's license. Unfortunately, Jeremy and Paul got into a fight over a missing microphone, blew up the band and blew the record deal.

One day at the Smoking Area at West High School, a guy wearing torn up denims with long blonde hair came up to me and said "I hear you play guitar." He said his name was Fly, and he did an Alice Cooper tribute act. I signed on immediately and we put together an Alice Cooper tribute band called DEDLOK with the Toth brothers, David and Michael, who played drums and bass respectively. Now Fly was a couple years older, very wild and rebellious, and our drummer David Toth was a mean tough son of a bitch, so I was finally hanging with the right crowd. We did the whole Alice Cooper shtick, cutting the heads off baby dolls and playing all those classic Alice hits and some originals.

I had a life-changing experience with that band on Halloween, 1976. We did a free gig at a place called A.R.C.H. (Arizona Retarded Children's Home) – they only called us because no one else would do the gig. There was no pay, and the audience was about a thousand mentally handicapped people dressed up like Frankenstein's monster, Dracula, the Wolf Man, ghosts and witches. Our band was sloppy, out of tune, raunchy and wild, and they loved us. After the gig, a mentally retarded girl came up to me and began stroking my shoulder, and she was crying, saying, "Thank you for playing for us, most people ignore us, but you showed us that someone cares..."

Then and there I knew I'd made it. I had experienced music's ultimate reward – making someone feel better by playing for them, making a small difference in their day and maybe in their life. All the platinum and prestige in the world is nothing compared to that.

We'd worked our way up to the Water Front Stage at Legend City, where the best bands got to play. One night a very sexy older woman came backstage and hit on me. She had a friend with her that hooked up with Fly. Not only did she have these huge amazing tits but she also had a CAR and I thoroughly enjoyed both of them...and the car too. I had fifteen years' worth of horny to make up for. If you grew up in the 70's like I did, you know that the only way to learn about sex was by your Mom or Dad sitting you down and telling you about the "birds and the bees." There was no internet, no cable TV, and the only naked women I'd ever seen were in the Playboy magazines that some of my older friends and bandmates would share with me. And one time, Fly and I climbed the fence behind K-Mart to peek at the dirty movies playing at the Big Sky Drive-In Theater but we didn't see much before the cops escorted us home. Well, my Dad sure as hell never sat me down for that talk, so the first time Lu Ann Shaver led me into her bed I didn't have a clue about what to do or how to do it. She was very patient and I was a quick study, and I must have been doing something right because she kept coming around.

There were a couple of local clubs that had good live music. Mr. Lucky's was the big country bar on Grand Avenue, but downstairs on the weekends they had rock bands, and there were a couple of other rock bars on the west side that we used to hang out in, now that I had an older girlfriend with big tits and a car. The drinking age was only 18 back then, nobody ever asked you for ID, and I was over six feet tall with an older woman, so no one questioned my presence in these fine drinking establishments. Those bands were polished, and playing great Top 40 rock like Boston and Kansas, very difficult stuff compared to the Alice Cooper, Foghat, and KISS that we were slopping through. I had not yet even been to my first rock concert, so seeing these working bands in the clubs at such an early age was a great education for me.

One night while sitting at a table drinking and soaking up the music, Lu Ann slipped me my first hit of LSD. She had told me about it, offered it to me and I was apprehensive and declined, not understanding the effects of the drug. I enjoyed smoking pot and had already developed into a fine young budding alcoholic, but dropping acid was like doing *drugs*. Eventually I had enough liquor in me and said OK, and she put a little square piece of paper on my tongue. I thought what the hell, it's only a little piece of paper, what can that do to me?

She and our friends kept looking at me over the next half hour, asking me "Are you getting off yet?" Determined to keep it together, I kept saying no, no effect, this shit doesn't do anything for me. And then about 45 minutes after I took it, Lu Ann leaned in and gave me a big deep kiss. She had a cute little mole on her face, and when she drew back from the kiss I saw the mole get up and run around her mouth and end up back where it started, and I had to admit that I was "getting off." No longer fit for public consumption, we went back to her place and enjoyed a long night of hallucinogenic sex. I don't even remember what excuses I told my parents back then when I would stay out all night, probably the old stock "spending the night at a friend's house" bullshit.

One night, my parents went out to eat at a Mexican restaurant, and I declined their invitation, claiming I had "homework." The minute they were out the door, I called

Lu Ann and told her to come over. Within a half an hour we were naked on the living room couch when my parents walked right back through the front door and caught us in the act. Apparently the line at the restaurant had been too long and my father didn't have the patience to wait. Mom was furious, and Lu Ann grabbed her clothes and made a quick exit. Dad never said a word to me about it, but the following weekend we were working together on a construction site when I overheard him telling one of the electricians, "You shoulda seen the tits on that woman," he said, and there was no mistaking the pride in his voice.

3

WILD FOREVER

I want to play hard – I want to sing loud
I want to live it up before I lay it down
'Cause everything changes when I'm with you
Don't want to look back on all the things we didn't do

Live every day like Friday night
Don't look back, just hold on tight
We've only got one chance to take this ride

And we can be wild forever
Nobody's gonna put those chains on me
I want to be wild forever – whatever it takes I'm living free
We might just live once, but baby you & me
We can be wild forever

("Wild Forever" – lyrics by RK 2013 – from the Ron Keel
album "Metal Cowboy" released 2014)

Sometimes I accompanied my folks to the Swap Meet on weekends. There was a vendor who had boxes full of vinyl record albums, and I would dig through them looking for new music.

This was the golden age of album artwork, and I bought a lot of records just because of the cover. So when I was shuffling through the box one Sunday afternoon and pulled out a disc called "High Voltage" by some band called AC/DC it took a split second before I clutched it in my greedy hands and forked out the asking price, which I think was two dollars. You could just tell from the image of a maniacal Angus Young on the cover, the cool logo with the lightning bolt, and the live shots on the back cover accompanied by the cleverly written letters, that this was going to be a raunchy naughty powerful rock & roll ride, and I couldn't wait to get home and spin it.

Some of my friends hated it and others loved it. It was so primal, so powerful – and what I loved most about it was the simplicity. Pile driving mega-riffs played and overplayed until they hypnotized you – and for a kid still in his first year of playing guitar, these were songs you could play along with fairly easily, with a minimum of study.

There were some other pivotal releases in '76. KISS' "Destroyer," "2112" by Rush, and Aerosmith's "Rocks" were epic and spent the whole year in heavy rotation on my record player. Another major musical moment around the same time was experiencing Led Zeppelin's "The Song Remains The Same" flick all alone in a local Phoenix theater, and immediately I had to have one of those doubleneck guitars with the 12-string on top and the six string on the bottom. I found a beautiful Alpine white Ibanez doubleneck at a music store at Metro Center mall – they were going out of business and I got the axe for $185.00 out the door with case. God I loved that guitar. Just writing about it makes me want another one.

The Dedlok lead singer Fly got kicked out of wherever he was staying, so I convinced Mom and Dad to let him stay at our house and it was all downhill from there. He was a loose cannon and a wild son of a bitch, and my parents correctly perceived that he was a bad influence on me, so they kicked him out. Right around this time Roy mentioned that one of his tile suppliers had a son that was in a rock band and they were looking for a lead singer who played bass, and he took me to meet them at a huge warehouse not too far from our house.

The guitar player Chris Hart was really good, he was kicking out the Bad Co. and Rush tunes like nobody's business. They had this huge warehouse to practice in that felt much more like an arena than our family room did, it was close enough to home where I could walk to rehearsal but far enough away that I could get out of the house and into some beer and cigarettes. It was musically superior to what we'd been doing in Dedlok – Fly was more of a character than a singer, and the rhythm section of the Toth brothers left a lot of room for improvement. With these new guys, I would be the lead singer again like I always wanted to be.

It didn't matter to me that I had never played the bass and didn't even own one. I bought a cheap bass guitar at Lederman's music store and traded a guitar amp for a bass rig, and was determined to learn the traditional way – with fingers instead of a pick. Chris came up with the band name – ZYZZX, a misspelled take on a road near the California border where he was from, and we started rehearsing every afternoon after school. The problem was, rehearsal started around four o'clock, Roy didn't get home from work (or from the bar he stopped at after work) until around six, and I was still too young to drive. So everyday around four, you could see me hauling my amp and my bass down the sidewalk on Thomas Road just east of 35th Avenue via a metal hand truck in the Arizona heat. We'd play for a few hours and I'd haul it all home after sundown; I needed my bass and amp to practice at night and in the morning before school.

That sophomore year in school I was loaded up with music classes – I had band, orchestra, and now guitar class. First day of school I went into guitar class and the teacher auditioned everyone to judge their skill level, and there were a few of us that could actually play already. He would send us into the soundproof practice booths where we would jam and show each other songs while the beginners were taught the basic fundamentals. There were a few guys that were way ahead of me, and for an hour a day I would soak up their chops like a sponge, learning tunes and licks. I also liked hanging out with my acoustic guitar at school; it was a chick magnet and a great icebreaker. I would come to school a half hour early and sit around playing, I would play at lunch, I would ditch classes to hang out in the music room and play guitar.

I don't really remember what happened with the magnificently breasted older girlfriend Lu Ann – I don't recall the breakup but it was probably just me being a horny teenager in search of the next conquest. There were a few girls at school I carried on with that year; I'd fall in love, go through a breakup, and write a sappy song. I don't remember what happened with the ZYZZX band either, but I know we never did a gig. I've always lived at a pace three times the normal speed of life, but those years in the late 70's seem to have been even more accelerated – from one band to the next, from one girl to the next, always in search of the next song or the next party or the next ejaculation. The girls, the music, and the parties are all blurred together in a perfect storm of reckless teenage abandon, and I guess that sophomore year adjusted my metabolic throttle to high gear and rarely have I slowed down since.

June 1st in Phoenix means it's hot enough to fry eggs on the sidewalk or the hood of your car (they actually do that on TV every year just to prove it). On that date in 1977 I somehow got booked at an "End Of School" party at a local Phoenix high school, one hour during lunchtime out in the courtyard, which meant high noon under the sun. We got there early, set up the gear, and around 11:30 went to the boy's restroom to change into our stage clothes. Of course I'm wearing black jeans and a long-sleeved black shirt. We went out to play the gig at 12:00, nice little crowd gathered around, and started the first tune. I went up to the microphone to sing the first line of the song, and when my lips touched the mic the damn thing was so hot it branded the mesh pattern of the Shure SM-58 windscreen into the tender flesh of my lips; I could actually smell my lips burning as I pulled away and struggled through the next line. It was so hot that day the glue that held the speakers together liquefied in my little Fender P.A. system.

Sometime during the show, a really pretty girl walked up to me with a camera and took my picture. I forgot all about my charred and branded lips – of course she liked me, she was taking my picture! – and I struck a pose. I still have the print of that picture, very damaged after all these years, but I still remember the moment and the girl. Her name was Sheri, and we were immediately inseparable.

She was sweet, smart, pretty but wild, a year younger than I. She was rock & roll to the core, her favorite band was Aerosmith and Steven Tyler was God. I used to sneak over and visit her when she was babysitting for a neighbor, and we learned about love together that summer.

My parents were just a little more stable than I've been, but not much – we'd been in Arizona for eight years or so, and it had been up and down. While my father's business had prospered due to the housing boom, his drinking and adultery had also thrived. Many jobs were in the outlying areas of town, and at the time there was only one freeway (I17) so it could take hours to get from our side of town out to Mesa, Scottsdale, or any of these areas where the custom homes were being built, and Roy could stop "by way of" a local bar or barmaid and use distance as an alibi. Of course my mother knew better, and thus conspired to extricate my father and I from the evil influences that surrounded us. She went to Texas under the auspices of visiting some old family friends, and when she got home a week later she proudly proclaimed that she'd bought a 15-acre farm in the middle of nowhere, 118 miles from Dallas, and that we were moving.

I hit the roof, refusing to abandon the city, my dream of rock stardom, my new girlfriend Sheri. No way was I going to go live on a farm in bumfuck Texas. As the folks began the process of selling the house in Phoenix and relocating to the small town of Mt. Pleasant, Texas, I began to plot running away and living on the streets if that's what it came down to.

In truth I had nothing really going on musically, just hacking away in garage bands. So when my Mom came to me with a copy of the Mt. Pleasant newspaper she'd brought home from her trip, and showed me a classified advertisement for a "band looking for lead singer," the tables began to turn.

Band looking for lead singer, along the lines of KISS, AC/DC – call DannyRhea XXX-XXXX

I called the number and spoke to Danny Rhea. By the end of the conversation, I knew I was moving to Texas.

It was partly the fact that he was really nice and really into the music. Part of it was I knew that immediately upon arrival I would have the best band in town, whereas in Phoenix there was a lot of competition from guys who were a few years older and a helluva lot better than me. And part of it was that restless spirit kicking in, just like it did with my parents – the excitement of relocating to a new place of adventure and opportunity. So I told Mom and Dad I would give it a try, but that if the band didn't work out I was coming back to Phoenix on my own.

The hard part was telling Sheri I was moving out of state.

Of course she was totally supportive, encouraging me to do whatever I thought I had to do to make it, and promising that she'd be waiting for me. So by the end of summer, I was enrolled in Mt. Pleasant High School, living on a farm with cows, pigs, chickens and ducks, and playing in my first good band.

I named the group "Nightfall," after my favorite Isaac Asimov science-fiction short story (I would later use that name for the Marc Ferrari classical guitar instrumental on "The Final Frontier" album). Danny Rhea (guitar), Bucky Allen (drums), and Randy Baggett (bass) and I rehearsed in an abandoned school auditorium in the woods. Bucky's family had money, his father has been a pro football player, and he had considerable pull in the community. So somehow this old abandoned school still had electricity, and we got to practice on a huge stage in an immense building with arena-style echo and no adult supervision. Danny was a great songwriter and I thought I was a good songwriter, and it was a wonderful atmosphere in which to create, so we decided early on we'd be an all original band and that we'd also try to put on a real show. We'd experiment with props like skulls that lit up and we'd put them on top of the P.A. speakers, any kind of trick lighting that we could come up with, and somebody made these Druid-like hooded robes that we would wear out on stage for the first few tunes. We started experimenting with choreography like KISS, and Danny and I had this part of the show where we'd both play behind our backs. And yes, we were the best rock band in town – in fact, we were the only rock band in town. One drawback was, other than that amazing huge abandoned auditorium in the woods, there was no place else to play.

We managed to get our first gig at the Bumblebee Lounge just outside of town. It was a lot smaller than our auditorium, and we were over the top loud and very extreme for the small crowd of beer drinkers and pool shooters in attendance.

We used to put on our own shows in the band shell at the local park. We promoted our own Halloween show at the local high school and sold tickets to that. There was just nowhere else to go, and Dallas was far away and tough to crack for a band of high-school kids from Mt. Pleasant.

One of the cool things about the year I spent growing up in Texas was, we had one hell of a school band. I remember some serious road gigs where our orchestra would travel to Dallas, Houston, Austin or some other major metropolitan area to compete with other high school bands, and we always smoked them. I believe it was a credit to the small town work ethic and the quality teachers and conductors we had there at Mt. Pleasant High School, but we had seventy kids playing the most difficult compositions in history to perfection. One of the proudest moments of my academic career was when I took two first place awards for two different instruments – one for playing lead guitar in the school jazz band, the other for composing and performing a 7-piece percussion ensemble piece. I actually had two gold medals for those honors, and paraded them on my guitar strap for a while until they fell off at a gig somewhere and were lost forever.

I got my first car the next spring when I turned sixteen – a 1972 Chevy Malibu. I loved that car, it was a mean silver and black heavy metal machine, and of course the first thing I did was install a "tape deck." For those of you to young to know the term, that was a stereo system that played cassette tapes, and I remember blasting Grand Funk Railroad, Ted Nugent, Rainbow and the like on the seven mile drive from home to school and back. With my own car, I could leave school grounds during lunch time and cruise through town, grab a chili dog at the local Sonic drive in. We used to like to hang out at the local pool hall, playing Foosball which I became deadly at and still love to play whenever I get the chance.

Danny Rhea got three tickets to see KISS at Tarrant County Convention Center in Dallas during the "Destroyer" tour. It was my first concert, Styx was the opening act, and we fought our way right up to the front row, in the middle of the frenzy when Gene, Paul, Peter & Ace took the stage, close enough to get sweat on and spit on. At one point, my outstretched arm managed to catch one of Gene Simmons' guitar picks.

While Nightfall was a step forward on my career path, there came a point when I realized it was not going to be my ticket to the arena stages I craved, and I moved on in search of the ultimate power trio. I was at the point where I actually believed I could cover all the guitar parts and lead vocals, digging bands like Rush and Triumph and wanting to create my own band in that mold.

Of course rock musicians were scarce in that neck of the woods, but I had heard tales of a bass player that lived out deep in those woods and that I should check him out. I got directions from somebody and drove out there – I mean *way* out there – to a house in the country and went up the porch steps to the front door.

"Hello, ma'am," I said to the lady who answered it. "I'm looking for a guy who plays the bass?"

"That would be my son, Gary," she said, and led me through the house to the back door. She pointed to a shed in the back yard. "He's out there." I went out there and heard loud rock & roll coming from inside the shed. When I knocked and Gary Presswood opened the door, I was in front of a wild eyed long haired rocker who pleasantly invited me into his man cave. Black light posters with hippie slogans and marijuana leaves decorated the walls, there was a bass amp with a Gibson Ripper bass guitar leaning up against it. We smoked a joint and I told him who I was and that I was putting together a new band and looking for a bass player.

Woody was an eccentric cat, a high school dropout who pretty much stayed in his shed in the woods and played bass and smoked pot. Not a lot of people skills, but a sweet guy when you got to know him. What was most amazing was that his record player/turntable motor was stuck on 45 revolutions per minute instead of 33 rpms and he didn't even know that he was listening to all his albums at a faster speed and higher pitch than they were intended to be played – and he had learned to play bass by playing along with those albums, thus developing lightning-fast lead guitar-like bass skills. The first song I ever heard him play was "I Got The Fire," the lead track on Montrose's killer "Paper Money" album, which is a pretty fast tune anyway, and here was Woody just tearing it up 20 beats per minute faster and four frets higher. I actually had to inform him that his record player motor was in hyper drive, and I also informed him that he would from now on be playing bass in my band.

We had a pretty smoking little power trio going on in the Texas woods, and we called it Touch. We did a few gigs at the park, with Sammy Hignight and then Jim Aleshire on drums. Our big gig came when I arranged a performance in the school auditorium for entire student body during the day, they actually let everybody out of class for an hour to watch us play. I recall we opened with Queen's "We Will Rock You." I loved any song with the word "Rock" in the title, and we played them all, and I was starting to write songs like "Born To Rock" and "Rock & Roll Man."

I remember the day music changed forever. You could hear it – and hell, you could feel it – in the parking lot when I pulled into school that morning. Everybody was blasting it on their stereos. By the end of first period, everybody was drawing the logo on their notebooks. And by the end of the day, you just weren't cool if you hadn't heard it and didn't just fucking love it. Of course I'm talking about the debut album from Van Halen, specifically the song titled "Eruption," which at that time revolutionized the music of my generation and set the standard for all that was to come in the 80's. As far as I'm concerned, that album created the mold for everything that followed in the ensuing decade, raising the bar and establishing the "state of the art" for both musicianship and showmanship. Van Halen's motto of "if it's worth doing, it's worth overdoing" would become the theme of the heavy metal scene that dominated the 80's.

4

LIVE

I used to hope I'd die before I got old
Living in the moment – never worried about tomorrow
I learned the hard way to just hold on to the good times
No matter what went wrong
As long as I'm alive, I got something to live for

Looking back on those reckless years
No regrets, no more tears
We got each other – and so much more

This is who I am, this is where I stand
Give it all I got, do the best I can
Gonna hold on for dear life
Just to make it through the night

I wanna live – I wanna rock
Wanna chase these dreams and never stop
I just wanna hold you and never let you go
I wanna live – I wanna fight
And hold on to this life like there's no tomorrow
I want to live

("Live" – lyrics by RK 2009 – from the KEEL album "Streets Of Rock & Roll" released 2010)

There is nothing like being young, wild, and free, out on the open road chasing down a dream.

That was me on the first day of summer 1978; seventeen years old and heading out on my own, ready to take on the world and claim my piece of rock & roll history. Sunrise couldn't come soon enough for me, and at dawn I loaded my guitars, gear, and luggage into my Chevy, kissed my teary-eyed mother goodbye, and hit the highway out of Mount Pleasant, Texas, with Meat Loaf's "Bat Out Of Hell" blasting on the cassette player. I'd seen Meat Loaf on "Saturday Night Live" and had to buy the album and cassette the next day, it was that powerful to me. I still love me some Meat Loaf, and all three "Bat Out Of Hell" albums rank in my Top Five of all time. "Bat Out Of Hell III" is actually my "if you were stranded on a desert island and can only have one album, what would it be" album.

My year of being a Texas farm boy – my junior year in high school - was over. I'd done as I'd promised my parents I would and given small-town life a shot and now I was headed back to Phoenix. I'd conquered every goal a young rock musician could in that one horse town - been in the two best rock bands that area had ever seen, drank their beer and smoked their weed, and fought with the roughest rednecks they had to offer, and now it was time to get serious about my career.

Though I was still technically a minor, my parents did the necessary emancipation paperwork that would allow me to be my own legal guardian on the condition that I would finish high school. They knew I was hell bent on the rock & roll dream and nothing could stop me, so they resigned themselves to the fact that I was wasting my life and my intellect on a fruitless fantasy that would only end in disappointment and poverty. I really think they gave up on me at that point, and for the next six years we would see each other little and remain distant both in proximity and at heart. I came back the following year for a couple of months, and I would try to visit at Christmas, but that sunny morning when I lit out for good was really my childhood's end.

At that same time, my sister Sherleen and her husband Dennis were on a cross-country road trip with friends, Bill & Georgia Duty. Bill and Georgia had a couple of sons not much older than me, Randy and Terry. While the elders continued their vacation, the boys, along with a friend of theirs named Mike, were parting ways in Arkansas and heading home to Phoenix. The plan was for me to hook up with them all in a place called Batesville, Arkansas, and Randy, Terry, Mike and I would caravan out to Phoenix, for safety's sake and strength in numbers. I had never done a long road trip like that on my own, and I was not mechanically inclined in case I had car trouble, so it sounded good to me. And I was told the youngest brother, Randy, also played the drums and I was thinking we might be into putting a band together.

That moment when I turned out onto the highway and heard the first strains of "Bat Out Of Hell" blasting through my speakers was one of the best of my life. The world was mine, I had it all out in front of me, and I felt like the king of rock & roll. I was invincible, I was happy, I was free at last. Since that day, I've always really enjoyed reliving that feeling every time I hit the highway alone with the music cranked up. I love being on the road with a band, and I love traveling with Renée, but I also treasure those solo trips because they remind me of that day and that feeling.

Five days later, I would arrive in Phoenix broke and ill, having lost my car, my guitars, and all my belongings along the way.

I made it to Batesville in time for supper with my sister's friends. After meeting Randy, Terry, and Mike the four of us snuck outside and got stoned out of our minds. We were at their Grandmother's house and she had cooked a huge feast, and I remember having a real hard time keeping it together at the table. The other guys were discussing a side trip to Memphis before heading back to Arizona, and I had little choice but to buy in. I was anxious to get to Phoenix and start my new life – Sherleen and Dennis were going to let me stay in a little guest house that was behind their home and I would spend the summer getting the new version of my band Touch off the ground. But for now, I was headed to Memphis.

I can only write about what I remember, and unfortunately I don't remember much about that wild-ass road trip over thirty years ago. We made it to Memphis, drinking beer and smoking dope the whole way. I remember being on Beale Street drunk as hell.

Since there were four of us and only two vehicles, the plan was to drive straight through from Memphis to Phoenix, taking turns sleeping and driving. My car was full of everything I owned, with no room for a passenger, so whenever someone else was driving it I was grabbing shut-eye in the back of the van. It was a long couple days and nights of partying and driving until on the afternoon of the third day. Mike was driving my car and I was passed out in the van; when Terry woke me up, my car was engulfed in a cloud of white smoke, and not the kind of smoke we were used to. We pulled over and ascertained that, 26 miles west of Tucumcari, New Mexico, my beloved '72 Chevy was fucked, probably the engine was blown but we'd have to have it towed back to town to be certain.

It took a little over an hour to get back to Tucumcari, find a tow truck, and get back out to where my car sat on the side of the road. I couldn't believe it when I walked up to the driver's side and saw the windows shattered, nothing left inside but broken glass. My two guitars – a sunburst Les Paul and a black Strat – were gone, along with my amp, my backpack containing my clothes and personal things, as well as the stereo with all my tapes, including "Bat Out Of Hell." I'm not sure why we didn't leave somebody with the car while the others went back to arrange the tow, but we were young, dumb, and stoned and that was a mistake I would never forget. I remember acting like it wasn't a big deal, playing the tough guy, and riding back to town in the van with the guys as the Malibu was towed to a local garage for evaluation.

I'm not sure where Terry met the Preacher's Daughter, probably at the restaurant where we went to eat and await the verdict on my car, but she was hot and blonde and claimed her father was a preacher, and the next thing I know we were all in her living room smoking pot. That's where I made the call to the garage and received the news that my engine was blown. I was down to my last few dollars, so purchasing a new engine in Tucumcari, New Mexico was not an option. I called my Dad from the Preacher's Daughter's kitchen to get his advice, and all he said was "I'll be there tomorrow."

And sure enough, Roy drove out immediately from Mount Pleasant to Tucumcari. We stayed the night on the Preacher's Daughter's living room floor (all of us but Terry, who spent the night in her bed) and my father arrived the next day, rigged a towing chain with a rubber tire between his truck and my car (so that every time he put on the brakes, the car would hit the rubber tire instead of rear-ending his truck), and headed back to Texas while we piled in the van and continued our journey to Arizona.

When we arrived at the Duty house in Phoenix that night, that's when it really hit me. My car was gone, I had no musical equipment, I had no money, no change of clothes. What had started with so much promise a few days before had turned to shit. Thanks to my sister and her husband, I wasn't homeless, but that little guest house they put me up in might as well have been a prison cell if it didn't come furnished with a guitar and some gear.

One thing that road trip had accomplished was to create a bond between me and Randy Duty, and we pretty much concluded that he'd be the drummer in the Arizona incarnation of Touch. He was a super guy, fun to hang out with, absolutely fearless, a hard partying motherfucker and a great mechanic. Last I heard, he owned and ran The Engine House in Phoenix, in fact he replaced an engine on my Ford Ranger in the mid-90's.

I went to work as a tile setter's helper with my sister's husband Dennis' company, Sunburst Tile, and Dennis' sweet mother loaned me $1800.00 to buy some new gear. I bought a Randall P.A. system, a Randall amp, and a beautiful wood grain Stratocaster guitar and I was back in business. After a year's worth of love letters from Texas to my girlfriend Sheri, I broke up with her not long after my return home, realizing that I was way too wild to be tied down. I would see her years later and re-ignite our teenage passion but again I would end up walking away. She was the closest thing I ever got to a high school sweetheart, but the guy that came back to her was not the same guy that had left a year earlier..

Whenever I needed to get my gear from Point A to Point B, I'd bum a ride from Dennis or Randy or somebody; if I didn't have to transport equipment I just walked or hitchhiked. Hitchhiking was a fairly safe and reliable method of transportation in the 70's – eventually somebody would give you a ride. We met a lot of interesting people hitchhiking, sometimes other musicians who would take you to their place to jam and get stoned.

Randy and I started working up some of my original songs with a bass player friend of his. I don't remember the guy's name, but he was a nice guy, good player, good looking long haired rocker dude and we had a blast putting together the tunes in Randy's bedroom at his parent's house. We played all the songs with the word "Rock" in title; I copped a couple of Danny Rhea originals just because I liked them so much – "Burning Lips" and "Believe Me." We were playing covers, Stones, Robin Trower, Montrose, "Hot Blooded" by Foreigner.

We did our first gig with that bass player in the dining room of the Duty house – cleared out all the furniture, set up the gear in the elevated dining area like it was a stage, and invited over every girl we knew. We did a couple more gigs after that, I don't remember where, but the last time Dude ever played bass for us was the Tambourine Incident.

Of course throwing things is a tried and true stage move for rock stars of all ages, whether veteran or novice – tossing your guitar or mic stand to a roadie and other such antics. I had a part of the "show" where I played tambourine; I didn't have a roadie yet so I would pick it up off the top of my amp and shake it during a drum/vocal break. When I was through with it, of course I flung it behind the amps like a Frisbee. This time, when I tossed it, I Frisbeed that tambourine right into Bass Player Dude's forehead – I saw it hit him, saw the surprised look in his eyes as his head jerked back, and then stared in horror as the slits opened up on his forehead and blood began to pour out. The guy was a trooper, because he played on without missing a note, and he just looked at me like "Why did you do that?" – like he wasn't even angry, just hurt. I felt really bad about that.

That's when we brought Gary "Woody" Presswood out from Texas to fill the now vacant position of bassist. He rode a Greyhound bus and moved into the little guest house with me.

Somewhere around this time I also started running with my old friend Josh Ertel. I had been friends with his sister Shawn during my freshman and sophomore years in high school, and Josh and I bonded because we were both outcast rebels who loved the band KISS. Josh wanted to play and sing and lived vicariously through me, and we shared a lot of common interests from substance abuse to the occult. I was the wanna-be rock star and he was my trusty sidekick. He helped us out hauling gear and trying to run sound ("If you hear feedback, turn this knob down"). We were like brothers, sharing the dreams and the hard times as they came. We got our left ears pierced together at Chris Town Mall and wore the gaudiest dangling earrings we could find.

My Dad replaced the engine in the '72 Chevelle Malibu for me, and drove it out to Phoenix so I would have my wheels back. He hung out for couple of days visiting me and my sister and her family, then he flew back to Texas.

After Gary arrived, we started doing more and more bar shows, playing a regular Tuesday gig at a very rough joint called The Zoo in Phoenix, on McDowell near 17th Street. I was seventeen, but looked older, and had no trouble booking our rock & roll power trio into the bar and nobody questioned me when I ordered drinks during our breaks.

The waitresses got up and danced on poles fitted into the centers of some of the tables. They danced for dollars when we took a break, and sometimes danced during the gig if they liked the song. We played KISS, Rush, Montrose, Rolling Stones, and a lot of the original songs I was writing at the time - edgy, simple, juvenile rock riffs with basic lyrics and melodies. The patrons were a cross-section of bikers and speed freaks; I recall the very last time we played there, some kind of a drug deal had gone bad between our bass player and a biker gang. We managed to get our gear loaded into my Chevy and were trying to make a getaway when the car wouldn't start. I remember looking in the rear view mirror and seeing a large group of very menacing characters approaching our vehicle, and thinking we were dead, when finally the engine turned over and I put the pedal down just in time.

One morning after a typical gig at The Zoo, me, Woody, and Josh were all crashed out at my place, hung over and sleeping on the floor of the guest house. I woke up to the phone ringing, and upon answering it I was very excited that somebody was actually calling about a booking. We usually had to pound the street hustling gigs, it was rare that someone actually called *us*.

The guy on the line said he had heard good things about us from the people at The Zoo, and that he owned and ran a club in Lake Havasu City, a couple of hundred miles away. There'd been a cancellation, and he offered us the Thursday through Saturday slot that week. Promised us $100 a night, meals, and a place to stay. I accepted without a second thought - we didn't turn down gigs, and this was an actual opportunity to get out of town. The promise of wild Lake Havasu women, a road trip, a threenighter, and three hundred bucks was a dream come true for us. It was lucky the guy had called the morning after a bar job or we may not have had gas and trailer money to get to Lake Havasu City; it was likely that by that evening what little we'd made the previous night would have been squandered on food, beer, cigarettes, and guitar strings; as it stood, we had just enough cash between us to rent a U-Haul trailer for the gear and fill up my tank with gas. I told the guy we'd see him that evening, that we'd go ahead and cruise up there, get the gear set up and checked, and be ready to rock & roll the following evening.

I remember the Chevy ran hot much of that journey, even with the rebuilt engine; it was summertime in the desert and we were towing a trailer uphill and had four people in the car.

That's a beautiful drive from Phoenix to Lake Havasu City, long and winding roads through gorgeous country to a bar that's no longer there on the town's main drag, a place known then as "The Old Ranger's Watering Hole." It was well after dark when we finally arrived. The place was, by the standards of the day, a decent venue - fairly good-sized stage and dance floor, adjacent to a steakhouse restaurant. I met the Owner, a big guy with a face full of craters and busted capillaries who at the time seemed friendly enough, albeit a bit imposing and we proceeded to load in. We were famished, so I inquired about the meals we'd been promised. The Owner flat out denied making such a promise, claiming he'd never told me food was included. I felt a fucking coming on, so I asked about the accommodations. He said he'd take us there when the bar closed. My request to receive a portion of our pay in advance was balked at - he insisted that we would receive payment in full upon completion of the third night, softening the blow by providing us with pitchers of draft beer.

At this point, we were at his mercy. We didn't have enough gas money left to get back home, so we couldn't tell him to fuck off and besides, we were there to play. So we sat up the gear, did a couple of songs to make sure everything worked, and drank free draft beer until closing time. We unhooked the U-haul trailer and left it chained up behind the building, and followed Mr. Bar Owner down a dark dirt road, all the while wondering where in hell he was taking us. Surely there were no hotels out here in the middle of the desert.

"Where the fuck is he taking us?" I asked.

"This is bullshit," Randy replied. He had a way of saying that word ("bullshit") with a short "u" as in "unbelievable." I picked that up from him that summer and retain that pronunciation to this day.

Our accommodations turned out to be a very small camp trailer parked about a hundred yards from his house. And I stress the point, very small. It did have electricity and a bathroom. Tired and drunk, we were just happy the day was over; we had a place to crash, and the prospect of making a favorable impression on the local female population at our gig the next night.

The next day, I knocked on the door of the Bar Owner's house to ask if we could use his shower. His wife graciously extended their hospitality. These people had a filthy houseful of loud messy kids - we had to pick our way through piles of trash, broken toys and dirty clothes to get to the bathroom which was a disaster area. I was just happy to be able to get a cleaned up - that is, until I got out of the shower and began to look for a towel. Assuming we'd be staying in a hotel, we hadn't brought towels of our own. The only towels available to us were the dirty ones scattered about the bathroom floor, and it became a challenge to search for those with the fewest skid marks on them.

Once we were all showered, we headed into town to get tuned up and ready for the gig. By now we were starving, not having eaten in a couple of days, and the Bar Owner was not going to deviate from his policy no matter what - if we passed out from starvation and didn't do the gig, he wouldn't have to pay us - but for some reason he had no misgivings about supplying us with pitchers of draft beer. Flirtations with a couple of waitresses led to them bringing us a huge platter of French fries, and we proceeded to feast on them until the platter was clean.

I recall the gig being okay - by that I mean nobody yelled at us because we sucked, the Owner seemed pleased with the turnout, and people were dancing instead of throwing shit at us. I of course immediately set my sights on the hottest girl in the house, a vivacious young blonde who was displaying her assets on the dance floor in front of me. I don't recall her name, but over the next three days I fucked a lot and ate a lot of French fries. I got so sick of French fries that I didn't eat another one for years, and still can't finish an entire small order of fries. I will purposefully not order a combo meal just to avoid getting French fries.

I am very thankful that all that sex I had that weekend did not have the same effect on me as all those French fries.

When the third night was over, it was like pulling teeth to get Bar Owner's attention long enough to get paid. Much to my chagrin, he took it upon himself to deduct about a third of our pay for the countless pitchers of draft beer we had consumed, and we had little recourse but to go back and trash his shitty little camp trailer. Randy was big, tough, drunk, and pissed off and he really took it out on our temporary home away from home. I was less pissed because at least I had been getting laid for the past three days, but I know we did some real damage to that trailer, to the point where it was probably no longer habitable.

The next day when we went to pick up our gear from the club, Bar Owner was standing at the load out door with his arms crossed, livid about the condition of his trailer and informing us that he was keeping our gear as payment. I ended up calling the cops, and when they showed up I explained to them that this guy had promised us accommodations and ended up putting us in a beat up camp trailer for the weekend, would not pay us until after the third night, and so on pleading my case. I think the cops had a beef with this guy too, because they made him stand aside while we loaded out, hooked up the trailer, and headed home with just enough gas money to get there.

I take no pride in admitting to the criminal behavior in which I engaged during this period in my life. I only hope the statute of limitations has long since come and gone and that the supermarkets and convenience stores in the greater Phoenix area have bigger fish to fry.

It wasn't my idea, and I won't say who's idea it was, but when you add broke and hungry to reckless and young things can get pretty hairy, and they did. The first time, I was the designated driver of the getaway car – hell, it was my car. We parked in a supermarket parking lot, and I kept the Chevy running with all the windows down while Randy, Woody, and Josh went into the store. I couldn't believe it when five minutes later they came running towards me, and before they even opened the doors they were throwing stuff into the car – it was raining cigarettes and bread and hot dogs – and the second the doors were shut I peeled out and we were gone.

It didn't take long to register that while only minutes before we had nothing, now we had smokes and food, they even grabbed beer and condiments. It became a regular method of shopping for us, mostly at convenience stores. Remember, kids, this was in the 70's, before Big Brother was watching our every move on networked video surveillance cameras. We would park around back or around the side, one guy would be the driver while two or three guys went inside. One would grab the beer, one would grab the food, one would go to the counter and ask the clerk for a carton of Marlboro. Just as we were about to put the stuff on the counter, one of us would ask the clerk for something that was back behind the counter on the far end – batteries, whatever – and when the clerk turned away to retrieve that item we would run like hell and dive into the car as it sped away. Thing was, it always worked and we never got caught, so this only emboldened us to expand our criminal horizons.

We became the kings of dine-and-dash, where you go into a restaurant, order, eat, and run out on the bill. I remember the guilt and embarrassment I felt when we pulled this at a place where my family had often eaten when I was younger, and we had the same favorite waitress - I'm sure she didn't recognize me, but I still felt bad about it.

The other guys were wild with it, intoxicated by the thrill, but I saw it as a means to an end. This was survival, a way to stay alive while learning songs and playing gigs. I didn't like it, but it beat the hell out of working construction with my brother-in-law.

There was a music store in town that displayed a number of fine guitars in a glass window right on the street, and a couple of the guys got the idea to add some of those instruments to our collection illegally. They would use the same brilliant strategy as always: bust the glass, grab as many guitars as they could, and haul ass. I flatly refused to participate, but did allow them to use my car. I waited at the house, watching TV and wondering if I'd ever see them or my car again. Within the hour, they came busting through the door with a half dozen guitars and basses – they had selected a beautiful matching pair of Ovation acoustic guitars for me, a six-string and a twelve-string.

The next time I got up the nerve to drive past that music store there were iron bars between the glass and the goods.

One day we were rehearsing in the Duty garage and received a call from Josh, who had been hitchhiking over to us from his Mom's house. He claimed he'd gotten a ride from some big time record producer, and the guy was interested in coming over to see our band. I told him to come on.

Jim Daley looked every bit the role, with his Tony Orlando mustache and confident air. When he and Josh arrived at the Duty house, we talked for a bit and then proceeded to play some of my original songs for him. He got very serious, moving to different locations in the room to hear different things, furrowing his brow, cupping his hands over his ears. We were watching him more than he was watching us; one time, he put his ear into the speaker on a cabinet that wasn't plugged in.

"That speaker's not hooked up," I told him after the song.

"I know that," he said. "I was listening to the reflection of the music resonating off the cone of the speaker." We were floored, convinced that we really were in the presence of a big time record producer.

He took my phone number, but never called. I took his number, and held on to it, and a few months later a call to him would change my life dramatically.

That summer seemed to last forever, but September came like it always does, and with it came the responsibility to fulfill my promise to my Mom that I would finish high school. I had one year to go, and after the summer of '78 that Senior year loomed like an impending prison sentence.

The first letdown was that I could not go back to West High because my new address, at the guest house behind my sister's place, was in a different district. I had hoped to make a triumphant return to my old stomping grounds sporting my longer hair, earring, and platform shoes; I would instead have to attend Central High, where I knew no one. I felt sure that I would win over enough of the female student body to make my senior year worthwhile, but when I went to enroll I was denied both entry in the school band and a position on the school newspaper. The senior band and the senior newspaper staff had paid their dues and come up through the ranks since they were freshmen, and I was the scary looking newcomer with the attitude. So I ended up getting math and English and science classes that would not have been required at my other school. I remember that one semester of Home Economics (girl class = cooking/sewing etc.) was also required at Central, and while I hated it at the time it was actually the most practical course on my fall schedule.

I was the only guy at that school with an earring, leather pants, a hopped-up Chevy and my own house. So the chicks that were into that kind of guy all had me on their radar. I remember bringing girls to the house at lunch hour, banging them, and then rushing to get back to school in time for Home Ec.

That fall, we landed some side-stage shows at the Arizona State Fair. These were the Holy Grail of gigs because you would play for a larger audience than in the bars, which meant more girls would see us play, and you got free admission to the Fair. They had flatbed carts to ferry us and our equipment from the parking lot to the stage. During one of these after-show rides, I spotted a girl who I thought was the most exotic beauty I'd ever seen, beautiful long flowing red hair, a smile full of life and energy, a full buxom body and olive skin. "Slow down," I told the cart driver. "Hop on!" I called to the girl without hesitation, and without hesitation she did just that. She was sixteen, a year younger than I. Her name was Maria, and I was in love again.

Maria lived in Mesa, around 83rd Street and Van Buren when it still had the feel of a rural neighborhood, practically on the edge of civilization and almost in the shadow of my favorite place on Earth, Superstition Mountain in nearby Apache Junction. Our dates consisted of walks in the nearby hills, holding hands and talking of dreams we wanted to share...some possible, some not. Maria was a devout Mormon, something she had picked up on her own and believed in with all her heart despite her family's criticism of her faith. Her father was a mean son of a bitch, an ex-military hardass with an evil stare and an arsenal of weapons under his bed. Maria also had a sweet mother and a little sister, but the family did not share her religious views. Those views prohibited us from ever consummating our love in bed, but they also endeared her to me that much more; I studied the Book Of Mormon, but I didn't get it and certainly didn't believe in it and knew that I would never be able to embrace it in order to be with her. But the fact that her faith was so important to her and she clung to her beliefs despite all opposition from her father, and even from me, made her angelic in my eyes and I was hopelessly obsessed with her.

Though I really meant to keep my promiseto my Mom about staying in school, it was taking a huge chunk out of my life which I thought, at the old age of 17, was rapidly slipping away. Our regular Tuesday night gig at The Zoo made it hell to get up for school at 6 AM on Wednesday mornings, and then usually we had a gig on Friday that required an early load in and set up, so I missed a lot of Fridays. By late October, I had already missed so many days that if I missed one more day that semester I would not be able to graduate.

That was the day I went to jail for the first time.

I started the day with every intention of going to school. I was up at 6 AM and dressed when David Toth, the old drummer from my band Dedlok, knocked on the door. He was a crazy and unpredictable motherfucker, and I'm not even sure why I was hanging out with him because it had been a couple of years since we played together, but he had the entire bed of his restored 1950 Ford pickup truck iced down with a couple of cases of Coors and wanted to go for a ride. I went with him for no good reason, and the only time I ever went back to Central High School was to officially drop out.

David and I went to West High, our alma mater. He parked in the student lot and were hanging with some old friends at the Smoking Area when Frankie, the chief bitch security guard, recognized us. She knew every kid at that school, she knew us, and she knew we didn't go to school there any more, and she told us to get the hell off school property. David stuck his middle finger in her face and said "Fuck you," she turned red and called for backup, I grabbed him by the shoulder and said "C'mon let's go," and I managed to get him to the truck. He'd probably started drinking a lot earlier than I had, and he was a natural born asshole anyway, but when we finally got back in the truck he went nuts. He was peeling out, burning rubber, throwing beer cans both empty and full at the security guards who were chasing us on foot through the parking lot, yelling at them and flipping them off. It was a wild scene, and we made it off school grounds but not far when a couple of police cars cornered us in a nearby neighborhood and drug us out of the vehicle at gunpoint.

They put us in separate cruisers with our hands cuffed behind our backs. I maintained my innocence, blamed it all on David for being a drunken out-of-control asshole, and tried to convince them I was a juvenile. I did not have any identification on me and whether they believed me or not seemed irrelevant, because they took me to the adult jail and booked me for trespassing and disturbing the peace. And that was the last time I ever saw David Toth.

5

I NEVER TOLD YOU

I never told you that I loved you
It'll be too late when I'm gone
I don't want to hurt you anymore
So I'll just pack and move along

("I Never Told You" – lyrics by RK 1978 – unreleased)

April 12 1979 – Alhambra High School, Phoenix, Arizona

November 1978 found me alone in the trashed little one room guest house behind my sister's home.

School's out forever. My car was breaking down from lack of attention and the abuse that comes with being the only car in a rock band. Woody and I got drunk and came to blows in the parking lot of some bar we were playing at, and that was the end of Touch.

At least I still had Maria. With my car broken down, I took to hitchhiking the forty-something miles out to East Mesa to see Maria on her lunch hour at school. Sometimes it would take up to six hours, depending on the goodwill of the drivers, so I would leave around sunrise and hope for the best. Just to see her for a few minutes, get a smile, a hug, catch up on life, a quick kiss and then a six hour thumb ride home.

On the stolen Ovation acoustic guitar, I wrote my first power ballad – one of the first songs I crafted that actually showed some promise – called "I Never Told You." It felt like I'd unlocked some magic combination, and for the first time I had a song which I really thought might be my ticket somewhere. Five chords picked slow, first-person lyrics about a nomadic troubadour headed out on the road without confessing his true feelings to the girl he's leaving behind.

I dug out that guy's business card – what was his name, Jim Daley? – that record producer that had come to our rehearsal and made such an impression on me.

"Hello Jim? This is Ron Keel – you came to see my band rehearsing a while back? Yeah, that's me. Hey, I have this song, and I really think it's a hit – I'm wondering if we could meet and I could play it for you?"

I was thrilled when he gave me his address and invited me over at noon the next day.

I brought Josh and the Ovation with me to his modest two-bedroom apartment, and he had the living room area set up with musical equipment and recording gear. He was cordial, shook our hands, introduced us to his wife Mary, and told us to have a seat on the couch. There were a couple guys with guitars hanging out, tuning up, and adjusting tones on a couple of small guitar amps. Soon they were joined by more people – a bass player, drummer, keyboardist, a sax player, and two female vocalists. I observed silently and patiently as they set up for a rehearsal in Jim Daley's living room; it seemed they weren't a band, although a couple of them apparently knew each other and may have worked together before, it was obvious this group had been assembled for this particular session.

Once everyone was tuned up and dialed in, Jim began to explain to them his vision for the song. It started with instructions to the drummer on what kind of backbeat he wanted – a laid back Latin funk groove with a deep sensuous pocket. Once the drummer had the feel Jim wanted, he turned to the guitarists and started describing the chord progression in musical terms like "arpeggio," "7th," "major," "minor," "staccato," "whole note," "rest," "dotted eighth notes" and so on – there was no sheet music, and Daley never picked up an instrument to show them anything, it was strictly verbal instruction. They started jamming, and he would cue the sax player for fills, sing the melody for the chick singers, use hand signals for transitions, pauses and crescendos. All the while, he totally ignored Josh and I on the couch as if we weren't even there.

For a young musician getting to observe this process, it was something akin to watching Michelangelo paint, as this guy literally composed and produced a masterpiece of a song right before my eyes and ears. Once they had the pieces in place, they rehearsed it relentlessly until it was tightened to perfection. It was clear from their conversations that he was planning on taking them into the studio the next day to cut a master recording of the song. It's been decades but I can still remember every chord, every word, because as Jim Daley was teaching those session musicians he was teaching that song to me too. It was called "Do You Love Me" (no relation to the KISS classic of the same name).

After about five hours, the rehearsal wound down, everyone packed up their instruments, said their goodbyes, and made arrangements to meet at the recording studio the next day. When they were all gone, Daley finally turned and for the first time since our arrival acknowledged our presence.

"I'm really sorry, guys," he said. "I'd like to hear your song, but it's been a long day, and right now I'd just like to spend some time with my wife. Thanks for coming over. I'll be in touch."

I was so blown away by what I'd witnessed that day, I didn't even mind getting brushed off like that. I grabbed my guitar and we left, and I felt like the Scarecrow getting a peek behind the Wizard's curtain. That was the first of many lessons I would learn from Jim Daley.

One day I was cleaning up the crib, trying to make the most of my small and lonely sanctuary. I remember finding a dime in the cushions of the fold out couch that was my bed, and walking through the cold to a local convenience store where I had seen these little sample bags of potato chips on sale for ten cents. Josh and I were both starving, and we took that bag of chips and split it between the two of us – literally "one for you, one for me," – and that was our meal for the day. We took to picking grapefruit from a neighbor's tree and eating them even though I hate grapefruit.

In the midst of this depressing time came a call out of the blue from Jim Daley.

"How would you like to do an album with me?" he asked.

Maria's parents went out of town for the four day Thanksgiving weekend, and she managed to concoct an excuse to stay home alone with the intention that we could spend some quality time together. Due to her devout religious convictions and my deep respect for her, there was no sex involved, just the intense passion and affection that comes from two teenagers sharing first love. She would cook for me – we had spaghetti for Thanksgiving dinner – and we made a bed of blankets and pillows in the middle of the living room floor where we watched TV, cuddled and talked, kissed and touched, and I got horny as hell but never crossed the line.

The backyard was dirt and rock, with an empty swimming pool where lived a big Gila Monster, the poisonous red-and-white speckled reptiles indigenous to the region. That Friday evening, the day after Thanksgiving, we sat outside and watched the striking November sun set behind the tall block wall that enclosed the yard. It was to be our last sunset together.

A little after midnight, we were cuddled up on our makeshift floor bed watching a particularly raucous episode of "The Midnight Special" that featured Aerosmith and Ted Nugent, when headlights pulled into the driveway. A look of panic came over Maria's face as we realized her parents had come home early.

"He'll kill you!" she cried. "Get out of here!"

I was wearing pants but no shirt and socks, and I scrambled to round up those items Maria's mother, father, and sister were walking to the door. There would not be time to sneak out the sliding glass patio door into the backyard; my only recourse was down the hall to her bedroom, the last door on the left, and hide behind the door.

Breathless, I heard her father's voice coming down the hall, and I knew he would show no mercy to a guy with no shirt hiding in his sixteen year-old daughter's bedroom.

"Come out from there with your hands where I can see them."

He was right on the other side of the door. I did as ordered, coming face to face with his .45 pistol leveled at my chest. I fully expected him to pull the trigger, and Maria's crying and pleading were probably all that kept him from it, but he led me into the kitchen at gunpoint and motioned for me to sit at the table while he called the cops.

We assured him that nothing had happened – that we were in love, and that we had never had sex, which was all the truth – but of course, he'd been seventeen once and didn't believe it for a minute. I was a few months shy of eighteen, which saved me from a statutory rape charge – such a charge would have been dropped anyway after subsequent tests they forced her into confirmed Maria was still a virgin. A lone Mesa police officer escorted me out of the neighborhood, and I was left with no option but to hitchhike back to Phoenix in the middle of the night.

Maria's punishment was a pile of dirt in the front yard, which the asshole forced her to shovel from one side of the yard to the other and back and forth, every day after school. She was not allowed to see me again, although I went to visit her school during lunch hour a few times after that. She began to complain of terrible headaches, and her family refused to take her to the doctor. She never lost her faith or her smile, and I was determined that nothing would come between our love, but she ended it because I would not consider converting to her religion. I was devastated. And I didn't get over that one for a long time.

Meanwhile, my musical development under Jim Daley's tutelage had been explosive, to say the least. He was writing and recording a progressive pop concept album, a space opera like "Major Tom" on steroids. The popularity of new movies like "Star Wars" and TV shows like "Battlestar Galactica" encouraged the project's direction, and my love of sci-fi and my off-the-wall playing style were well suited to the strange mix of songs Jim was composing. It was an amazing creative process, and no style of music was out of bounds as we orchestrated songs which would weave in and out of each other with intensely complicated transitions, and Jim's faith in me and appreciation of my enthusiasm was mirrored by my desire for recording experience, knowledge, and a chance to go into a real recording studio and make records.

He embraced the role of mentor, and proved to be an incredible coach. He kept a big bucket of marijuana at the house, and he would use it as motivation for me. He would assign me homework and reward me with dope: three ZZ Top songs was worth a joint, while one Al Dimeola guitar solo would net me three fat ones. I was an avid student, and enjoyed these challenges like a dog at obedience school.

Around this time, my sister's marriage to Dennis hit the skids and they split up, officially ending my stay in their guest house. Sherleen and I planned to share an apartment, but when that didn't work out Jim Daley took me in at his place and I ended up sleeping on that same couch where a few short months before I had first witnessed his magical production skills. I spent Christmas of 1978 there. He made me get a "real job" – my first, other than helping my Dad or my brother-in-law on a construction site – at the local car wash. For ten hours spent soaking wet out in the cold, I would be rewarded with a twenty dollar bill, and go home and work on music all evening.

Jim always had something in the works. He would take me in the studio to do jingles for Mexican radio; we actually did a version of "Do You Love Me" in Spanish. He really liked that I could play bass and drums as well as guitar, and would use me as his entire band for these sessions because it was cheaper than hiring professional musicians. He had me doing all kinds of recordings that winter, thrusting Spanish lyric sheets in my face and coaching me on pronunciation although I had no idea what the hell I was singing about. It was an incredible experience. Jim believed in me and assured me that I was going to be a star one day, and I became his musical conduit – he was a brilliant composer and producer who could not play an instrument, so I translated his ideas into songs and we made an amazing team.

I loved the rehearsals, the songwriting and composing, learning how to be a producer and do sessions, but I was really itching to get back on stage, back into a band situation. I convinced Jim to put a band together with me, and we started working with a drummer named Mike Polvani, bassist Beaver Brown, and guitarist Dan Deihl. We recorded an album's worth of material at a really nice studio called Desert Sound; Jim sang lead vocals on his tunes, and let me sing lead vocals on four of my songs. Jim started to hint that we should set our sights on L.A., painting Southern California as a land of opportunity and if you wanted to succeed in the music business, a move to Los Angeles was the way to go. This would resonate within me for a couple of years until I actually did make the pilgrimage from Nashville to L.A. with Steeler in 1981.

I had to drag Jim kicking and screaming onto any kind of stage; even though he had the music in his heart and soul, he had no taste for performing live and this is where we started to drift apart. It wasn't enough for me just to be a musician, I had to be a rock star and I had to get my ass back on stage. Jim and I did a couple of gigs where you were required to include *disco* music in your repertoire – yes, I must admit it, disco was yet another musical style that I have 'experienced;" although I never liked it, it was easy money for a guitarist: just mute the strings with your left hand and go chunka-chunka waka-waka while working the wah-wah pedal.

As I learned more about the business side of things, I realized that it was going to take money to make money to finance my career – equipment, supplies, recordings, photos and presentations, clothes, beer. So when my father called and offered me a summer job back in Texas, laying 2000 square feet of ceramic tile in the newly built high school where I had spent my Junior year, Josh and I packed up the Chevy and went back to Mt. Pleasant.

It was ball busting work but the pay was great. We mixed 27 tons of concrete by hand that summer, hauled it in there one wheelbarrow at a time, and Roy and I laid the hell out of some 6"x6" Italian tile. I was using a rack which held 12 pieces of tile at a time, and making a buck a foot for every foot I laid, so I'd spread the thin set (tile adhesive), put the rack down, and lay one tile, two, three, four, and say "Dollar." One, two, three, four, "Dollar." I was literally racking up the bucks, listening to Journey and Ted Nugent on the boom box. We'd start drinking early and work until we felt we'd done a day's worth, then head back to my parent's house seven miles out in the country. I had keys to the job site, so after dinner, I'd head back there with my guitar and my amp and some more beer, to write songs and sing and play. The acoustics were amazing, just like an arena, and I would rock out alone, eyes closed, and pretend I was in a sold out coliseum.

Rockabilly legend Burton Harris had a recording studio in Mt. Pleasant, just a four track reel-to-reel but he had a couple of soundproof rooms and a drum set. I took some of my pay from the tile job and financed a four-song demo there; I played drums, guitar, bass, and sang. It was really primitive and sloppy, but it was *mine*. One of the songs I cut was the ballad that had led me to Jim Daley, "I Never Told You."

I got ahold of a Dallas phone book, and on impulse I looked up "Record Companies." I felt that at 17 I'd paid my dues and was ready for a record deal, and I got excited to see "Capital Records" and other labels listed in the phone book, so I started calling them.

"Hello, my name is Ron Keel – I'm a musician and a singer, and I'd like to set up a meeting with the person in charge of record deals."

"I'm sorry, we don't have A&R staff here, this is a distribution center where we stock and ship albums to the record stores. You'll need to go to New York or Los Angeles for that."

Undeterred, I kept going down the list, racking up a long distance phone bill on my parent's tab. Different record company, same answer. Finally I got to the "M's" and called MCA Records.

"Hello, my name is Ron Keel – I'm a musician and a singer, and I'd like to set up a meeting with the person in charge of record deals."

"Hold please." They put me on hold?

"Hello, this is Brad Hunt."

"Hello, my name is Ron Keel – I'm a musician and a singer, and I'd like to set up a meeting with the person in charge of record deals."

"That sounds great; you want to come in Thursday at four o'clock?"

The next day I went and bought myself a brown sport coat and matching jeans, a nice new pair of boots, had some color 8x10's made of some live photos, and typed up a document of introduction. I made some extra copies of my demo on cassette with nice printed labels. And Thursday I drove the 118 miles to Dallas, and walked into MCA Records to make my pitch.

Brad Hunt had a nice office, he seemed important, and he was really cordial to me. He popped my tape into the player and listened to it.

"Who's in your band?" he asked.

"I don't have a band, I played all the instruments on this stuff."

"Are these your songs?" I told him that I had written those songs myself. He looked through my portfolio with the beautiful color 8x10 photos and the document of introduction, and he looked up at me and furrowed his brow, and asked "How old are you?" I told him I was 17.

When the music stopped, he said, "Look, kid. This is just a distribution facility, where we stock and ship albums to record stores. I can't help you.

"But I believe you're going to be a star someday, and I know somebody who *can* help you." He dialed the phone. "Hello, Leon?" He was calling Leon Tsilis, an A&R man at MCA Records in Nashville. "Yeah, Brad Hunt at the Dallas office. I've got a kid in here right now named Ron Keel who's going to be a big star. Would you meet with him?"

I stood there as he listened for a response, and then he hung up the phone. "He said OK."

And I moved to Nashville.

Of course my sidekick Josh came with me. I cashed out and Roy finished the tile job in Mt. Pleasant without us.

Just outside Jackson, Tennessee, we picked up a long haired hitchhiker who said his name was Captain Trip. And he was. He was a roving pharmacy with an arsenal of illegal drugs, one of which was called Hash Oil – liquid hashish, which when spread on a rolling paper would turn the shittiest weed into a euphoric experience and we rolled into Nashville stoned out of our minds.

We ended up in Printer's Alley, at a bar with a Chinese Elvis impersonator, drank ourselves stupid, picked up some women and found a cheap hotel. In the morning, Captain Trip talked me into buying a bunch of vials of his Hash Oil and went on his way.

I went to a rental service to find an apartment, and ended up renting a room in a house on Music Row, 17th Avenue South. This Slumlord catered to musicians who had come to Nashville to pursue their dreams; some of the spaces were little more than plywood cubby holes where you could climb in and sleep, each floor had a shared bathroom, and you could choose your accommodations to fit your budget. Since I had some money saved from the Texas job, I paid for a few months up front in an upstairs apartment with a view of Music Row – it was inspiring to look out the window and see the signs of the various record companies, publishing companies, and recording studios.

Leon Tsilis, the MCA rep whom I'd gone there to meet, ran me around the tree a few times before finally passing on me because I was "too primal." It was the first time I'd been passed on, but of course it wouldn't be the last, and I looked out at the lights of Nashville and believed that my big break was just on the other side of one of those doors, so I stayed. Seven years later MCA Records ended up putting a few million dollars into my band KEEL, and I ran into Leon backstage a couple times in the Hollywood years.

We did a lot of drugs then, maybe more than I did in later years as a rock star. I'd barter Hash Oil for pills on the streets, and sometimes we'd sit around the table with a baggie full of different pills and just eat them, not even knowing what we were taking. I would jam and write with the other singers and songwriters in the adjacent houses, and I started making the rounds on the street trying to meet people in the business.

A guy named Chuck Chellman at a publishing house called Adventure Music gave me my first publishing contract – he really believed in me, but nothing ever came of it. I was in uncharted territory, not knowing how to get where I wanted to go; I became a recluse in that apartment, with the guitar and the drugs and Josh. The money started to run out, and I took to selling Hash Oil in Centennial Park. I guess I should have added "drug dealer" to my history in the introduction of this book.

The only two places I went during that period were the Idle Hour, a bar on Music Row, and the music store down the street whenever I would need a guitar string. The Chevy broke down and I ended up selling it for next to nothing. I was lost and dying inside, and I know I didn't write any songs worth a shit while living in one of the most inspirational musical locations on the planet. I was still hirting over Maria, and didn't even have the desire to get laid. I just wanted to be high all the time. At some point even my buddy Josh had had enough, caught a Greyhound back to Phoenix and I was on my own.

From time to time I would hang with one of the songwriters who lived next door, his name was Bill and he was a Jimmy Buffet kind of guy, always had a good song and a good attitude. We'd jam and get high, mostly I would play solos over his tunes. He had a 1949 Ford Coupe parked out back which he would tinker with, trying to get it to run. He kind of took me under his wing and treated me like I was somebody.

It was my 18th birthday, and there I sat alone, already burned out and headed for worse, when a knock came at the door. It was Bill, holding up a six pack of Schlitz beer.

"I got the Ford running," he said, grinning from ear to ear. "Let's go for a ride!"

"Naw man, I'm just gonna hang here. Way to go, getting that heap started."

He wouldn't take no for an answer, and eventually I caved in and we hopped in the Coupe with the six pack and headed out on the town. He pulled into the back parking lot of a place called the Silver Dollar Saloon, and we sat there and drank a beer. I told him man, I don't want to go in there. My clothes were pretty ragged, and I was dog-ass broke, without a dollar to my name by this point and rent was due. He was cool, didn't pressure me, so we had another beer in the parking lot. The back door of the bar was open, and I could see people in there partying, shooting pool, playing foosball, drinking, it looked like fun. But I just couldn't do it. Two more, and then the six pack was gone. And still I refused to go into the bar. And he was cool with that too, and went to start the car, but the engine wouldn't turn over.

He kept trying, shaking his head. And there we sat.

A girl walked out the back door, a tough looking chick with blonde hair, leather pants, tight white tank top over a killer rack, tattoos...and as she walked by the car I stuck my head out the window and said, "Got any jumper cables?"

I ended up marrying her a year later, on my 19th birthday.

Her name was Kathy Wolfe. The jumper cables worked. The Ford started up, and then Bill shut it down and said "We're going in." So with my first ex-wife in tow, we entered the Silver Dollar Saloon. There was a guy up in a loft with a wooden railing, playing an acoustic guitar through a little PA system, with a tip jar out front. When he took a break, I introduced myself and asked him if I could play a song or two, if he'd empty out his tip jar and let me sing, and whatever was in the jar when I finished, that would be my drinking money. He emptied out his tip jar, handed me his guitar, and I went up there and sang "Shooting Star" by Bad Company and "Turn The Page" by Bob Seger.

And by God, I'm still drinking.

6

GIMME THAT

Gimme that song that takes me home
Gimme the music – bring it on – gimme that
Take me back where I belong
Give me a reason to carry on – gimme that

Give me a war that I can win
Give me something to believe in – gimme that
Yeah, gimme that

I want a cause worth fighting for
I want a life worth dying for – gimme that
Yeah, gimme that

("Gimme That" – lyrics by RK 2009 – from the KEEL album "Streets Of Rock & Roll" released 2010)

Tabu

At first, Kathy was really good for me. I needed some kind of stability, even if it was unstable; without an anchor I may have drifted away aimlessly into obscurity, or worse. Our relationship was fraught with drugs and violence but it was during that time that I became the Ron Keel everyone first saw and heard in Steeler, and a lot of that was because of Kathy Wolfe.

Because I was in a relationship now, and because I was starving and the rent was due, I got a real job. One of my drug buddies was a waiter at a seafood restaurant called The Sailmaker, and sitting around the kitchen table one day popping pills he told me they were looking for a dishwasher. He took me in the back door and introduced me to the kitchen manager, a tall white guy a few years older than me named Sid. "Put this on," ordered Sid as he handed me an apron an immediately led me to the Hobart. Apparently I was hired.

The Hobart was a huge $30,000.00 stainless steel mechanical "U"-shaped cockpit. Large surface area on the left where the busboys would pile up plastic tubs of plates, bowls, silverware, glasses, leftover food, whatever the customers left; up above that was a slanted shelf that held the Racks, at waist level all along the left side was a trough in which to dump the food scraps, the trough led into the industrial-size garbage disposal, then in the center of the "U" were the sinks, and on the right was the Hobart dishwashing machine, which grabbed the racks of dirty dishes and sent them through the wash and rinse much like a miniature car wash.

The Sailmaker served about 2000 meals per day and I got hired in the middle of a rush – my predecessor had walked out earlier in the day and I was in the right place at the right time. There was a mountain of bus pans piled high, the entire dishwashing station was a filthy disaster area of food and crap, and as I tied my apron Sid gave me a crash course in how to operate the Hobart. Pull a Rack, set it in the staging area, scrape the food off the plates into the trough and then into the garbage disposal. To save time, this was all done without utensils; I scraped the plates with my fingers, and used my hands to feed the scraps into the garbage disposal. He showed me how to regulate the temperature, where to put the soap into the machine. When the dishes came out the other end you had to inspect them all to make sure they were clean; it was never good when our high-end customers found a piece of dried chicken on the rim of their drinking glass. Once you determined they were clean, then you stacked them up stocked them where they belonged, glasses here, plates there, salad plates in the freezer. By the time I got back to the Hobart the mountain of dishes would have piled up and I'd start all over again.

The job was literally the absolute bottom of the food chain, for which I was paid the minimum wage of $2.65 per hour before taxes. I soon found out that nobody lasted long at that position; they either couldn't handle it or they got promoted to Salad Prep which was the next step up – the crown jewel of the Sailmaker dining room was a huge boat-shaped salad bar with masts and sails and

21 items which had to be prepared and maintained adhering to a rigid set of standards.

The dishwasher's job appealed to me because I was in my own world manning the Hobart; far away from the customers, and isolated from the rest of the kitchen staff, the only people I had to deal with were the bus boys who brought the tubs of dirty dishes and the waitresses and waiters who brought dishes when the bus boys got backed up. But the coolest thing about it was, the Hobart was so damn loud I could sing all day and they could barely hear me over the roar of that dishwasher. So I would sing, and wash the fuck out of thousands of dishes, and when I'd get caught up I'd clean up the entire area, get the stainless steel all shiny, and then I'd go outside for a smoke break. Behind the dumpster for a few hits off a joint, then a cigarette, and by the time I got back into the kitchen the tubs full of dirty dishes would be piled high again.

It was a two mile walk down West End from home to work each day. It was tough work, long days, and I ended up with about 90 bucks for a 40 hour week. I'd sometimes pull a double, doing the day shift and the night shift. Pretty soon I was learning the other kitchen positions, and then the minimum wage went up to $3.10 an hour, and I made Sid an offer to do both dishes and salad prep, which was really two full time jobs, for a solid $5.00 an hour. I would chop lettuce and veggies and prep the 21 salad items, make coleslaw, keep fresh stock of hundreds of pounds of salad stuff that lived in the adjacent fridge in ten gallon bins, and then when the dishes piled up I'd return to the Hobart and knock those out. Because I had long hair, they made me wear a ball cap for a while, and then a hair net which I hated and refused to wear most of the time unless the health inspectors popped in. I remember one day during a surprise inspection I got caught with nothing on my head and Sid had to fire me in front of the health inspector; I threw down my apron, went to the theater next door and saw "Star Wars: The Empire Strikes Back" and when the movie was over I went back to the kitchen, put my apron back on, and went back to work.

Kathy was a living contradiction. A few years older than me, she was a thoroughbred race horse trainer and English-style rider, a profession that demanded total discipline and focus and she was very good at what she did. I would go with her sometimes and watch in amazement as she controlled those massive temperamental beasts around a complex course, jumping fences and streams. She was also admirably disciplined in her drug use; pot only on week nights after work, saving the hard stuff for the weekends. After work on Friday she would decide upon our drug or combination of drugs for the weekend, contact whatever dealer specialized in that drug of choice, and we would go shopping. One weekend it would be this stuff called "Crystal T" which when snorted would make you deathly sick crawling on the floor; sometimes it was LSD, other times mushrooms and Quaaludes. For twenty bucks we could zonk out for the entire weekend and be back to work on Monday morning. She had a marijuana leaf tattoo on her breastbone right between her tits which she had to cover with a flower when we got married.

She also had a very sweet and cute side, playful and childlike, in stark contradiction to her angry violent alter-ego. She wasn't just violent with me, she was hell bent on self-destruction as well; she had been incarcerated in a number of mental institutions for multiple suicide attempts. And she was no sissy chick looking for attention, taking a few sleeping pills and crying out for help - she really wanted to die a painful death. The insides of her forearms were brutally scarred from palms to elbows from slashing her wrists multiple times with razor blades.

I think we'd only been dating a week when she first bared her fangs; it was Friday after work and her drug of choice was not available, so I suggested we just do some different drugs, and she turned quickly with evil in her eye and yelled "Don't you start any shit with me!" I was startled and maybe should have walked away, but I took it like a man and didn't say a damn thing. I really did care about her, and we were both outcasts and misfits together against society. But she would fly into a violent rage at the drop of a hat, and I would be on the receiving end of another verbal, and sometimes physical, tirade.

There was a little corner music store down on Music Row back then, and whenever I broke a string on my guitar I would walk down there and buy a replacement. It was too expensive to buy a whole set of strings, so I would dump a handful of change on the glass counter and ask Art Beard for an "E" or a "G" or whatever string I needed.

Art is another in the long list of guys that worked at a music store that really helped me out along my journey. One day I went in for a string, and he mentioned that he was quitting his band that night, they were going to need a new guitarist, and would I be interested in auditioning. He even offered to drive me there.

I had not been in a band or on a stage in a year. Kathy encouraged me to give it a go; she made me dress up (leather jacket, jeans, black boots and a silver 70's scarf around my neck, big hoop earring) and did my hair, and I rode out to Kriss Shelby's house that evening with Art Beard and a fresh "D" string on my guitar.

Kriss "Famous" Shelby was (and still is) a tall, talented, good looking black man; there were a couple of other black guys in the band, Kevin, the organ player who was the musical director, and "Little" Bill on bass; a handsome well-built white dude named "Big" Bill Reece sat behind the drums. I still hear from Kriss and Bill every now and then, and Art Beard too. Actually, I hear from Kevin every now and then too, but that story is a few pages ahead.

Kriss' living room was set up for band rehearsal, amps on either side of the drum set and Kevin sitting behind a big Hammond B3 organ. There was an awkward moment while Art quit the band and introduced me, asking them to give me a chance. These guys, Art Beard and Kriss and Big Bill, they are still playing around Nashville separately and together, and last I heard Art was still quitting the band.

My audition consisted of fumbling through a few of their originals, many of which were a cross between Pink Floyd and Motown. I loved the way they sounded, they were all great players and singers, and just auditioning made me realize how much I missed being in a *band*. After a few tunes, Kriss left me in the living room while the guys went into a bedroom to discuss my fate. While the other fellows weren't sure if I could cut it, it was Kevin who stood up for me and convinced them I had 'it' and his endorsement got me the gig.

We called the band Tabu, and for the next nine months we created music without prejudice or boundaries. It was all-original music, although sometimes we'd jam a cover tune for fun, and anything that anyone wrote was embraced, accepted, learned and played. Everything from Kevin's ethereal keyboard masterpieces ("Wizard Of Oz") to commercial pop-rock ("Baby You Know") to soul-flavored vocal tunes ("The Heat"), and man could those three black guys sing. They taught me so much about singing, and about blending harmonies.

Kriss had a master plan for the band which didn't include playing local gigs, so we just wrote songs and rehearsed in his living room through the long cold winter of '79-'80. We went into the studio and recorded a seven-song demo which I have always thought was a very strong collection of songs that never got released.

After a while it became obvious that if I broke up with Kathy she would either kill herself, kill me, or both. So I left the place on Music Row behind and we moved into an apartment together.

It was a closer walk to work for me, and we had two bedrooms, which meant I could use the spare room for music - plenty of room for my one guitar, a little amplifier, a tape recorder and a notebook.

So when the 70's ended and the 80's began, I was in Nashville, washing dishes at the Sailmaker, smoking a lot of pot, living with Kathy Wolfe in a two-bedroom apartment on White Bridge Road, doing a lot of drugs on the weekends, and playing in a punk-funk-rock band called Tabu.

Kathy and I were also avid concert-goers, always managing to sock $13 away for a pair of tickets to see the shows at Nashville Municipal Auditorium. The average ticket price for an arena show then was $7.50; some (Blue Oyster Cult) were a buck cheaper, some (Heart) were a buck more. I'm sure at that time in L.A. people were starting to dress up all rock & roll to go to concerts, but in Nashville I was one of the very few guys who was decking out in leather and scarves, poofing up my hair, and wearing gaudy cheap jewelry. Plus Kathy was a striking site with her blonde hair streaked with black, all tattoos and leather. So we got a lot of attention in the beer line at Nashville Municipal Auditorium, people would come up and ask if I was in a band, and where was I playing. I actually hadn't been on stage since before I left Phoenix the year before, and going to those concerts made me insatiably hungry to gig, so I started pressuring Kriss and the band to get out of his living room and onto the stage.

Tabu was rehearsing during an early February snowstorm, one of those nights when not everybody could even get there because of the road conditions, so it turned into a jam session. During "Funk 49" by the James Gang Kevin started missing notes – and Kevin *never* missed a note. He got this blank look in his eyes, swayed a little bit, and then planted his face on the keys of his B3 organ and played his last chord.

Little Bill, who was a paramedic by trade, tried to save him but he was dead on the spot at the age of 23. I heard he suffered a simultaneous cerebral hemorrhage and heart attack brought on by a hereditary disease no one knew he had. A sweet and beautiful man and musician who was just getting started, a musical genius that had fought for me to be in the band, gone just like that. Though it was a painful shock at the time, Kevin taught me one of the greatest lessons of my life that night:

This might be your last song. Play it like you mean it. A blessing and a curse, that lesson: I've never been able to not give it my all whenever I'm playing or singing, no matter what the situation. I see so many people in my business just hacking through a gig, mailing it in to collect a paycheck, and I think about Kevin and that winter night and how he died in a living room in front of half a dozen people but he was playing his ass off like that song was the most important thing in the world.

Kevin's death fucked me up pretty good; whenever something like that happens you have to rethink your own life and situation. I thought the band was finished before we had ever done our first show, and my relationship with Kathy had gotten more and more difficult after we moved in together. There were fights because we were on drugs – and there were fights because we weren't on drugs. The violence escalated, and she was a tough and powerful woman from having to control spirited thoroughbreds that weighed in excess of 1000 pounds – so when she fought, she fought like a man. I never hit her back; I would just take the pounding and get through it. I'd walk into work at the restaurant the next morning with a black eye and a split lip, and the guys in the kitchen would ask what happened. I'd make up a story about getting in a bar fight the night before and laugh it off. "You shoulda seen the other guy."

She was insanely jealous. I only cheated on her once (the night before we got married), but she thought I was nailing every waitress at work. The only thing I was nailing at work were as many Tequila Sunrises as possible after my shift, to cushion the blow of going home to her each night. And while she encouraged my music she would also throw a tantrum when I went into the spare room with the guitar and try to write a song. I'd be in there trying to hammer out a couple of riffs and she would yell "Put that God damn thing down and get your ass in here!"

So I'd had enough. A couple of days after Kevin died, as soon as she left for work I quickly packed up what little I had, called a cab, hopped on a Greyhound bus and I was back in Texas the next day.

I didn't have a plan; I just wanted to get the hell out of there, away from that woman and away from that restaurant, out of that town. It wouldn't be the last time Nashville chewed me up and spit me out, and it wouldn't be the last woman I ran out on. What really hurt was missing Kevin's funeral. I called Kriss to let him know what I'd done and where I was, and he understood. We talked a couple of times over the next few days. "You know," he said, "Kevin would have wanted us to keep going." He said he'd found another keyboard player and asked me to come back. So within a week I was back in Music City, back in that abusive relationship, back in that kitchen making $5.00 an hour, and there was a new guy in rehearsal behind that same Hammond B3 organ where Kevin had taken his last breath.

Kathy and I were married a month later, on March 25th 1980 – my 19th birthday.

Kriss had been telling me about a lady friend of his who had seen the black and white Tabu promo photo and she'd made in clear that she wanted an intimate experience with the tall white boy who played guitar. I'd never been with a black girl, and I was hungry for the soft touch of a stranger before marrying a woman with a strong right hook. The only time and reason I could ever be out anywhere without Kathy was the night before the wedding, when tradition says you're not supposed to sleep together. Kathy was to spend the night at her parents' house, so I had Kriss arrange a rendezvous between his friend and I.

He even drove me to her house. What a true friend.

She was beautiful, a dark skinned goddess, very intelligent and soft spoken. Her house – and her bed - were warm and comfortable. We talked, we had some wine, we made love in the candlelight. It was one of the most romantic experiences of my life, in sheer contrast to the life I was living outside her door. I never really understood why I even walked out that door, and back into that life and down the aisle the next day – I guess it was the path I had to follow to get where I am today, and now all these years later I'm OK with that.

It was a small church ceremony with a half-dozen people, Kathy's parents, her two brothers, and my Dad drove out from Texas to be there. Mom refused to attend. And the preacher made six. Kathy used a flower to cover the marijuana leaf tattoo between her breasts. The only thing else I remember was thinking "What the hell am I doing, and how am I going to get out of it."

Tabu finally made it out of Kriss' living room and onto a stage, for one night only, at a club called Flanigan's at 100 Oaks Mall. I remember my stage wardrobe was a striped multi-colored bathrobe cut off at the hips and tied with a scarf. It was really comfortable, but I'm glad that was before YouTube and camera phones. The world was a much safer place back then.

7

SPEED DEMON

Can you feel the thunder – see the white line shake
Feel the heat of my motor – is it too much to take
Ain't got no caution – got no emergency brake
No time to slow down, 'cause there's too much at stake

I'm a speed demon – running from another day
Hear the highway screaming to take me away

("Speed Demon" – original lyrics by RK 1980 – from the
"Homegrown" album featuring Lust released 1981)

Lust – Battle Of The Bands – Nashville 1980

On September 14th, 1980, Kathy and I were at a Rush concert at Nashville Municipal auditorium. Opening act Saxon had made a strong impression on me; I had never heard of them but loved their power and simplicity. I was in the lobby, all decked out in my dime store rock star gear, leaning up against a pillar having a smoke, when three long haired guys came up to me and asked me if I was a rock singer.

"Yeah man," I replied. "I am."

They introduced themselves, Keith Maxwell, Mike Easley, and Tim Morrison. "We have a band called Lust, and we're looking for a singer. Can we get your number?" I gave it to them, and went back inside to see Rush.

We had a little clock radio by the bed and it was always tuned to KDF, the local rock station. We'd wake up every morning to the pop hits of the day, and listen at night while we were getting high or having sex. On Sunday nights they had a show that featured local bands, and they were having some kind of Battle of the Bands competition and I was lying in bed listening when these massive power chords came crashing through the tiny speaker. The DJ announced the name of the band – Lust – and the name of the song – "Hooker." It was a great riff, like a cross between Judas Priest and AC/DC, the players and the recording sounded awesome, and I was thinking, is this those guys I met at the Rush concert? The DJ encouraged people to call in and vote for their favorite band – the bands with the most votes would move on to the next phase of the competition, which was a live gig in front of music industry judges - and I called and put my vote in for Lust.

I came home from the restaurant the next day stinking like leftover seafood and the phone was ringing.

"Hey man, it's Keith Maxwell, from Lust, we met at the Rush concert."

"Hey! Was that you guys I heard on the radio last night? That was great, man."

"Yeah, that was us – listen, we made it into the top 10 and we have to perform on stage next Sunday night for the finals, and we need a lead singer, are you interested?"

I asked him what happened to the singer who did the "Hooker" session, and he explained that their drummer, Mike Easley, had sung on the track. They had been together for two years but had never found a frontman, had never done a gig, and now they had six days before the live band competition.

I turned them down. I'm not sure what I was thinking or how I rationalized it – I had never sung that heavy stuff and really didn't know how, I didn't think I could be ready in such a short amount of time, the only gig I'd done in the past year and a half was with Tabu in a makeshift bathrobe, so I thanked him and passed.

He called back on Tuesday to work on me some more. "Come on man, we really need a lead singer and you look like a rock star." I thanked him again and passed. And that night Kathy started working on me, telling me I should give it a try, what the hell did I have to lose, I was a dishwasher in a seafood restaurant, this could be my big break.

On Wednesday, Keith called back again, asking me if I'd given it any more thought, he said they were holding auditions that night and wanted to make sure I wasn't interested.

"I'll be there," I told him.

They were rehearsing in a school auditorium in the middle of the woods way out in Murfreesboro. I washed the stink off of me, Kathy dressed me up in tight pants, boots, a flowing white shirt, scarves, earrings, did my hair, and we spent the next couple of hours driving through the woods looking for some damn school. No GPS back then, kids. I was getting angry and frustrated and I was already over an hour late for my audition when we finally pulled up to the place and heard the loud music coming from within.

I looked through the round Plexiglas window on the auditorium door, and saw the band on stage, and some good looking guy singing with them, and he sounded really good. I turned to Kathy. "I'm too late. They already got somebody, let's get the fuck out of here."

"Just go in there, God damnit, we drove all this way out here, you have to at least let them know you're here and why we're late." She literally opened the door and shoved me in.

We grabbed a couple of folding chairs and joined a small group of their friends who were hanging out watching. They looked down at me from the stage and raised their eyebrows, and glanced at each other. The lead singer looked up from the lyric sheet he was holding and saw me.

When the song ended, they said hello, and I told them we got lost trying to find the place. Keith told me they'd made their decision, and this guy was going to be their singer, and I said that's cool, you guys sound great, mind if we just hang out and watch. That's when the bass player, Tim Morrison, spoke up.

"Look at this guy, we gotta at least check him out!" And after a little debate between them, they invited me on stage. The singer left the microphone on the stand for me and handed me the lyric sheet. I knew I couldn't out-sing him, my only chance was to out "rock star" him, so I read through the lyrics as the band kicked into that "Hooker" tune, then I wadded up the lyric sheet and threw it down onto the stage, I assumed my best rock star stance and started flailing the microphone stand around and screaming loud angry shit that vaguely resembled the lyrics. I was strutting around, putting on a show, interacting with the guys in the band, and playing it like I was on stage at the Garden. When the song was over, they apologized to the other dude and gave me the gig.

That Sunday night I was back on stage at Flanigan's, where just a few months ago I had done the lone Tabu gig, but this was a whole different animal – now, I was fronting a HEAVY METAL band. Dressed in black spandex, leather jacket and boots, blonde streak in my hair, and whatever bling I could muster, I walked out onto the dark stage and could see the place was nuts to butts, packed to the gills. As soon as the band launched into the first power chords of "Hooker" I grabbed the mic stand with a vengeance and screamed, and for the first time in my life I experienced the unbelievable thrill of seeing an audience with their fists in the air, banging their heads, going wild over the music. None of the other bands had gotten that reaction, and we didn't even have a following – this was just the first gig. It was the power of the music, Heavy Metal was the voice of that generation, and it was 1980, and that night in Nashville Lust delivered a blistering 20 minute set that left the judges no choice but to award us First Place in the KDF Homegrown Battle Of The Bands competition.

Suddenly we were in the studio cutting two songs which would appear on the "Homegrown" album, a compilation of the top five bands, and since we'd won first place our songs would be the first tracks on each side of the vinyl. We were cutting "Hooker" and the first version of "Speed Demon," which was nothing like the version I would write and record with KEEL four years later – the only similarity was the title and basic theme about driving too fast.

I was so nervous and freaked out about having to sing in the studio that I actually made myself sick, puking and running a high fever. I'd been in the band for less than a week, I had gotten this far just on sheer charisma and attitude, and I was nowhere near ready to enter the studio and lay down two master vocals.

The guys recorded the music and then it was my turn to sing. They dimmed the lights in the recording room for vibe, and I put on the headphones and went up to the microphone. The whole band, and the producer and engineers were all in the control staring at me. And I choked. Everything that came out of my mouth sounded like shit, and the producer made me more and more uncomfortable with stupid motivational tactics like, "Try to imagine there's a hot chick bent over in front of you, and you're banging the hell out of her and singing at the same time." It didn't work.

We left the studio and went back to our real lives, washing dishes and making pizzas, and I made lame excuses for my shitty vocals by saying I was sick, I'd only been in the band for a week, the producer was a jerk. The guys in Lust all worked at the Pillsbury pizza factory in Murfreesboro, and I remember moving our rehearsals from the school auditorium to a double wide trailer. These guys had Marshall amps, and I bought this little Peavey PA system to sing through, but the guitars and drums were so loud that you couldn't hear me. After my dismal performance in the recording studio, it's probably a good thing they couldn't hear me or they might have realized I didn't know how to sing and kicked me out of the band immediately. But I thought I could sing, and I really wanted to be heard, so I started screaming these piercing high notes, mimicking Rob Halford from Judas Priest at the end of "Victim Of Changes," and those notes would cut through. That double wide trailer in Murfreesboro, Tennessee was where I developed that high screaming style that would be my trademark for rest of my career.

All the encouragement Kathy had been giving me evaporated now that I was in a band that demanded pretty much all of my time when I wasn't working the day job. I'd get off work, take a shower, drive to Murfreesboro to scream in the trailer for hours, and come home late. And I was driving her car because I didn't have one. So she got increasingly pissed off and belligerent, and the angrier she got, the later I'd come home because I didn't want to hear it.

One day I turned on the little radio that we had beside the bed and did a double take. The voice coming through the speaker was mine – the song was "Hooker." My excitement suffered a quick and painful death when I realized how terrible my voice sounded, and what should have been a moment of triumph – my very first time on the radio – turned to disappointment when I realized the whole town was listening. "Hooker" turned out to be a huge hit on local radio; it seemed that every time cranked up the car, there it was – the clock radio alarm would go off and there would be my out of tune groaning voice. I used it as a motivating factor and swore to myself that the next time I went into the studio, I'd be ready. I dedicated myself to becoming a great singer, and stopped playing guitar completely the entire time I was in Lust to focus on developing my voice. AC/DC's "Back In Black" had come out the previous summer and had a profound impact on all of us, especially me. I loved Brian Johnson's raspy tone and started to try to incorporate that into my style. I still knew really nothing about singing, it would be a few years before my knowledge and skill caught up with my passion and drive, but I was developing a style which combined elements of my favorite rock singers like Rob Halford, Paul Stanley, Robert Plant, Brian Johnson, and David Lee Roth.

Lust had booked a gig at the Mainstreet Music Emporium in Murfreesboro. I told Kathy that rather than drive home late after rehearsal and then back the next morning for load-in at the club, I was just going to stay the night out there with one of the guys on our crew. I had gotten a ride, leaving her with the car so she could come out to the show the next day. After rehearsal we got some burgers, did some drinking, and I ended up back at my buddy's house with him and his girlfriend. We did some more drinking, and they went to bed and I passed out on the couch.

Mainstreet was the happening club in the band's hometown and we were hot because we were ON THE RADIO, so the place was packed. About halfway through the show, Kathy started glaring at me from the audience with murder in her eyes, so bad that I had to avoid looking at her from the stage, and that just exacerbated her anger, so that as soon as the show was over she stormed up to the front of the stage and started in on me.

"You bastard, I know what you did last night!" she yelled. "I heard that girl in the bathroom talking about how you slept with her! You lying cheating son of a bitch, fuck you, go to hell, I'm leaving you!" This is in front of the entire band and audience; she left me no choice but to say "Go ahead." What she'd overheard in the lady's room was our crew dude's girlfriend making a casual remark about me staying the night the previous evening, and Kathy's jealousy caused her to twist that into a fuck fest. So we split up, and I quit my day job moved into the double wide band trailer.

Since I was broke, I lived off bags of frozen sausage my bandmates smuggled out of the pizza factory. I got pretty tight with our bass player Tim Morrison, who was a good guy, really smart, and a helluva bass player too. We used to sit around in the candlelight playing with the Ouija board, and some pretty crazy things started happening, like noises in the house, stuff getting moved around. There were two spirits that spoke to us through the board, an evil male presence who called himself Zegas and a benevolent female spirit named Jeda. I know I wasn't moving the pointer, and I don't think Tim was either.

I had started hearing about another rock band that was making some noise around Nashville called Sniper and went to check them out at a bar called Cantrell's. I was blown away – these guys were dressed up, rocking out, and putting on a show, whereas in Lust I was the only one doing that. The other guys were pretty much just standing in place on stage, wearing T-shirts and jeans. Lust was like AC/DC without an Angus – Sniper was scarves and animal prints and lots of shiny accessories. The guitar player, Michael Dunigan, was really over the top – he was the first guy in Nashville to have a Floyd Rose tremolo bar and he was working the whammy like Eddie Van Halen. The singer, his name was Bruce something, he was good, probably better than me except I had that high piercing screaming thing going on. There were only two rock bands in the area at that time in the fall of 1980, us and them, and I got to know the guys in Sniper from going to their shows and hanging out at concerts.

On August 5th of that year I was seated next to Bruce – hell, we weren't seated, we were standing on our chairs – at a Van Halen concert. David Lee Roth had taken the rock star frontman persona to an entirely new level with his athleticism, wit, piercing screams, everything. At that time, he was the best that had ever been in my opinion – nobody could scream like that, jump off the drum riser and do the splits in mid-air, prowl the stage and with all that he had the intelligence to craft raps that elicited deafening cheers from everyone from the front row to the cheap seats. To this day, that was probably the best rock concert by a lead singer I've ever witnessed.

Headed to the parking lot after the gig, Bruce and I walked side by side, with a marked contrast in our attitudes. I was inspired – fired up to raise my game to that level. Bruce was beaten. "I'll never get there," he said. "I'm going to quit my band."

"Can I have 'em?" I joked.

I remember being at that Lust trailer the night we heard John Lennon had been shot and killed. The Beatles had changed my life with one song when I was two years old, and I was one of millions that held out hope that someday they'd get back together. You never forget those days when your heroes die; I remember what I having for supper when Skynyrd's plane went down. And I remember the night Lennon died in the winter of 1980. It was just Tim Morrison and I at the trailer, sitting around on the couch, watching the news coverage. It must have triggered something in him.

"They're going to kick you out of the band tomorrow," he said to me. "Ken (Kennedy, guitarist and songwriter) doesn't think you'll ever be able to cut it in the studio." The backlash of hearing my horrible rendition of "Hooker" on the radio all summer had taken its toll. I believed in myself probably to a fault, but I couldn't say that I blamed them. I'd never been kicked out of a band before, and my pride wouldn't let that happen, so I thanked Tim for the heads up and asked him to let them know I quit the band.

Homeless and without a band two weeks before Christmas, I decided to give it another shot with Kathy. We got another apartment together, about a mile away from the previous one, and I got my job back at the restaurant which was now an extra mile's walk from the new place, in the snow. The kitchen grease on the floor would quickly wear holes in my boots, and by the time I got to work my socks were soaked with melted snow. I knew Kathy and I wouldn't last, but I was cold and lonely at Christmas and even with her violent mood swings it was better than being homeless.

I decided I would follow up on my conversation with Bruce and steal his band, which I did. Michael Dunigan, Bobby Eva, Jeff Palmer and I were really the only four guys in Nashville that wanted to dress up, rock out, and put on a show and it was absolutely natural that we'd end up in a band together. I was way too full of myself to join Sniper; I was adamant that we start over, with a new name and new songs. I'm pretty sure it was our sound man Allen Isaacs who suggested the name, which I wasn't sold on until Bobby, who was also an artist, drew up the logo and showed it to me at the next rehearsal, and when I saw that, we had ourselves a band name.

Steeler was born.

8

AMERICAN METAL

Sundown in the city – ten thousand voices screaming loud
A dark arena filled with energy and smoke
This is our music and we're proud

We're the spark – and you're the fire
And nothing's gonna take us higher than American metal

("American Metal" – original lyrics by RK 1981 – unreleased)

Steeler hit the ground running, doing as many shows in our first week (3) as I had done in the entire two years I'd lived in Nashville (3). Our debut was at Cantrell's on February 17th 1981, a cold and blustery Tuesday night. We were hell bent on putting on a SHOW - we'd gotten a sheet of metal and covered it in black tape, and then Bobby meticulously took a razor blade and cut out the band name so it looked like a metal Steeler logo on a black background. We made extra lights out of coffee cans. We carted around this huge 50 gallon barrel contraption that was a smoke machine, and were always hunting for dry ice for it to make the smoke. Jimy Isaacs, our soundman's brother, was in charge of pyro and guitars, in that order. Jimy and Allen had been childhood friends with guitarist Michael Dunigan, and loved rock & roll as much as we did and they were a huge help, learning on the job, putting up with us, believing in us. When Allen started running sound, I think he had two knobs – VOLUME and TONE – and he went on to become a very successful recording engineer and producer in Japan. Jimy learned the stage and went on to work with some of the biggest in the business, including Don Henley and James Taylor.

Jimy had rigged these pyro units on either side at the front of the stage, and each one had three barrels pointing straight up. One was a flash for the opening of the show when we struck into the first chords of "American Metal." I'd written that song in response to the "New Wave Of British Heavy Metal" which was taking the world by storm – Judas Priest, whom I'd loved since "Stained Class" in high school, was now headlining U.S. arenas. Def Leppard's first album had made a huge impression on us because it combined the power of metal with commercial songwriting, and their follow-up "High & Dry" was, in my opinion, the most influential album of 1981 because it proved a commercial hard rock band could have legitimate mainstream success and opened the floodgates for all of us. So "American Metal" was my way of staking our claim in the heavy metal minefield.

The second pyro barrel was for flames. We had a "devil" song called "Hounds of Hell" during which I would raise my hands up and these huge towers of flame would rise up from those barrels. And then then at the end of the show, we would do a reprise of "American Metal," and a deafening concussion bomb would explode out of the third barrel.

The only picture I have of Kathy, my first ex-wife, is from that debut Steeler show. We're on stage rocking out, and she's in the audience, turned around in discussion with Michael's girlfriend. Shortly after, a violent fight got ugly and she put her fist through the glass top on the screen door at our apartment. That was it for me. I decided that being homeless was better than being dead, and I packed up everything that meant anything in a small bag, put the strap on my shoulder, and walked away for good.

And I really was homeless. Sure, sometimes I would crash on a friend's couch, or there was the occasional sympathetic female fan. But there were times when those options weren't available, and I had a place behind a dumpster in a grocery store parking lot that became my home away from homeless – it was great because next door there was a gas station that was out of business but the toilet still worked, so I could take a proper shit every morning, wash my face, brush my teeth. I was still working at the restaurant, but instead of renting an apartment I used what money I could scrape up to file for a divorce.

One morning after a particularly uncomfortable night behind the dumpster, I did my bathroom ritual and headed across the road to the fast food joint to grab a bite. I know I looked like hell, torn up jeans and leather jacket, long hair and big dangly earrings. I walked by a table with three guys sitting there having breakfast, they looked like construction workers. As I was in line ordering, they started making comments about my long hair, whistling at me like I was a girl. I was used to that kind of prejudice and discrimination, but that morning I wasn't in the mood. I walked back by their table on my way out, a bag of fast food in my left hand, flipped them the bird with my right, said "Fuck you," and walked out. I got about ten feet into the parking lot and the biggest loudmouth was at the door, coming after me, talking shit.

I turned around and met him halfway and laid him out with one punch to the left side of his face. His buddies, who had followed him out, looked at me in disbelief and said nothing.

I'm proud to say that's the last time I ever had to punch somebody. I was twenty years old and had had my share of fist fights growing up, but I've never been a violent guy. I'm sure it would have happened during the wild years to come if I hadn't had a posse of road crew always around to drag me away from trouble.

Steeler performed 32 shows all across Tennessee that summer, from a frat party in Cookeville to a big opening slot (for southern rock band Grinderswitch) at the Tennessee Theater, which was where all the mid-level touring bands like UFO were playing. We were starting to get a lot of attention, because we were like an apple tree in a cornfield, there was no other band like us in that part of the country at that time.

Keep in mind, this was in *Nashville*. Four guys in spandex, leather, and animal prints with scarves and gaudy jewelry, running around the stage like madmen doing all this choreographed moves we stole from KISS and Judas Priest, metallic Steeler logo shining in the coffee can lights, smoke pouring over the edge of the stage, bombs going off, Michael jerking the whammy bar like he was trying to kill his guitar, Bobby slamming out thunderous beats on a huge double-bass drum kit, Jeff playing the bass behind his head, and me screaming like somebody was ass-fucking me. In *Nashville* in 1981.

The next step was to hit the studio and record a demo. Inside, I was still vocally reeling from the Lust session and still had no clue how to execute in the studio, and the four song demo we cut for a hundred bucks wasn't much better. But now I had "the scream" to fall back on during songs like "American Metal," and these were songs I'd written or co-written, rehearsed, and sung live. The demo got some play on KDF, on the Homegrown show. No, I don't have a copy, the last cassette tape of that fell through the cracks a long time ago.

A few hours before a headline show in front of thousands at the Cumberland Speedway in Crossville, we were sitting in the hotel parking lot smoking a joint. I was in the passenger seat and realized there was a carful of girls parked on our right, and I recognized the one behind the wheel as Tim Morrison's girlfriend. Her name was Helen. We struck up a conversation, and she came back to the hotel with me after the show.

That gig was one of the coldest of my career – outdoors at the speedway, and I was dressed in spandex pants and a thin vest. You could see my breath when I was singing like I was exhaling smoke, and our fingers were numb, but we were headlining a speedway show and kicking ass, and Helen was there to warm me up afterward. She told me how she'd recently broken up with Tim and I fell for her fast and hard; she was a tall beautiful redhead with a heart of gold, way out of my league, and for some reason she really seemed to like me.

We had a manager, a good looking clean-cut guy named John Chamberlain that had managed Sniper and had come with the package when we rebuilt that band into Steeler. Using him as a reference, I managed to rent an apartment for $119 per month and got off the streets. I couldn't afford furniture, so I used milk crates for chairs and boxes for tables. I pilfered a door from a trash pile and put that on milk crates to make a bed; whenever Helen and I would be making love we'd throw it off balance and fall onto the floor, laughing and fucking and laughing some more.

John Chamberlain was the initial casualty of Steeler's growing pains, the first to exit from a revolving door that would plague that band throughout its history. I don't remember how or why it happened, but we ended up with a really ugly road dog of a manager named Larry Owen, who was a sweet enough guy, and managed to get us some gigs. We called him Yoda because he looked like the character from Star Wars only less teeth.

Larry was just as broke as we were and he ended up living at my place on couch we'd scrounged up from somewhere, and he taught me The Great Pizza Scam. He'd find out what time the corner pizza parlor closed the night before, and then call them up using a fake name. "Last night, I ordered two large supreme pizzas and picked them up about 9:55, and when I got home with them, we realized they weren't even cooked, you must have shut your ovens down early or something. Man, my family was really disappointed. I brought the pizzas back but you were already closed, and I just thought I should call and let you know." He'd pause and listen for their response, and I couldn't believe it the first time he pulled it off. "Uh huh. Oh. Well, okay." He hung up the phone, looked up at me and smile his crooked-toothed Yoda smile, and told me to walk down to the corner and pick up our pizzas. Nine times out of ten, the manager of the pizza parlor would apologize and offer us free pizzas. And they would throw in extras, like salad and Cokes. And we would eat for free. We started pulling the scam at other take-out joints, Chinese food, whatever, and managed to stay well fed that summer.

Helen lived in Cookeville, over a hundred miles away, so we would usually see each other on the weekends. One night I was at a party and missing her bad, and while everyone else was inside having a good time I went off outside by myself and wrote a song called "Serenade."

Daybreak – heartache – I'm leaving you once more
A lonely smile across the miles is what I'm living for
Swiftly through our fingers, the sands of time will flow
And much too soon I'll have to go

But I'll sing to you again
Across the midnight wind
Forever I will sing this serenade

("Serenade" – lyrics by RK 1981 – from the Steeler album released 1983 – © 1983 Varney Metal Music Co. used by permission)

I credit this as being the first really good song I ever wrote. I sang it in falsetto, which seemed perfectly natural for me at the time. It was a soft love song so I couldn't scream it out full voice, and for some reason I didn't even consider singing it an octave lower. A lot of bands in the 70's had used falsetto, like the Eagles and the Bee Gees, and we'd used it on some of the Motown-flavored music we'd done in Tabu. I guess I didn't realize that this was STEELER, not the fucking Bee Gees. In 1983 when we recorded the Steeler album, producer Mike Varney got his classic "what the fuck is that" look of incredulity on his face when I started singing in that falsetto, but he let me have my way. The song was a heart-melter live, an amazing contrast to our metal music, and has stood the test of time – I still do it in my solo shows, but now I sing it like a man, an octave lower than the original.

The next casualty of the rock & roll minefield was our bass player, Jeff "Hart" Palmer. Jeff was really good looking, always going off with a chick and we wouldn't hear from him for days. He was a great performer, flailing away on stage, playing behind his back, but he was sloppy and played with a pick – after experiencing Tim Morrison's precision grooves with all fingers on the bass, I felt that was what we needed to beef up our sound. After a few days sitting around rehearsal without Jeff because he was out partying and fucking, I called Tim Morrison and offered him the spot.

"Man, I'd really like to do it," he said. "But I know you're seeing Helen, and I'm still in love with her. I can't be in a band with you, and be around her."

If I were asked to describe the key to success in one phrase, it would be "Do whatever it takes." People that impose restrictions on what they will and won't do, what they can and can't do end up missing opportunities that could have been their big break. So I did what it took.

I loved her and I let her go.

Years later Marc Ferrari fed me a song title called "I Said The Wrong Thing To The Right Girl," and I drew upon my time with Helen for the inspiration for the lyrics. She was so sweet when I broke up with her, and she understood. We reconnected in later years when I was again in between marriages and once I again I did the right thing at the wrong time, or the wrong thing at the right time, I'm not sure.

And so Tim Morrison joined Steeler and we were immediately better. I've always said that bass is the meat of the musical sandwich, the bridge between the drums which provide the foundation and the guitars and vocals that soar wild and high. And instead of playing bass like lead guitar, with a lot of notes and licks, Tim loved to lock into a solid 8th note groove and keep it simple.

Yoda booked us into a place called Uncle Sam's in Knoxville. We had a local opening act called "Candy

Crème & The Wet Dream," kind of a punk/pop band with a chick singer who was hot as hell, and I was so enthralled watching her move and sing that I didn't realize the place was empty. We went on stage and performed for nobody but the opening act and the waitresses, but we did our show – all the moves, all the pyro. It was one of those gigs where the bar separates the stage from the crowd, and I jumped the 5-foot canyon in between in my platform boots and was standing on the bar screaming my guts out. I wasn't showing off for the hot chick singer, I wasn't trying to prove anything, I was just living out the lesson Kevin taught me when he died at the keyboard: play it like you're never gonna play again.

Of course I hooked up with Candy Crème, a spitfire with centerfold looks and an attitude to match. I encouraged Yoda to book us in Knoxville as often as possible, and we started playing regularly for several nights at a time at a shithole called the Bundulee Lounge. We drew a good crowd, we kicked ass, and I had mornings, afternoons, and nights with Candy.

Steeler did a great instrumental version of "Tubular Bells," the theme from "The Exorcist." For all our Def Leppard/Van Halen party rock vibe, there was definitely a devilish side to us as well, with the "Hounds Of Hell" and the smoke and flames and the Exorcist theme.

Michael Dunigan's family had money, and a lot of it – their family was heir to the Murray-Ohio bicycle empire, and Michael was set to inherit a couple of million dollars when he turned 21 (which was still a few years away). His father Bill expressed an interest in investing in the band, and brought us together for a meeting to address how we could best utilize their family's assets to ensure the band's success. I felt strongly that no matter how much attention we would get in Nashville, we were still a novelty in the country music capital of the world – what we needed, I suggested, was to relocate the entire project to Los Angeles.

I saw the New Wave of British Heavy Metal coming, and I sensed that a similar revolution would occur in the U.S., either in New York, L.A., or even both. I heard my old mentor Jim Daley in the back of my mind telling me "You gotta go to California," made my case, and the decision was made. We had the music, we had the magic, and now we had the money.

And we were headed to Hollywood.

9

COLD DAY IN HELL

Dream stealer – disbeliever – don't take a chance on me
A high risk – a shot in the dark
I come easy, but I don't come free

Shot down – kicked in the teeth
Call me crazy, call me a fool, yeah
Lay the odds – roll the dice
But don't tell me I'm breaking the rules

("Cold Day In Hell" – lyrics by RK 1981 – from the Steeler album released 1983 – © 1983 Varney Metal Music Co. used by permission)

I was hypnotized by the lights of L.A. as the plane descended into the promised land. Dunigan money had sent Michael and me west to spend a week in Hollywood scouting out the scene and formulating a battle plan for Steeler's relocation. We got a rental car and a centrally located hotel room, bought two maps of the Los Angeles Metropolitan area, and stopped at a few convenience stores to pick up copies of the local music magazines and papers. I hung one copy of the map on the wall of our hotel room, found the addresses of every rock club within 50 miles, and marked them with a red dot on both maps.

It's important to note that we weren't focused on Hollywood or the Sunset Strip, and I believe that played to our advantage. We were coming to Los Angeles to get a record deal, not to be another local band; the goal was to book enough gigs to establish the band locally, generate some revenue to offset the investment, and build a following like we had in Nashville while pitching ourselves to record labels. But of course, after putting some dots on the map, it was obvious that Sunset Boulevard would be ground zero for this mission.

The first stop was Gazzarri's on the strip. We paid our money at the box office and walked in.

A band named RATT was on stage – Stephen Pearcy, Jake E. Lee on lead guitar, Matt Thor on bass, Dave Alford on drums, and Chris Hager on guitar. They were playing "Lights Out" by UFO and we were just blown away by the scene, the band, the babes everywhere, and we knew we'd come home. Moving from one club to another, we'd catch DuBrow (Kevin's band in between incarnations of Quiet Riot), White Sister, Dante Fox (Great White), Bitch, and so many more. Walking down Sunset Boulevard it was as if we'd fallen down the rabbit hole and landed in rock & roll heaven.

The next week was spent calling clubs, setting up appointments, driving all over the Los Angeles metropolitan area meeting with club owners and trying to set up bookings. The only Hollywood gig we could crack was the Troubadour, who gave a us a slot at midnight on a Monday. The procedure was they'd give you a stack of color-coded $1.00 admission tickets; you'd hand them out to people and receive a buck for each ticket turned in at the door that was your color. Gazzari's, that first club we'd gone to, had a 'unpaid audition' policy of making every potential new band trying out there on a Sunday night for free. The owner, Bill Gazzari, fashioned himself like a mobster and called himself the Godfather of the Sunset Strip. I made the first of many trips up the back staircase at the Whisky that week to drop off a promo kit to a secretary through a locked steel gated door. She promised to pass it on to the person who booked the bands. There was no way I could have foreseen that that person was my next ex-wife.

The only traction we could get was at clubs in the outlying areas, where the competition wasn't quite so stiff. Michael and I were nice-looking intelligent guys, with a very strong promo pack – custom printed band bio, individual bios with photos, a professional black and white 8x10, a personal letter from Bill Dunigan (we called him "The Colonel" after Elvis' manager, he got a rush out of that). Plus, we were willing to do whatever it took – play for free to prove ourselves, pimp tickets, take out ads in the local magazines, all of which we could do because we had financial backing. By the time we boarded our flight back to Nashville, we had secured a half-dozen confirmed shows and learned the lay of the land.

We used the investment money wisely, purchasing a new sound system, matching red Marshall stacks for Michael and I, a huge bass rig with a massive speaker cabinet for each side of the stage. We bought a black van (Steeler 1) and a big box truck (Steeler 2) and a CB radio system to connect them ("Breaker breaker Steeler 2, Hoover Dam up ahead, let's check it out,"). The only thing holding us up was my divorce – I wasn't about to leave town without those divorce papers in my hand.

We did four shows in a row on our "Farewell To Nashville" tour – three nights at the Fairground Sports Arena and one final gig at Flanigan's. Flanigan's had this wooden rail separating the stage from the audience, and I was up there balancing precariously in my thigh-high platform leather boots when I looked off to my left and saw a very cute tall brunette giving me the eye. I was so taken with her that I slipped off the rail and landed on my ass in a tangle of cables.

She was a Canadian girl named Jeanette, and before I left for L.A. and she went back home to Ontario, we managed to get serious enough to begin a long distance romance. This was the third girlfriend in a row that lived in another town – Helen had been a hundred miles west in

Cookeville, Candy to the east in Knoxville. Jeanette stayed in Nashville almost until we were ready to head to Los Angeles, and after that we talked on the phone and wrote letters.

Early one sunny fall morning, Steeler One and Steeler Two were loaded for departure in Bobby Eva's parents' driveway, and Michael, Bobby and I with our crew – Allen and Jimi Isaacs and our newest recruit Steve Raff, who ran our light show - waiting for Tim Morrison to show up. Tim had to make a stop along the way, to pick up something from my soon-to-be ex-wife Kathy Wolfe. He got out of the car with a big smile on his lips, waving my divorce papers, and we all laughed and hugged and cheered.

I painted the fingernail red on the ring finger of my left hand as a reminder.

And then we went to California.

The landscape was a blend of grays, from the dark asphalt to the thick light gray cloud of pollution, and all the shades of concrete in between, on the chilly October morning when Steeler One and Steeler Two rolled into Los Angeles carrying seven kids in search of a dream. It seemed nothing like the land of sunshine and opportunity I'd promised everyone; instead of a fresh saltwater breeze there was the stifling stench of smog, and the traffic jam on the freeway did not remotely resemble the Sunset Strip I had described upon returning from our scouting expedition. It felt like we were at war, heading into enemy territory, but we were young and fearless, confident that we would not only survive but we could *make it* here. We were going to conquer this town.

Let me be perfectly clear that although we had financial backing, there were strict guidelines I had to adhere to and every dollar had to be spent wisely and accounted for. There was a hard limit to what we had to work with, with the emphasis on music and business, not comfort and security. We would rather have flyers printed or take out an advertisement in a local music magazine than have our bellies full. Expenses like fuel, lodging, musical supplies such as guitar strings and drum sticks, promo packs and marketing all took precedent over normal stuff like peanut butter and toilet paper.

So we crammed all seven of us into one sleazy hotel room for thirty bucks and bought a newspaper. I took the same map I'd used during our previous visit, with all the clubs and venues marked on it, and tacked it up on the wall. I opened the paper to the classified ads, looking at properties for rent; we had to find a place where we could live and work that we could afford.

The run down three-room warehouse at 1907 Palm Grove Avenue is no longer there, but in later years it became an almost legendary location in Hollywood 1980's folklore. I lived there for three years; it was where Steeler died and KEEL was born. When we got signed to our record deal and moved away Poison took it over and used it as their band house, but it will always be affectionately known as the "Steeler Mansion." In later years I would go back to visit from time to time, and piss on the front door.

I don't recall even looking at another rental option that first day; when the Slumlord showed us the place and set the rent at $300.00 a month, I said "We'll take it." That neighborhood has come a long way in recent decades, and is now a much nicer middle-class area than it was in 1981. The fact that it was an all-black neighborhood did not bother me in the least; I was not prejudiced and didn't expect our new neighbors to be prejudiced against a bunch of long haired white boys playing loud heavy metal music. But the truth is, it was a very low income section of town with a lot of drugs, violence, and other crime, and we were never safe there. It had been a little over 15 years since the infamous Watts race riots, which happened about 15 miles away, and those memories floated just beneath the surface in the hearts and minds of the local residents. We would soon find out that to leave the door unlocked at any time was to invite trouble and danger.

The warehouse was divided into three large rooms with 20 foot ceilings. There was access via the front door off of Palm Grove, which allowed entry into the Central Room, and there was a gated loading area with access to all three rooms around back by the alley. The only window was a thin little strip way up high on the street side of the Central Room. The West room had a filthy cockroach-infested kitchen area, and if we would sign a one-year lease, the Slumlord agreed to put a makeshift shower with a fiberglass pan and steel walls in a closet of the East Room, which we chose to be our rehearsal area.

I signed the lease, and we stayed in the fleabag motel a couple more days while the Slumlord readied the Steeler Mansion for habitation. I've never been a praying man, but before we moved in I did a walk through alone, touching the walls, asking for the negative energy to disperse and for the positive energy to keep us safe and help us succeed.

Our furnishings came from trash heaps and yard sales as we learned to keep our eyes peeled on the sidewalks while we drove around. We scrounged for scraps of carpeting and nailed it to the walls of the rehearsal room to deaden the sound. Every wall was a mad mosaic of different color carpet, foam, whatever we could come up with. I found some wood and constructed a semi-private area on the street side of the Central Room, with a curtain for a door and a sheet of ¾" plywood for a bed. A makeshift desk of wood crates and planks became my office. We got a P.O. Box in Hollywood to use as a business address, installed a telephone, got a business account under the name Metal America Productions at the Bank Of America on Sunset Blvd, and proceeded with our systematic takeover of the Southern California rock scene.

Steeler's first West Coast show was on October 26th, 1981, at H.J.'s on Lankershim Boulevard. It wasn't exactly Hollywood, but hey, it was North Hollywood, close enough. We treated that gig, and every gig, like it was a headline slot at Budokan – every detail was covered, from the hair and makeup to the P.A. and pyro, the choreography, everything.

And there was only one guy in the audience.

We'd just gotten to town, didn't know anyone, and had not yet gotten our promotion machine cranked up. The local magazines were full of advertisements for hundreds of bands playing a metropolitan area of over four thousand square miles, so nobody had noticed the word "Steeler" in the fine print of the local listings. Undaunted, we did our show the only way we knew how – balls to the wall, screaming vocals and guitars, flames and explosions, all for the one short-haired guy with the beard that sat out there in the back of the room taking it all in.

After the show, he came up and introduced himself as Joe Benson, host of the "Local Music Show" on KLOS, one of the big rock stations in town. He gave me a business card and I gave him a Steeler promo kit with a copy of our demo tape. Joe gave us our first regional airplay on his show a couple of weeks later; it was such a thrill to hear it cranked up on the radio together at the Mansion. Over the next few years, Joe Benson gave us (and a lot of other bands) invaluable support and radio play. He was the first to play our "Cold Day In Hell" single a few months later, and in 1984 KEEL made our radio debut on his program as well. All because we kicked ass on stage for just one guy that very first gig, proving my point that you have to always give 100% no matter what.

One night very early on, we were all in the rehearsal room working. When we took a break we opened the back door to let in some fresh air, because the combination of mildewed carpet and a bunch of sweaty guys would generate an awful stench in there. Then we went about the business of taking a break – burning a joint, toweling off. At one point Tim Morrison wandered in.

"Man, you guys aren't gonna believe this," he said. "I was just out in the alley getting some air, and there was a black dude back there hiding, grabbing his leg. He said 'I don't mean ya'll no harm – I just got shot in the leg robbing a place down the street and needed a place to hide out.' I told him he couldn't hide here, and to move on."

As we shook our heads in disbelief, Michael came out of the rehearsal room in shock. "My guitars are gone!" he screamed. And sure enough, two empty guitar stands remained where just minutes before his two expensive Stratocasters had rested. And these were custom axes, modified with Floyd Rose tremolos, hot rod pickups, custom finishes, all done with Dunigan money, literally one-of-a-kind instruments. Someone had come in the open back door and grabbed them while we were in the next room.

We realized that Tim's hider in the alley had been lying about which house he'd robbed – he hadn't been shot in the leg, but was pulling Tim's leg with that excuse – he'd really been in the process of robbing us! So we fanned out in all directions, scouring the neighborhood looking for someone that matched Tim's description (basically a black dude in a long coat). After circling the block to no avail, I decided to head back to the Mansion – after all, we'd just been robbed, and it didn't seem prudent to leave the place unattended and full of gear.

When I got back home, I tried to think it through. Tim had shooed the guy off and watched him walk away – obviously he hadn't been carrying Michael's guitars when he left. So I thought maybe he had stashed them close by. An inspection of the loading area off the alley in back led me to Michael's guitars, which had been hidden behind the hot water heater. I brought them back inside and explained to the guys as they came back one by one from the neighborhood search.

Later that night, Steve Raff and I were out back in the darkness of the loading area where I had found Michael's guitars, and I was smoking a cigarette, marveling at how someone could just sneak into the Mansion with all seven of us present and steal two guitars from right out from under our noses, when I felt something crunch beneath my feet. I reached down and picked up a leather wristband with metal spikes on it, and recognized it as my own. I noticed other items lying about, a shirt here, a belt there. After retrieving a flashlight from inside, an inspection of the area revealed that all of our travel bags were strewn about, their contents scattered on the ground.

There were shelves along the wall of the Central Room where we all kept those bags lined up and ready for the next gig. While we had been in the next room practicing, the son of a bitch had come in through the unlocked back door and grabbed all of them, then taking them out back only to realize they contained spandex pants, leopard and zebra skin tops, cheap costume jewelry and spiked and studded heavy metal accessories purchased at a Hollywood gay men's store. I don't think a single item was missing. After rehearsal, he had come in through the door we opened to air the place out and snatched Michael's guitars, and had still been in hiding out back when Tim discovered him.

We made it a house rule that the doors were to remain closed and locked at all times. Over the next couple of years, the times that rule would be forgotten would always result in loss or threat.

My long distance relationship with Jeanette fizzled when she sent me a love letter laced with the "maybe it's time you considered getting a real job" dialog. I became the proverbial kid in the candy store, finding and fucking the hottest women in the audience on a nightly basis. Usually along with the pussy came food, drugs, and a temporary escape from the squalor of the Mansion. All the guys in the band were doing it; sometimes these became semi-steady relationships when you found a good one. For a while I dated a drop-dead gorgeous latino girl, Donna Sanfillipo, who broke up with Jack Russell to be with me. One night Steeler was playing at Radio City in Anaheim, and Dante Fox (Great White before the record deal) was at the club next door and Donna and I went over there and stood together in the audience. Jack was furious, and after the show he caused a scene outside, jumping up and down on the roof of a car (I don't think it was his car) while screaming at the top of his lungs. But he never said anything to me, and we became friends in the course of time, doing a lot of shows together in the 8o's and in recent years.

Steeler became a staple at the Troubadour, playing as often as they'd let us, taking the midnight slot on off nights, but other than that we couldn't crack the Hollywood clubs. Gazzari's had mandatory auditions on Sundays for any new bands that wanted to play there, and we went to try out, but they wanted us to load in up two flights of metal stairs on the outside of the building and our PA speakers were too big, so Steeler never did play Gazzari's. We focused on the suburbs, bringing the big show to small out-of-the-way clubs in Pasadena, Orange County, and other outlying areas, and the audiences were starting to get bigger and wilder. We would put out printed mailing list cards on all the tables for people to sign up, and send out a weekly flyer promoting the gigs. We were driving all over SoCal stapling flyers to phone poles, distributing discount tickets, and spending way more on local print ads than we were on groceries.

Several times a week I would climb the steel staircase to the second floor offices of the Whisky A-Go-Go and ring the buzzer. The secretary would come to the locked gated doorway, and I would perform the now-familiar ritual of passing her a manila envelope containing a Steeler promo kit. I was constantly updating the promo kit with live photos, advertisements, lists of upcoming shows, anything I could use to spice it up. The secretary would take the envelope, hopefully to deliver it to the person in charge of booking the bands.

I was confident we deserved a real shot in Hollywood and could hold our own against the competition in terms of entertainment value. But the industry and the media still viewed this heavy metal mania as a passing fad, and at that time even bands like Motley Crue were not yet being taken seriously. My frustration with that lack of respect manifested itself into the first good metal song I ever wrote – a simple and powerful riff dressed with an angry vocal message entitled "Cold Day In Hell." We had songs like "American Metal" and "Beyond Your Dreams" that were pretty strong, but with "Cold Day" I had taken it upon myself to write an anthem that really captured what Steeler was all about.

These days, an up-and-coming artist can write a song in the morning, record it in his bedroom in the afternoon, and by that night he can share it with the world via the internet. It's no longer a real accomplishment to have a CD – you can burn them from your computer. But back then, it really meant something to have a tangible piece of product in your hand, a RECORD that you could sell, send around the world, and shop to managers and record companies. Earlier that year, the Crue had released a 45 rpm single on their own and it seemed to have paid off well for them, and I felt we needed to do the same thing with "Cold Day In Hell," so I went to the Colonel and asked him for $700.00 so we could record and press our own 45 vinyl single.

He said no, which was very frustrating to me – he'd trusted my decision to bring the band to L.A., and I felt we were on the verge but needed this product to get to the next level. Although he denied my request for the funds, he sent us $100.00 each as a Christmas present that year. We unanimously each pitched in our Christmas money to come up with the $700.00 we needed to make the single, and I immediately booked us into Sunset-Gower studios in Hollywood and we cut "Cold Day In Hell" and "Take Her Down" in one afternoon, recording the band live and overdubbing the lead and background vocals. Bobby Eva did the artwork for the front and back cover, color was too expensive so the whole package was in black & white.

While Tower Records was a landmark on the Sunset Strip, Oz Records up in The Valley was where you'd go to find the rare and imported metal releases thanks to a man who would spearhead the Southern California version of the New Wave Of British Heavy Metal and become largely responsible for the genre's explosion in the years to come. Brian Slagel was a heavy metal enthusiast who worked at the store, and by importing those British and European releases he opened the floodgates for that music in our region. He published his own magazine called the "New Heavy Metal Revue." He was at every gig, really pushing and supporting the scene. He told me that he wanted to put together a compilation album featuring the hot L.A. metal bands and asked if Steeler would contribute a track. You had to love Brian and his enthusiasm and love of the music – he wasn't some suit in an ivory tower, he was one of us, and I offered him our recording of "Cold Day In Hell" for his compilation, which was to be called "Metal Massacre." I had two stipulations with Brian during these negotiations – one brilliant, one not so much. I got Slagel to agree to make "Cold Day" the opening track on the compilation, which also featured the first recordings by RATT and Metallica. Brilliant – anyone who listened to the album would hear Steeler first. I also insisted that our track would only be on the first pressing of the album; it was an effort to maintain control of our work, but in retrospect yanking your track off of an historic ground-breaking compilation is not a smart career move.

Our expenses grew with the mailing list as we relentlessly printed flyers, licked the stamps, and serviced our mailing list. The war between bands for space on the Hollywood telephone poles is well documented and entirely true – you would rip down a Crue flyer in a heartbeat and put up one of your own. You would tape them up in the window of any business that would let you. You would stuff them between the pages of the local music publications. You would pass them out to people waiting in line at clubs to see other bands.

And still, several times a week during my post office/bank/music store run, I would drop off the latest version of the promo kit through that locked gated door at the top of the Whisky stairway. Finally it paid off with a phone call from the Secretary, offering us a late night slot on Wednesday February 17th, 1982. Although the last band was technically the "headliner," midnight on a Wednesday with a couple of unknown bands before us on the bill was a tough way to make our debut at the crown jewel of legendary Hollywood venues; but I took the gig anyway.

It worked out that we'd be able to pick up the 1000 "Cold Day In Hell" singles from the manufacturer in time for that show, so we made it into a kind of "release party" and promoted it as such. That night, our fans from the outlying areas like Orange County, the Valley, and Pasadena came out in full force and helped us pack the place, we had an actual "record" in our hands, and Steeler had officially "arrived" in Hollywood.

We started working with the management team of United International, made up of entrepreneur Jim "Jay" Warsinske and attorney John Malpezzi. One week after Randy Rhoads died in a plane crash, I turned 21 at a gig in Pasadena – right in the middle of a song, the band just stopped playing. I turned around, livid, as they all put down their instruments, tackled me onto the stage, and the guys in the crew poured Jack Daniel's down my throat.

STEELER
By Brian Slagel

The return address on Steeler's press kit reads "Horseshoe Lane, Nashville Tennessee." At first look it would seem that this band must be country. One listen to them, though, would put all of those thoughts right out of your head.

Steeler are a pro 4-piece outfit who hail from, yes, Nashville, Tennessee – not exactly a breeding ground for HM. In this case, an exception is made. Steeler combine burning metal with an excellent stage show. Lead vocalist Ron Keel fronts the attack with a Halford-like range, as well as moving about as if he were shot out of a cannon. Guitarist Mike Dunigan provides some wild leads. He and Keel (who also plays guitar on some songs) do some great dual guitar work, especially on show stopper "Hounds Of Hell" (which is accompanied by some great pyrotechnics). Bassist Tim Morrison and Robert Eva provide a thunderous backbeat to all the goings-on. Steeler have just released their first single. Available on Ravage Records, this limited pressing (unfortunately, only 1000) features "Cold Day In Hell" b/w "Take Her Down." "Cold Day In Hell" is a certain classic. Its heavy power chords and wild singing display Steeler's talent to the fullest. The song is also an excellent commentary on the music industry in L.A. This was the first song the band wrote in L.A. and the lyrics are right on target. The L.A. A&R people are always telling bands to "soften" their sound. Steeler's response to this was that it would be a cold day in Hell when they would "soften" their sound. Many people complain that HM bands don't write "meaningful" or "social commentary" songs but "Cold Day In Hell" should put those people in their place. This is only the beginning for Steeler. They have attracted some major interest and hopefully, they will record an album soon. Yes, there is heavy metal in Nashville and that city should be proud of these metal mongers.

From "The New Heavy Metal Revue" – February 1982

10

QUIT WHILE YOU'RE AHEAD

You took my heart – stole my love
Sold the house and you sold my truck
You took the best years of my life
And you took the kids
I think you better quit while you're ahead

("Quit While You're Ahead" lyrics by RK 1999 – unreleased)

"'Cold Day In Hell' rips like an arctic blizzard through a blazing furnace, and when the two elements clash it's a cauterizing case of metal meltdown."
Geoff Barton - "SOUNDS" Magazine – March 13 1982

For a long time I dreaded writing this part, to the extent that it's delayed the completion of this book for many years. I love talking about the music, the struggles and the journey, but I can't tell my story and just skip over the seventeen years I spent with Dee Dee.

This portion of my tapestry is woven with twisted threads of infidelity and co-dependence which made headlines and network television, entwined in crime and scandal that eventually tore us apart and inflicted wounds that will never heal. Although she contributed a chapter of lies to a book which is nothing more than a tabloid-style glorification of the groupie lifestyle, with a bunch of trash-talking tramps, I am going to choose the high road for the sake of my children. My son and my daughter are the most important people in my life, and those of you who are parents will understand my discretion in matters relating to the Second Marriage. My life is an open book, and I am fair game, but I am honor bound to do what is best for my kids and my telling of this tale must be crafted with them in mind. Dee Dee is the mother of those children and as such will be treated with due respect. We both fucked up big time; I plan on admitting to my adultery, lies, alcoholism and drug use and keeping hers personal. I ask for the reader's understanding in this matter.

After hitting a home run with that first show at the Whisky, they gave Steeler a slot opening for RATT. After the gig I was upstairs talking to their guitarist Robbin Crosby and this petite blond walked up between us, grabbed my crotch and smiled, and walked off. I had no idea who she was. Robbin and I both towered well over six feet and were in the middle of a conversation, and she was such a tiny thing I didn't see her coming. But I watched with interest as she walked away.

Stephen Pearcy, the voice of RATT, was having a fling with the woman who booked the Whisky. One day he went to the upstairs office there and apparently copped an attitude during a discussion with her, and when he said "Whatever – I'll see you tonight," she replied "No you won't. I have a date." He said "Oh yeah – with who?" All those promo kits I had dropped off there paid off, because when she looked down at her desk, there was a black and white Steeler 8x10 promotional photo on top of a pile of paperwork. She pointed at me and said "With him."

Stephen laughed it off and said, "Well, Steeler steal her away."

That afternoon, our manager Jim Warsinske rushed over to the Steeler Mansion and said he had to talk to me.

"Dee Dee, the woman who books the Whisky wants you to call her," he said. "She says you have some unfinished business."

I wasn't sure what he was talking about. If they wanted to book a gig, he would be the guy to talk to. But he raised his eyebrows and gave a couple of quick nods of encouragement, and I called her.

"I want you," she said, and followed that with a long pause.

"To meet me here tonight. Ten O'clock." And she hung up.

When I showed up at the box office, the girl behind the glass was expecting me and gave me an admission ticket and a complimentary bar tab. I went upstairs where the cool people hung out and slammed a couple of Jack and Cokes on the house. She was later than fashionably late – she always was – but eventually when she arrived and introduced herself, I recognized her as the petite blond who had grabbed my crotch not too many nights before.

That's how it began. She was married but unfulfilled, eleven years older than I was, and one of the most influential people in Hollywood. She had money, power, fast cars, she was intelligent and charming, frail yet strong, and she wanted me. She courted me, seduced me, and gave me confidence, opportunities, and lavished me with gifts. I resisted going on a first date with her because of two reasons: she was a married woman, and I couldn't go out and have fun (unless it was business) and leave the guys in my band and crew languishing in the roach-infested squalor of the Steeler Mansion. My stipulation for going out to see a movie with her was that we had to bring all the guys with us, so she footed the bill for all seven of us to go see one of the "Halloween" flicks at a Hollywood theater.

Slowly I fell into a relationship with her. She bought me cool clothes to wear on stage and around town, she bought me my first wireless microphone which freed me up to roam wildly about both on and off stage. She let me drive her Trans Ams and Corvettes and paraded me around Hollywood, introducing me to bands she had been instrumental in helping like Van Halen and Motley Crue, as well as prominent music industry executives. And I liked it.

Distance grew between the guys in the band as we spent more and more time with girlfriends. I don't blame the girls, and I don't blame the guys – but I do blame the Steeler Mansion. In the beginning, that building had helped us forge an "us-against-the-world" mentality and the cockroach wars and shared peanut butter sandwiches served to bond us as brothers; but poverty and physical danger get old quickly to a group of wannabe rock stars and within six months we'd had enough. As I spent more and more time with Dee Dee cruising Sunset Boulevard in sports cars and eating at fine restaurants, Bobby and Tim found comfort and escape with steady girlfriends who got them out of the house often. Dunigan found his solace in marijuana and the more he smoked, the stranger his riffs became.

One night Michael and I were the only ones home, passed out on the couches in the Central Room when something – either a noise or a feeling – woke me up.

Standing over Michael's couch, looking down at him, was a rough looking black man in a long coat, with his hands in his pockets. I got the distinct impression there was a gun in his right hand, the sight at the end of the barrel bulging out his coat pocket. I sat up slowly and calmly asked him what he was doing here. He made up some lame story about looking for someone, and he must have the wrong place, but he made no move to leave. Michael woke up startled, but luckily made no quick moves and he and I looked at each other with an understanding. I sensed imminent danger, and we were unarmed except for my bow and arrows which were out of reach anyway, so I did the only thing I could. I asked the guy to sit down and smoke a joint with us.

We made small talk as I rolled up a fat one, and I steered the conversation to music which is the universal language. As we passed the joint around, the black man used his left hand, never taking his right from the jacket pocket. After he got high, he wished us well and made his exit, leaving Michael and I shaken and shocked. We'd gone to sleep with the door unlocked.

We had a rule that if a girl was coming over, she had to call first. We told the girls this was because we couldn't have them interrupting any "band business," but the truth was we couldn't have them interrupting us fucking other women. One night Tim's girlfriend Valerie called from the pay phone down at the corner market, and Tim told her to come on over.

She didn't make it.

As she hung up the pay phone, two black men grabbed her and threw her into their car. They robbed her, and probably intended to rape her as well, but thankfully did not for some reason. The driver shoved her head into his crotch, pulled out a gun, and pointed it at her head. Just as he pulled the trigger, the other guy grabbed his arm and said "No man, don't do that!" The bullet went into the driver's leg, and the passenger tossed Val, traumatized but alive, to the curb. The bullet wound led to the arrest of the perpetrators.

So it's no surprise that we all wanted to spend as much time away from that place as possible. But no matter where I spent the night, I was back in my makeshift office the next morning, taking care of business, writing songs in the afternoon, screaming my guts out in rehearsal in the evening. But the chemistry was dying, and my leadership skills were not up to the challenge of maintaining it. Instead of working with Michael to write better songs together, I began to write more on my own, which paid dividends with songs like "Backseat Driver" and "Hot On Your Heels." Motley Crue had just become the first band on the scene to get a major label record deal, and the pressure was on to measure up if we were ever going to do the same. I would look at guys like Tommy Lee and Bobby Blotzer and realize that our Bobby was not on that level; guitarists like Eddie Van Halen, Randy Rhoads, and Jake E. Lee had set the whammy bar really high and I knew Michael was progressing in that direction.

I was fearless as a frontman and would perform amazing physical feats on stage, and I had perfected hitting and holding those high piercing inhuman screams which dazzled audiences. Those traits masked the deficiencies in my voice and songs and enabled me to exceed my limitations; people *loved* us, we were packing the clubs and starting to get some great press around the world. But I knew my actual singing ability needed to catch up with my confidence and charisma, so Dee Dee found me a vocal coach and funded the voice lessons to the tune of $40 an hour, which was a lot of money back then.

Elizabeth Sabine was a tiny Aussie lady who was sixty years old when I first walked into her studio for training. I was trying to improve my craft and lead by example, showing the band that I realized I needed to elevate my skills in order to compete at the next level. It only served to expand the growing chasm between us, as I felt that I was doing everything possible to succeed and the other guys were not.

Bobby had become the most distant from us and the least proficient at his instrument, and by unanimous decision between the band and management he was fired and replaced by Mark Schwarz, who'd recently made the pilgrimage to Hollywood from Texas. Mark was our Tommy Lee, strong, athletic, flashy, powerful, who played with passion and authority. Immediately the band was much improved musically, infused with new life and vigor. It felt like a new start, full of promise and potential, but looking back it might have been the first nail in the coffin. The bond between the boys who'd banded together in Nashville was broken, and in Mark I found a kindred spirit who was driven, smart, business savvy, with a relentless work ethic; he and I felt the same things and wanted the same things, and that only created more distance between us and the other two guys.

Our managers managed to get us some free studio time with a credible engineer and we cut a new four song demo: a new version of "Cold Day In Hell," and also "Serenade," "Out To Get You," and "Make Up Your Mind." On June 30th we did an "industry showcase" at S.I.R. Studios in Hollywood; these are gigs in a controlled environment where there are no screaming groupies or other "distractions" (read: "motivations") and the audience consists of a bunch of stiff suits sizing you up while you prance and rock out as if you were playing Madison Square Garden. This was easy for us because we'd always done it that way in rehearsal – and it had only been a year since we'd been playing to empty clubs anyway. While we did get some interest from Ron Fair at Chrysalis Records (they had UFO and Uriah Heep), we failed to secure a deal.

United International – our managers, Warsinske and Malpezzi – had presented us with a management contract about two inches thick which had been bounced back and forth between L.A. and Colonel Dunigan's attorneys in Nashville to no avail. Jim and John were very serious, detail oriented, and they thought big, which I liked; but Dunigan had invested a considerable sum in the band as an investor and we couldn't sign the management deal without his blessing. This was the second nail in the coffin, and created tension between Michael and me because our relationship wasn't just singer/guitarist, it was singer/investor's kid, and I started thinking I might have to split with Michael in order to make it in this business. No matter how much capital was invested, we were out on the front lines of a rock & roll war and I had to make critical decisions that would affect the outcome - and I couldn't do that with my hands tied by Nashville attorneys who didn't understand what was happening in L.A.

So we lost our management because our investors prohibited us from signing the management agreement.

But there were a lot of "managers" sniffing around the Hollywood bands at the time; some would go on to become icons in the industry, others would get the boot as soon as the bands became successful, like Motley Crue's first manager Allen Coffman, who reportedly spent millions to get them a record deal. Mark Schwarz (who was then going by the name Mark Scott, but would later use the name Mark Edwards) hooked us up with a British cat named John Collins. John's claim to fame was that he managed Dennis McKay, who had produced Judas Priest's "British Steel" album; I've already mentioned what a huge influence that album was on me, and it was cool being managed by the guy who managed the guy who produced that epic release.

Feeling our recording demo was not good enough to get us a deal, John Collins arranged for us to record at an incredible state-of-the-art studio in the Hollywood hills. On a winding road in a very affluent neighborhood, some Arab sheik had spent seven million dollars to create the world's ultimate recording facility; three stories of soundproofed isolation rooms all connected by video cameras and wired into a control room encased in a shielded copper dome, with a massive mixing console and walls lined with the latest signal processing equipment. The house/studio was unoccupied, and listed for sale with a one million dollar price tag. I tried to get Dee Dee to buy it for me but that was a little out of her range.

We started cutting tracks, and had some good tones happening, but the studio was so far beyond the skill level of the recording engineers that it took forever to get anything done. We would sit and wait for hours while they tried to figure out how to work the equipment. I was able to lay down a couple of pretty strong lead vocals on "Backseat Driver" and our cover of "Let's Spend The Night Together" – that was the only cover song Steeler ever did, and I would eventually include it on the first two KEEL albums. The Sabine vocal training and the luxury of not being pressed for time enabled me to get some much-needed studio experience and record a couple of quality vocals which helped to boost my confidence. Unfortunately that space age recording studio got the better of us and the property was sold before we could complete the project.

It turned out that Judas Priest allegedly owed "Stained Class" producer Dennis McKay a sum of money for production fees or royalties, it was never clear. John Collins made a deal with Priest: they would forfeit that debt in exchange for Steeler getting the opening slot on a leg of Priest's "Screaming For Vengeance" tour, and suddenly overnight we were booked on tour with the most iconic heavy metal band of all time. This was the break of a lifetime, and would include a concert at The Forum in L.A. which would certainly lead to a major label record deal. It was announced in the media, and we started gearing up for a month on the road touring arenas.

Our big pre-Priest tour gig was our debut at The Roxy on Sunset Boulevard - which Dee Dee also booked because it was owned by the same family as The Whisky - two shows in one night opening for Motley Crue. I remember Tommy at soundcheck, showing off his brand new Mighty Mouse tattoo (one of his first).

Steeler was subjected to every restriction a headliner could possibly impose on an opening act: 30 minute set. Very few lights. Major sound limitations. And by the time our drums were set up on the floor in front of Crue's gear, there was not enough room for me to stand centerstage between Mark's kick drum and the front edge of the stage. I really had to turn my feet sideways to stand up there. I was undaunted and determined to make a strong impression on the sold-out crowd, but at some point in the show I got frustrated by the lack of room and decided to improvise.

I haven't been there in years, but back in the day the Roxy had a VIP balcony up right off stage left. I went over to the balcony singing to the people up in there, and put my left hand on the brass rail around the top of it. It felt good in my hand, so when it came time for the guitar solo I put the microphone in my teeth and used both hands to climb up there. Standing on that rail, balancing myself in those black thigh-high leather boots, I realized I could reach up and grab onto the pipes and electrical conduit running across the ceiling. Of course I did that, hand over hand like on monkey bars, and when the guitar solo was over I took the mic out of my teeth and hung there above the audience, mic in one hand and pipe in the other, and screamed out the final verse and chorus. When the song was over, I monkey-barred back to the balcony, off the railing and jumped back onto the stage. One of the craziest and coolest things I've ever done on stage, I'm surprised no one got a picture of it. I could have killed myself or really hurt somebody, but the show did end in bloodshed; it turns out when I jumped down off the balcony, I broke the heel off of my right boot, exposing the little nails that hold the heel in place, and when I went back out to the middle of the stage all the fans were pressed up hard against it with their hands on the edge of the stage, leaving me even less room to stand. The nails protruding from the bottom of my boot ended up embedded on the top of the hand of a good looking young lady in the front row, and I didn't even know about it until the show was over.

As I was backstage drying off, chugging beer and whiskey and marveling at the monkey-bar feat, someone came back and notified me that I had stepped on some girl's hand and turned it into handburger. In shock, I asked them to bring her backstage, and sure enough, it looked pretty bad. I helped her wash it off, put some ice on it, got her bandaged up, asked her what I could do to make it up to her. She settled out of court for a kiss and some photos with the band.

While there are no photos from the overhead hanging escapade, there are some cool pics of that gig, including one where you can see a fist protruding up out of the crowd with a star-shaped tattoo on the forearm. That was Mark Workman, before we met, someone who would become very important to me in the months and years to come.

We got stocked up on supplies, guitar strings, drums heads, sticks, vehicle maintenance, and promotional materials in preparation for the Priest tour. We'd spent pretty much all the investors would allow when the first advertisements for the L.A. shows started to circulate, announcing "Judas Priest with special guest Coney Hatch."

John Collins assured us it was just a misprint, that we were truly on the bill and on the tour. I don't know what he had to gain by stringing us along, but he kept telling us not to worry about it, and to get ready for the road. Then the story changed, yes, we were losing some of the dates, but the Southern California shows were solid, and the Long Beach Arena gig was the one that was going to get us a record deal anyway, but maybe we'd have to be third on the bill below Coney Hatch.

Sheri, my high school sweetheart, was living in the L.A. area at the time and had come out to a few gigs. She had always been so sweet, she had believed in me, she had supported me, she'd been faithfully waiting for me during my Junior year in Texas and I'd broken up with her for no good reason other than to sow my teenage oats. I was spending the night with her three days before the Judas Priest concert at Long Beach Arena, which John Collins still insisted we were opening. Early the next morning, Sheri's phone rang. It was for me - Mark Schwarz.

"Judas Priest is playing in Fresno tonight," Mark said. "You and I need to go there and try to talk to the band in person."

I kissed Sheri goodbye for the last time and headed for the airport.

Upon arriving in Fresno, we rented a car and went straight to Selland Arena. With no credentials other than balls and bravado, we talked our way into the building and backstage where Judas Priest had just finished soundcheck. Suddenly there we were in the same room with them, as guitarist Glen Tipton greeted us.

"Glen, we're Steeler," Mark said. "John Collins and Dennis McKay arranged for us to be your opening act on some of these tour dates and we need to talk to you about that."

Tipton looked down and shook his head, then turned to one of his crew. "Get these guys some tickets and passes," he said, and then looked back at us. "We'll talk after the show."

True to his word, there were tickets and backstage passes for us at the box office. It was painful to watch Coney Hatch in what should have been our spot. I'd never heard of them (until I saw the Judas Priest tour advertisements) and I was not impressed. KEEL ended up signed to the same European label as them (Phonogram) a few years later and I ended up wearing out their second album, "Friction," but that night in Fresno I was anything but a fan.

It was the first time I had ever seen Judas Priest and I was blown away. Rob was having vocal problems, so I stood right in front of the stage and screamed every song at the top of my lungs, and I know they heard me. Backstage after the show Glen didn't want to speak there, but gave us his hotel information and asked us to come to his room.

He was very gracious, inviting us into his room and sharing his time and cocaine with us. He apologized for the situation, and informed us that they were involved in a legal dispute with Dennis McKay and could not honor the agreement. We begged to just be third on the bill for the Long Beach show, but he explained that was impossible because of union and overtime expenses at the venue.

Relief mixed with devastation after we left Fresno. At least we knew the score, there was no more speculation, but we also knew a huge opportunity had just slipped through our hands. It was with heavy disappointment that we broke the news to everyone else. We were broke, sitting on enough supplies for a month-long road trip, with no gigs in sight because we'd suspended all bookings in anticipation of that tour. And once again we were without a manager, because our relationship with John Collins imploded in the aftermath of the Judas Priest fiasco.

Dee Dee cushioned the blow by giving us three consecutive nights at the Roxy December 15-17, but it was a Band-Aid on a bullet wound, and on December 17, 1982, that incarnation of Steeler did their final concert performance. The band of brothers that began our journey in Nashville nearly two years before would disband on Christmas day; and although a group called Steeler, with a singer named Ron Keel, would go on to make history and record a groundbreaking album with one of the greatest rock guitarists of all time, something special died that Christmas.

11

GUITAR SOLO

(It's a guitar solo – we don't need any fucking lyrics here. Shhhhhhhhh, listen.)

Mike Varney has done more for guitar-driven music the past thirty years than anyone else on the planet, and fans of this genre owe him just as much gratitude as the virtuosos whose careers he has launched. In 1981, he founded Shrapnel Records and started exposing young hotshot guitarists on his "U.S. Metal" compilation albums, much like Brian Slagel had done with the L.A. bands on "Metal Massacre." A track on a "U.S. Metal" album and a mention in Mike's monthly column in "Guitar Player" magazine could arm a fledgling axe-slinger with enough ammo to land a big-time gig.

I had sent Varney a copy of the "Cold Day In Hell" single months earlier, and his response had been polite. He had complimented the vocal and the song but just didn't care for Michael Dunigan's guitar work, suggesting that he would sign the band and produce an album for us on his label if we had a lead guitarist he approved of.

Everybody but me went home to Nashville or Texas for Christmas 1982. I were busy plotting a career course for Steeler that included parting ways with Michael Dunigan and Tim Morrison, which happened on Christmas day. I met with a bass player named Rik Fox at the Rainbow and I was immediately sold on the guy, he just reeked of rock star and had a formidable presence and charisma. We had a lot in common, like a true appreciation and a love for early KISS, and we both believed in putting on a show. He would sometimes play bass by banging it on his forehead, and I thought that was so cool.

Dee Dee and I spent New Year's Eve in San Francisco. I'm not sure if her husband didn't know about us yet or was just looking the other way or what. On January 1st 1983, we drove to Mike Varney's apartment a couple of hours north of the Bay Area to meet him in person and listen to guitarists. He's a really nice guy, with a childlike passion for music and an amazing knowledge of all things guitar and guitarist, and we sat in his living room surrounded by shelves containing thousands of cassette tapes sent by aspiring guitarists around the world. Like kids at Christmas, we unwrapped them one by one and evaluated how they would fit into the Steeler mold; to be honest, most of them sounded the same, a lot of flash and dash, amazing technique and chops but nothing really stood out to me. Until he played a tape sent in by some kid from Sweden.

It was obvious that Yngwie Malmsteen had a special gift. If you're reading this, you've probably heard him play and you know what I'm talking about, but on New Year's Day 1983 nobody had ever heard anything like that and it was apparent that he had the potential to reach the status of Eddie and Randy. I decided immediately that he was the guy, we didn't need to listen to any more tapes, and Yngwie and I started communicating via phone and sending letters and music back and forth via regular mail.

A lot has been said about my relationship with Yngwie; he and I added fuel to the fire with a public war of words in the 80's. Our total experience working together consisted of four months in 1983, the album sessions, and nine shows; for both of us, it was a brief period in careers that have spanned over three decades now, but that moment was frozen in time by the album that launched us both into the international spotlight. In many ways Malmsteen and I have pursued parallel paths – we're both very dominant personalities, and our desire for total control over our projects may well have kept us both from realizing our full commercial potential. He is responsible for creating an entirely new genre of rock music called "Neoclassical," while I helped break down the barrier between heavy metal and country music, and though we've both sold millions of albums I don't think either of us reached the heights we intended to or should have.

While those four months were filled with stress and tension, there was never any real conflict. We did not fight or argue, but it was a frustrating situation simply because it didn't work. Steeler was my vehicle and I had my hands firmly on the wheel – we had a style, we had a format, and before anyone had heard of Yngwie I had proven that format worked. We were headlining and selling out all the primary local venues, "Cold Day In Hell" had been played on the radio around the world, and we were getting international press and major label interest. I could have chosen any guitarist Mike Varney presented to me that day and we would have had a record deal without the complications of bringing someone all the way from Europe. Whoever I chose was being given a great opportunity to step right into a band that had already paid its dues, fought our way to the top of the scene, and had secured an independent recording contract with Shrapnel Records. It was my house, and I didn't need someone to come in and rearrange the furniture.

Changing the name and musical direction of the band was not an option for me because of what we'd already accomplished and I was firmly committed to my vision. Yngwie had his own vision, and now I can respect that with the perspective of maturity and security in what I've achieved with KEEL and on my own. And I have absolutely no doubt that had I done that – changed the name of the band and adapted my style of music to his – and even if we had gotten along perfectly as friends and musical partners – he would still have quit the band the minute Graham Bonnet called him to join Alcatrazz. Malmsteen idolized Ritchie Blackmore and the opportunity to join a signed act fronted by the ex-Rainbow vocalist would have been too good to pass up no matter what.

On the phone and in his letters, he assured me that he loved Steeler's style and direction and that he was looking forward to coming to America, working together as a team, and making it to the top with me. Once he arrived, I began to have my doubts as to the truthfulness of those statements.

Mark Schwarz, Rik Fox and I met him at LAX and saw him take his first steps onto American soil. The tension was immediate; there was no happiness or excitement, and instead of a smile we got a blank stare. I chalked it up to jet lag, and an 18 year old kid enduring his first trans-Atlantic flight and being overwhelmed in the moment. As he picked up his luggage, I noticed that he had "666" stenciled in white on his black suitcases and guitar case, which was kind of alarming. While I'd flirted with the occult and sang songs like "Hounds Of Hell" while caressing flames out of the pyro system, painting the actual number of the beast on your stuff seemed a little excessive. When I asked him about it, he gave me that blank stare and said "I am the anti-Christ." Which made the van ride back to the Steeler Mansion a little uncomfortable.

I totally understood the culture shock of coming from his background into our backyard, which was the rock-n-roll equivalent of a foxhole in a war zone. Comforts were few and challenges were many, and there were way more cockroaches in the kitchen than there were quarters in the piggy bank. I never promised a limousine ride to the Hyatt Regency, all I could do was offer an opportunity to play in one of Hollywood's premier rock bands and make an album with Mike Varney. We moved Yngwie into Tim Morrison's room, which was the kitchen, and put him in the only bed available which was Tim's old waterbed. It was a shithole in the ghetto, but I'd spent over a year there and survived and hoped that the experience of us all struggling together would form a similar bond to the one I'd had with the original band members.

From my makeshift office I called Mike Varney to let him know that Yngwie had arrived in Los Angeles. I was straight up with Mike, and told him that things were a little strange but we'd all adapt. Varney, a devout Christian, was alarmed by the "666" stencils on the luggage and the "anti-Christ" comment.

One thing that impressed me immediately was Yngwie's dedication to his instrument. Before he opened his eyes in the morning, he reached out for his Stratocaster and started playing it before sitting up or getting out of bed. As he was pouring his first bowl of cereal with his right hand, his left was working the fretboard. And he rarely put it down.

He could not bring his Marshall amp to the U.S. because of the difference in voltage, so we supplied him with one and went into the rehearsal room to make music and history.

You hear legendary rock-n-roll tales like the first time Page & Plant jammed together, or the immediate chemistry between Steven Tyler and Joe Perry. Let me assure you there was none of that when the revamped Steeler lineup cranked it up that day and launched into "Cold Day In Hell." Yngwie had a distinct and unique style, and part of that was overemphasizing the vibrato on the power chords. Part of what makes those riffs cool is the stark strength gained by hitting the chords and holding or choking them with just the right amount of vibrato when called for; with Yngwie, every power chord was dramatically overdone by excessive jerking of the left forearm.

Another impression I recall from that first rehearsal was the utter lack of fun. An important element of Steeler had always been that Van Halen-esque fun factor, and having just enough smiles to offset the tough-guy grimaces; in all the time Yngwie played in the band there were far too few smiles. I was so shaken after that first rehearsal that I decided we'd made the wrong decision and I apologized to him, but this wasn't going to work out.

Mike Varney understood and was supportive as we turned the entrance to the Steeler mansion into a revolving door of hotshot guitarists that came and went over the next few days as Yngwie sat on the couch formerly known as Michael Dunigan's bed and watched and listened. I felt bad for him but we had gigs booked and recording plans and I was under the gun to right the ship that had run aground on a sandbar of neoclassical noodles.

After three days of auditioning all the other noodlers, Yngwie came to me and said he knew what I wanted and that he was ready to do it. Of course the guy was a musical prodigy and could play whatever he wanted however he wanted, and he'd decided he'd rather play it my way than return home to Sweden. He went into the rehearsal room, strapped on his Strat and played the most wicked metal power riffs laced with blistering solos, it was incredible – I was screaming at the top of my lungs, Mark was slamming the drums, Rik was pounding the bass on his forehead, and Yngwie was rocking out and laying it down.

We didn't audition any more guitarists after that.

Plans were made to move forward with the album sessions, but before Mike would produce Yngwie's guitar tracks he would have to get a Green Card to sign the record deal and legally work in the United States. We put that process in motion using Dee Dee's money and connections. It was the first time I imported a player from overseas, but not the last, and it's always frustrating how difficult it is when you want to play by the rules and do it by the book, but millions of people come here illegally and seem to have more rights than those of us born here.

Sometime during the transition between lineups, we'd developed a friendship with Mark Workman, the guy whose tattooed arm can be seen thrusting his fist out of the crowd in that photo from the previous fall's Motley Crue gig at the Roxy. Workman's original pitch was that he would make buttons for us – they were round, a couple of inches wide, with a white Steeler logo in the middle. We sold them for a dollar each. Then he started working ways to get T-shirts, which we'd never had before, and suddenly thanks to him we had merchandising. Our light man Steve Raff had stayed behind in Nashville after the personnel shakeup; Workman was so passionate about the music that we put him behind the lighting board at a gig, and he played the lights like it was a musical instrument, flashing in time with the music, creating dramatic scenes and blackouts and really adding to the show.

He worked at some audio-video place that had all the coolest new technology, and one day he brought over this thing called a VCR – "Video Cassette Recorder." It was a self-contained unit which played a VHS video tape onto its built-in little 3-inch screen. All seven of us huddled around in fascination watching a movie called "The Warriors." It was the coolest thing ever, you could watch a movie any time you wanted, you could hit "pause" and "rewind," unbelievable. Workman had an oriental girlfriend that used to cook for us, and he secured our first "endorsement" – a deal with a salon called "Long Hair Rocks" which enabled us to get free hair care. Up until that point, we'd trim our own hair or have some drunk chick butcher our locks; the deal with "Long Hair Rocks" was the equivalent of an image makeover and gave Yngwie and I the look we had in that now-legendary photo session with famed rock photographer Neil Zlozower (Rik Fox and

Mark Schwarz already had killer hair; Rik's Angelic coif and Mark's cool curls came naturally).

Mark Workman went on to become one of the most sought-after concert lighting directors in the business, designing and operating complex arena-sized light shows for major headliners around the world. He's also been a road manager and an author, among many other things, and most importantly a true friend who always had my back and probably saved my life more than a few times. He also wreaked his share of havoc, but didn't we all?

Subsequent rehearsals failed to capture the fire of that one magic day when Yngwie played American metal like his future depended on it. We slipped back into the tense and conflicted atmosphere but we had gone too far to turn back now. We were broadcasting on different frequencies and were just not in tune with each other – writing together was impossible, and not one good song came from that partnership. "Abduction," the instrumental show opener and prelude to Side 2 of the album, was cool but doesn't really qualify as a "song." "No Way Out" was a feeble attempt at putting some of Mark's lyrics to Yngwie's music because I was having a hard time matching my words with his riffs. The rest of the material were my songs most of which I'd written on my own since arriving in Los Angeles; the only surviving tunes from the Nashville era were "Serenade" and "Hot On Your Heels."

In addition to rehearsing for upcoming shows and album sessions, Mark and I assumed the management duties and had to rebuild the band's business and infrastructure. Everything from the banking to the business name and address to the marketing and promotional machine had to be restructured now that we were on our own.

Yngwie's American stage debut was at the Country Club in Reseda, opening for Hughes/Thrall on March 11th, 1983. Legendary rocker Glen Hughes had teamed with guitarist Pat Thrall for that project which was getting a lot of publicity, and I wanted to premiere the new lineup in the relative security of being an opener for a hot new national act. Before, during, and after Yngwie's tenure with the band, Steeler was always well-received by audiences - we never failed to get fists in the air and people singing along – but after Yngwie's first few shows you started to see the crowds divided into Steeler fans and Yngwie fans. Some fans wanted to rock out and bang their heads to the metal, and others wanted the guitar solo to last forever. It understandably went to Yngwie's head, and it all came to a head one night at a show in San Francisco.

Underground bootleg tapes of Yngwie's Swedish band Rising Force had surfaced in America and his reputation had preceded him to the Bay Area. When we walked on stage that night, Yngwie's side of the stage was jam packed with his fans, many of which were holding up banners and signs that said "YNGWIE IS GOD." The show proceeded in embarrassing fashion (embarrassing for me, I'm sure Yngwie was enjoying himself) as he took the praise to heart and turned the entire gig into a guitar solo, characterized by one distinct moment : during "Down To The Wire," a song that I didn't play guitar on so he was counted upon to hold down the rhythm chords, I looked over during the pre-chorus and he had his guitar off, scraping the fretboard back and forth on the monitor speaker, with utter disregard for the song. I tore into him after the show, and he understood and apologized, but I drove a wedge between us that night that would never dislodge. If you ask any entertainer to choose between his critics and his adoring fans, the adoring fans will win out every time.

I remember one night we were playing at the Roxy, and Ronnie James Dio came backstage to greet us after the show. I was a huge fan of his from Rainbow to Sabbath to his solo work, so it was really exciting to meet him. His diminutive stature is as well-known as his larger-than-life voice and presence (that means he was a short dude) and here I was, towering over him at 6'4", shaking his hand, and I said "Ronnie James Dio! You are the man! I've always looked up to you!" And after realizing what I'd said, we both cracked up laughing. I guess it broke the ice, because Ronnie chose KEEL to be his opening act on the entire European leg of his "Sacred Heart" tour.

When the time came to record the album, Yngwie still had not received his working visa but the decision was made to proceed in hopes that the paperwork would be official any day. We were on a very strict budget of $3000.00 – 100 hours at $30.00 per. Mike Varney would produce the sessions with Allen Sudduth engineering, at Prairie Sun Recording Studios in Cotati, California, about an hour north of San Francisco. It was a great place to record because it is located in a rural area away from the city and its distractions.

We spent the first couple of days recording the drums, bass, and my rhythm guitars. With Yngwie's green card still in limbo, we proceeded on to the lead vocal tracks and after the first couple of takes I realized I didn't know what the fuck I was doing.

The vocal training with Sabine had helped in so many ways – my strength, range, and endurance had vastly improved – but the physical training conflicted with the style I was going for. The voice I heard in my head was a perfect blending of Paul Stanley, Rob Halford, Brian Johnson, and David Lee Roth, but the voice I was hearing on the tracks sounded like none of the above. Sure, there was attitude in spades, and the inhuman high piercing screams, but I had no real control over my instrument or the melodies which I was trying to execute.

Unsatisfied with my lead vocal results, we moved on to the background vocals and I knocked those out with Peter Marrino, a longtime friend of Varney's and an amazing vocalist. Peter would go on to front his own band, Le Mans, on CBS Records as well as singing on a number of notable Shrapnel releases.

In the nick of time, Yngwie was granted his working visa and they began recording his guitar tracks. Mike Varney was producing the album, and he was the guitar guru, so I pretty much tried to stay out of the way although it was difficult. I'd peak into the control room every now and then but mostly I would sit in the band quarters listening to the rough mixes of my vocal tracks, trying to figure out how I was going to fix them. I implored Mike to give me another shot at singing the tunes, and he agreed that whenever Yngwie's guitars were wrapped up, I could have whatever time was left over to re-do some lead vocals.

On the last day of tracking, we had until 1:00 AM to wrap it up. While Yngwie continued to record all day, I paced the floor, impatiently checking in on their progress. 6:00. 7:00. 8:00. Eventually around nine o'clock, they announced that Yngwie was finished and I went to work, screaming through take after take, singing most of the entire album again without even listening back to what I'd done because there was no time for that.

When the Steeler album was released on September 25th, 1983, we did an in-store autograph signing at Tower Records. It was very awkward because by that time, within just a few months of the recording sessions, the band had once again gone through a furious round of personnel changes, and on the day the album came out I was the only guy in the band that was actually on the record. So there was Greg Chaisson, Bobby (Eisenberg) Marks, and Kurt Jaymes autographing over Yngwie, Mark, and Rik.

Yngwie had gotten the call from Graham Bonnet and left the band to join Alcatrazz. We parted on good terms, I wished him well, and breathed a sigh of relief that it was over. We parted ways with Rik Fox then as well and brought on board guitarist Mitch Perry and bassist Ron Murray and continued to sell out venues throughout Southern California. Mitch was – and still is – a superb guitarist who's gone on to tour with a ton of superstars including Cher, Johnny Winter, and Lita Ford.

When Juan Croucier left Dokken to join RATT, Don Dokken pegged our bassist Ron Murray for the gig. One night we were playing at Perkins Palace in Pasadena, and Ron had been out in the crowd checking out one of the other bands. While trying to talk and fight his way backstage, a security guard slammed his left hand in the door, doing extensive damage to all four fingers. I believe he received some minor cash settlement, but Dokken moved on with Jeff Pilson and Steeler continued with a myriad of guitarists and bassists.

In the chaos, confusion, and frustration I parted ways with Mark (Edwards) Schwarz. Mark went on to form Lion with vocalist Kal Swan and guitarist Doug Aldrich, securing a major label deal and a couple of notable single releases, including songs in "Friday The 13th Part 4" and the original animated "Transformers" movie.

In September of 1989 Mark was seriously injured in a motorcycle accident which left him unable to ever play drums again. Once back on his feet, he put his drive and his business skills to work and became a Wall Street rock star, making a fortune and jet-setting around the world in his private planes. He still has a rock & roll heart and we share a comfortable friendship and the occasional long talk on the phone to catch up. On September 25th 2013, to commemorate the 30th Anniversary of the Steeler album release, I had Mark, Rik, and Varney on my "Streets Of Rock & Roll" radio show; we celebrated that milestone and voiced our appreciation to the fans that made it one of the biggest selling independent heavy metal albums of all time. I extended the invitation to Yngwie through his management and publicity people but received no response.

In July of 2013, Rik Fox and I once again shared the stage as he joined KEEL during a concert appearance at the Whisky. The Whisky had been shut down for remodeling during the Malmsteen/Fox era, and KEEL had never played there back in the day, so it was a special moment when Rik joined us for "Cold Day In Hell." Then the band left us alone on stage for an acoustic version of "Serenade."

Michael Dunigan went on to play in some other bands but never got to the next level. He opened his own record store in Nashville, and was shot four times while being robbed at gunpoint. He made a full recovery, and I ran into him again when I first moved to Las Vegas in 2006. It was a friendly reunion and I was very happy to see him healthy.

Around 1989, I was walking down the street in L.A. when some guy in a suit and tie burst out of an office building door and ran after me. It was Tim Morrison, now an insurance salesman, who had recognized me on the street. We hung out a couple of times and then lost touch again, but I always loved that guy and never forgot how he stood up for me at that Lust audition and said "Look at this guy, we gotta at least check him out!"

I saw Bobby "Robert" Eva a few times through the years in my visits to Nashville, and he stayed in the business, producing concerts and such.

When KEEL was at the Record Plant in 1984 recording "The Right To Rock" with Gene Simmons producing, Yngwie J. Malmsteen was in an adjacent studio working on his debut Rising Force album. We would run into each other in the lounge, or at the vending machine, and it was cool – by then we were both signed to major label record deals, so the chips had slipped off all our shoulders. We even staged a photo session at the studio where we faked punching and choking each other.

12

MY BAD

I admit it's my responsibility
It's my fault we're all in the calamity
I caused the downfall of society
In my hands – the fate of all humanity

Bad judgment – but it's my call
I fucked up – and now we're taking the fall

It's my bad – my fault – I'm to blame for what's going wrong
It's my bad – my sin
I'm to blame for this mess that we're in – it's my bad

("My Bad" – lyrics by RK 2013 – from the Ron Keel album "Metal Cowboy" released 2014)

Dee Dee's husband had by now found out about us and given her the "it's him or me" ultimatum. It ended up being me, and she introduced me to her four children – Amy, who was around 12; Marlon, 8; and two little boys, Jeff and Erich. I started spending some nights at her house in Santa Monica after her husband moved out. I loved the kids, hell I was a kid myself, and love them still.

She introduced me to a booking agent, Tim Heyne at Tapestry Artists, who started helping us out. He'd worked a lot with Y&T and was ready to make the progression from agent to manager, and his guidance kept Steeler at the top of the local club scene even though we were getting zero interest from the record companies. He became Steeler's final manager, and we became his first management client.

That final Steeler lineup – me, Greg Chaisson (who went on to be in Badlands with Jake E. Lee), Kurt Jaymes, and Bobby Marks - was stable for over six months, from before the album came out until the final show in San Diego on March 4th, 1984. We wrote and rehearsed vigorously, knowing that if we were ever going to get a shot it would be based on the new lineup, the new show, the new songs – the Steeler album, which became a classic cornerstone of that style and time, was a useless slab of vinyl to me when it came to pitching for a deal. And now *everybody* was getting signed, it seemed every day you'd hear so-and-so got a deal with Warner Brothers, RATT got signed to Atlantic, those guys inked a deal with Electra, Quiet Riot got signed to Pasha/CBS, and Steeler was not being considered.

One day after rehearsal, I was walking the two blocks down to the corner liquor store for a quart of beer and a pack of cigarettes. After two years at the Steeler Mansion, the white boy musicians were a fixture in the neighborhood and I didn't feel threatened in the least. Many of the local shop owners knew me – I took my heavy metal boots to the old black cobbler on Washington for repairs, we'd eat at Roscoe's Chicken and Waffles and drink at the Red Rose, a little corner bar halfway between the Mansion and the liquor store. So I was surprised when a wild-eyed black man came stumbling out of the Red Rose – I'd seen him around, on the street – and he came up to me screaming and spitting in my face.

"You're the devil!" he cried. "And your music is the music of the devil!"

He pushed me in the chest. I could see he was absolutely fucked up, probably on PCP which was pretty rampant in that neighborhood at the time. I kept calm, told him to be cool and just kept on my way, but heads started to turn and a crowd began to gather as he followed me to the store, yelling the whole time. "You're evil! And that music you play is evil!" I could feel the sentiment turning against me with each vehement phrase, like a tide of negative energy rolling down Washington Avenue which, by the time I entered the store, had reached a fever pitch.

I wasn't afraid, but I knew I was in danger. I made the mistake of going to the pay phone and calling the land line at the Mansion. Workman answered.

"Hey man," I said, "there's trouble on the street and I don't think I'm going to make it back in one piece. If I'm not home in ten minutes, call the cops."

"What is it? What's happening?" Mark asked. I explained to him what had happened. "Did he touch you?" I replied, no, he just shoved me in the chest, no big deal. "I'LL BE RIGHT THERE."

"No, man, that's just going to cause more trouble. Maybe he's already moved on."

And he had. As I exited the store with my can of beer and pack of smokes, the whack job was now focused on a group of older ladies waiting at the bus stop. I probably would have made it home unnoticed, but then I saw Workman marching down the sidewalk with the boom arm of a cymbal stand gripped tight in both hands. As luck would have it, we met at the bus stop, right behind the troublemaker. "Is that him?" Workman asked. "Yeah, but let's just get the fuck out of here before – "

And before I could finish, Mark Workman had swung the cymbal stand like a baseball bat right into the guy's head. Now Workman is a big strong tough son of a bitch, but that direct blow to the skull did nothing but piss the guy off, and soon the two of them were grappling with the boom stand, wrestling for control. Cars on the street were screeching to a halt, a crowd of people had assembled around us, and I had no choice but to try to separate Workman and the wacko by putting my hands on the metal bar as well.

I heard the pounding of heavy footsteps on the sidewalk behind me, and turned just in time to see a huge man closing in on me, his massive fist already in mid-swing. I went down hard, unconscious before I hit the ground. I remember waking up with my face on the sidewalk in a pool of my own blood, my body twitching in some kind of a fit. There was a huge open gash on the back of my head, where I'd probably been kicked while knocked out. My necklace had been torn from my throat, the earrings ripped from my ears.

At this point Dee Dee was driving down Washington to pick me up for dinner, and she saw the crowd, and some guy on the ground, and not realizing it was me she drove on to the Mansion. Everything after that is fuzzy – I don't remember how I got back to the Mansion, or how the incident was resolved, but I'm glad nobody else got hurt. I'm lucky I survived that day with just a concussion and a wicked scar on the back of my head; nearly 20 years later, a chiropractor was looking at some X-rays of my neck and asked what the hell had happened to me around 20 years ago? He noted signs of severe neck trauma approximately two decades old, calcified deposits that needed to be operated on by going through the front of my throat, to which I said HELL NO.

And that was it for me at the Steeler Mansion. The desire to hang tough with the boys had been beaten out of me on the street that day, and I moved in with Dee Dee and her kids. I kept the place as a rehearsal facility and lodging for any band and crew that needed it, and I still kept an office there and a bed for nights when I would stay and fuck around.

Severing my bond with that building put just enough distance between me and Steeler to make me realize that the two – me, and Steeler – were not inseparable. I was Ron Keel, and I had a life, and a dream, and I could not let Steeler get in the way. So one night I took a copy of the Steeler album and traced the "EEL" from the logo onto a piece of typing paper, and created a "K" to put before it, and KEEL was born.

I told Tim Heyne I was putting a new band together called KEEL and he gave me his full support, agreeing to manage the project. I informed Greg Chaisson of my plans, and said the door was open but with this new venture I was going to call all the shots; KEEL was not to be a democracy, but a virtual solo project that would be built to withstand the personnel changes that had plagued Steeler. Greg declined, not wanting to relinquish control or authority, but asked that I consider his younger brother Kenny Chaisson for the bass position. Greg's endorsement and one conversation with Kenny was enough to secure him the gig. The Chaissons hailed from my old hometown of Phoenix and that was certainly a factor in recruiting Kenny and guitarist David Henzerling (aka David Michael Phillips) for KEEL – they would be fresh faces, unknown on the L.A. scene, and after growing up there myself I believed the harsh Arizona soil was a great place to cultivate musicians. Also, unlike bringing someone over from Sweden, there were no visas involved and if it didn't work out it was only a 250 mile trip back where they came from.

I discussed the new project with Mike Varney, who agreed to sign KEEL to the same album deal he'd given Steeler, so immediately as the band was forming we had a major independent recording contract on the table. Mike also took the liberty of passing my phone number to a new guitarist in town named Marc Ferrari.

I came home one day to a string of voicemails and handwritten messages: Marc Ferrari called. Call Marc

Ferrari. Marc Ferrari, recommended by Mike Varney. Please call Marc Ferrari. Marc Ferrari called again.

I immediately loved his persistence and called him back. Now he collects and drives expensive sports cars, but back then he was on foot when I picked him up on a street corner in Hollywood. He'd recently relocated from Boston and was everything I was looking for in a partner for KEEL – hungry, ready to do whatever it took to succeed, willing to take my direction while asserting his own creativity, really good looking and like Kenny and Dave he was a fresh face in town, and a musical breath of fresh air. After all the hot shot guitarists who came to L.A. with something to show, Ferrari's guitar playing had something to *say* – solos with real melody that reminded me of Michael Schenker or Thin Lizzy. Marc actually accompanied Dee Dee and I to the final Steeler show, where I was up front with everyone that this was the end of that chapter for me.

Drummer Bobby Marks was not a fresh face on the local scene – he'd been in RATT at one point, but I first saw him in one of my favorite Hollywood bands, Sarge. That band included other RATT alumni Chris Hager and Matt Thorr, who would go on to become Rough Cutt. Sarge was fronted by Steve St. James, a really good frontman and singer, and their shtick was they'd dress up in Army gear, full on loaded for battle with helmets, fatigues, ammo belts, fake grenades, guitars shaped like M16's, it was really cool. But what I loved about Bobby was that while everybody else was trying to be Neil Peart or Alex Van Halen with twelve rack toms, he had just one massive rack tom mounted right between his bass drums and that rack tom was the heavy artillery in that band, and when he hit that drum it was like a cannon being shot off. He was more into being powerful that he was being fancy, and he was a really nice guy on top of all that, so when I split with Mark Schwarz I brought Bobby Marks in to be the final drummer in that band, and kept him on to be the first drummer in KEEL. Bobby on the drums, like Tim Heyne behind the management desk, provided me with just enough stability to start fresh but with a solid foundation.

Ferrari had an apartment in Hollywood, but the other guys all lived at the Mansion. Kenny and David had quit their jobs, left their homes and girlfriends, and taken a chance on being in my band, so of course they were welcome to share the squalor and the danger of the 'hood. After the Phoenix guys arrived but before we ever hit a note, I assembled them for our first band meeting.

I asked them for total control over every aspect of the band. I asked them for absolute dedication for three months, and in return offered them the opportunity to immediately catapult to the top of the local scene and play the best gigs in front of packed houses. I offered them a chance to make an album with me on Shrapnel Records. "If, in three months," I told them, "you're not seeing results, if you're not happy with what we're doing, then you can go your own way. But give me three months of solid commitment." They all agreed to my terms.

And then I started getting the calls from Black Sabbath.

I'd been working with a local sound man named Jon Graves, who was breaking into studio production and started producing the final Steeler sessions as well as the initial KEEL demos. He introduced me to Mikey Davis, a recording engineer at Pasha Studios – Pasha was ground zero for the big 80's metal sound, owned and run by Spencer Proffer who had just helped make Quiet Riot a household name by producing "Metal Health." Mikey was the understudy to Duane Baron, who had engineered that album and was the king of the massive drum sound everybody was searching for at the time. Mikey and I hit it off big time, we loved working together and we loved the cocaine. He had the keys to the studio, so I would wait outside, parked across the street, for everyone but Mikey to leave. Sometimes it would be one in the morning, sometimes it would be four in the morning, but as soon as the coast was clear he'd give me the signal, I'd go in the back door, and we'd line up some blow and work until just before nine when the secretaries arrived. I notched some invaluable mic hours during those sessions, singing and screaming and snorting coke, learning to get comfortable in the studio and gaining confidence, finally starting to hear the same voice on tape that I heard in my head.

Ian Gillian had just left Black Sabbath, and Spencer Proffer had signed on to produce their next album. The times were changing – heavy metal had been reinvented by the British and shoved into the mainstream by Quiet Riot, and Spencer had a vision for Black Sabbath that included radio hits and heavy rotation on MTV. Spencer was also drunk on his own power; his exploitation of Quiet Riot's publishing rights and royalties is common knowledge and he thought himself more powerful than the mighty Sabbath. He was going to choose their new singer himself, and present them with a batch of "radio-friendly" songs composed by another one of his bands, a Canadian group called Kick Axe.

Spencer would come into the building in the morning around 11:00 and Mikey Davis would still be in there, gakked out of his mind on blow, mixing the KEEL demos. As the story was told to me, the more he heard the more he liked, and he asked Mikey for my number.

He called to explain the situation and offered me the opportunity to audition for Black Sabbath. As part of the deal, he would act as both my manager and producer, and he presented contracts to that effect which I signed with Tim Heyne's blessing. Proffer wanted to record my voice on some of the songs he had in mind for the new Sabbath album, and enlisted Dana Strum to produce the four song session. Strum also got Jake E. Lee to come in and give me a pep talk, and explain what an incredible opportunity this was and what it was like when he got the gig with Ozzy.

Strum was incredible at pulling some amazing vocals out of me. A lot of it was showing off, taking the Ron Keel screams to new extremes, but it was shit that nobody else could do at the time and it worked. Spencer Proffer loved it, presented it to the band, and I was instructed to go to Tony Iommi's hotel room to meet with him and Geezer Butler.

Tony is a legend, someone whom I admire incredibly and respect immensely, but I beg to disagree with the passage in his autobiography regarding the sequence of events that led to me joining Black Sabbath. The way Tony tells it, they were given a cassette tape that had one singer on the "A" side and a different singer on the "B" side. I can assure you that was not the case. For one thing, if any other singer had been in to record those songs at Pasha Mikey Davis would have known about it and told me. Second of all, Spencer's ego was way too big to give the band a choice or a say in the matter – it would have been totally out of character to offer them two different options.

Over the course of a few days, I met with Tony and Geezer several times and they arranged for me to meet with Don Arden, their manager. Tony told me in no uncertain terms that I was the new vocalist in Black Sabbath, and gave me a set list to learn that opened with "Neon Knights." Don Arden told me to say nothing to no one, that the news was strictly confidential, and that an announcement would be made in conjunction with the release of a new band photo with me in it.

Through this process I had been up front with Marc, Kenny, Bobby, and Dave and let them know the status of my negotiations with Sabbath. Here I was finally with my own band, a great group of guys, all my own songs, my vision – but the opportunity to join one of the most iconic acts in rock history, the band that had literally invented heavy metal, was something no one in my position could have turned down. After the meetings with Iommi, Butler, and Arden I sat KEEL down and told them it was official, that I was the joining Black Sabbath. The guys were all very understanding and committed to making our first and last show, scheduled for April 7th 1984, the best it could be. After giving them explicit instructions to SAY NOTHING – this was all strictly confidential – I went out to Dee Dee's Trans Am, and turned the key in the ignition to head home to her.

"Good evening Los Angeles, you're listening to KLOS radio and we've got some big news," boomed the voice over the car speakers. "It's just been announced that Steeler vocalist Ron Keel is the new singer for Black Sabbath." I was thrilled but shocked to hear it not two minutes after I'd told the KEEL band it was all hush-hush, wondered who had leaked it, and if there would be any repercussions. When I got home, it was all over MTV. Soon it was in print. No one ever accused me of leaking the news, and Black Sabbath and their management didn't seem to mind.

I made a tape of the Sabbath songs in the order that Iommi had given me and during the day, I would practice that show. I had it down to where I was pure evil, delivering the Ozzy, Dio, and Gillian material with total authority and confidence. Workman would sit in on some of these rehearsals and encourage me. I had hoped to get into a rehearsal situation with Tony, Geezer, and their drummer at the time (former ELO drummer Bev Bevan), but Bevan was unavailable and I never got to stand center stage with Black Sabbath.

It had been only four weeks since the final Steeler gig; the concert at Perkins Palace in Pasadena on April 7th was originally intended to be a Steeler show, but it evolved into the debut of KEEL when I decided to make the move. That event was produced by Dee Dee Lewis and Mark Workman, who had worked very hard to make sure everything from promotion to production was done first rate. They'd done everything from renting the hall to printing the tickets. Among the 1,700 plus in attendance were Tony Iommi, Geezer Butler, and Lita Ford (who was dating Tony at the time); they came backstage before the show, all smiles and handshakes, met the band, and wished me well. By then everyone had heard the news, and it was a foregone conclusion that this was to be our debut as well as our farewell. Also backstage was Carmine Appice, who then and there recruited Dave Henzerling to be one of the guitarists in his new band, King Kobra, since I was joining Black Sabbath anyway.

KEEL took the stage with a vengeance and it felt and looked like we'd been together forever. Blending the new material with the Steeler songs the local audience knew and loved, we put on a triumphant show that I am still proud of to this day.

And I never heard from anyone in the Black Sabbath camp again.

They severed their ties with Spencer Proffer, who ended up never producing a Sabbath album, and I was caught in the crossfire. To this day I don't know if it was the business thing or my performance with KEEL, or a combination of both, that cost me the job. I asked Lita Ford once what was said about me on the limo ride home, but she didn't remember. Sabbath and KEEL were two different shades of metal, darkness and light – KEEL was built to be a good time band with a lot of smiles, high fives, audience participation, choreographed guitar moves, there was definitely a "party" element that would have been uncharacteristic for Black Sabbath, and maybe they thought that was the only role I could play. Had we the chance to share a stage in a rehearsal or concert setting, I have no doubt that I would have at least recorded and toured with them, but it was not to be and I didn't waste any time rallying my troops for the next KEEL show, two weeks later at The Roxy.

13

LAY DOWN THE LAW

I know the difference – I know right from wrong
I know what it takes to make it, proud and strong
A will like tempered steel – sweat muscle and blood
A desire, a promise, a threat – and you better make it good

You've got to face it – reach out and take it

Lay down the law
You never know when you'll get your last chance
Lay down the law
You never know when you'll see your final glance

("Lay Down The Law" – lyrics by RK 1984 – from the Steeler album released 1984 – © 1984 Varney Metal Music Co. used by permission)

Kenny Chaisson   Dwaine Miller   Ron Keel   Bryan Jay   Marc Ferrari

Gold Mountain

Management:
TAP/KO Entertainment
(818) 980-0551/888-7833

KEEL

A&M
RECORDS
Printed in U.S.A.

Just as I was plotting the transition from Steeler to KEEL, we found out Dee Dee was pregnant with child #5 – my firstborn. I was happy and excited; I enjoyed my role with her children and looked forward to carrying on the Keel bloodline and experiencing the pregnancy, birth, and all that comes after.

What came next for KEEL was filling the vacant guitar position with less than three weeks before our next gig, a headline performance on April 28th at The Roxy. I didn't have time for a long audition and evaluation process – our show was all original music, extremely choreographed and rehearsed, and the new axe man would have to get in the game quickly. Now that the Sabbath experience was in my rear view mirror, I was ready to put the pedal down and I knew all eyes and ears would be on us for our Hollywood debut. In fact, I don't recall auditioning anyone other than a tall handsome kid named Bryan. He was fast and fluid, with an amazing dexterity, and the wildness and unpredictability of his style really complemented Ferrari's rootsy approach. This Bryan guy seemed very easy to get along with and willing to make the same commitment as everybody else, and he looked like a star, so I put him to work. We got right down to the business of showing him the tunes and hammering out the show.

"Ron ran rehearsals like musical boot camp, very regimented, serious, and structured. Not to say it wasn't fun, we enjoyed each other's company and all that, but it was clear that when we were rehearsing, it was with the objective in mind to tighten up the band and get it into fighting shape...we became a well-oiled musical monster in a short period of time."
Marc Ferrari

I stood Marc and Bryan side by side and made them both lower their guitar straps so their axes were slung low, in the saddle where I thought it looked the coolest. I oversaw every aspect of the performance, every chord, every note, every beat, every shake of the head and thrust of the fist, and they never questioned me.

There was a part in the show where I brought out a bottle of Jack Daniel's and as I introduced each individual guy in the band, we'd each take a swig and I'd say "Marc Ferrari on lead guitar!" or whatever. The first time we ran the show with Bryan, it occurred to me that I didn't even know his last name, and as the guys were grinding away on the groove I leaned over and yelled into his ear, "What's your last name?"

"Hongola!" he yelled back. Sounded like Tarzan herding elephants to me.

"What's your middle name?" I shouted.

"Jay!"

"On lead guitar, Bryan Jay!" And he became Bryan Jay. That was how committed to making it he was, he even let me change his last name without even asking him.

We had recorded a two song demo, "Lay Down The Law" and my new version of "Speed Demon" (the one we all know and love today). I took Bryan into the studio to replace Dave Henzerling's solo on "Speed Demon" and during his first KEEL recording session he came up with the classic solo that he still plays today. Mike Varney included that version on his fourth "U.S. Metal" compilation album which was actually KEEL's first album appearance; there are four KEEL versions of "Speed Demon," which appear on as many different albums: the original demo appears on "KEEL IV: Back In Action," the demo with the Bryan Jay solo appears on "U.S. Metal IV," the best version appears on the "Lay Down The Law" album, and we re-recorded it finally for "The Right To Rock" album. The song is still a staple of every show we do and was once voted the second favorite KEEL song (after "The Right To Rock") in an online fan poll.

For the demo of "Lay Down The Law" I fell back on my Meat Loaf influence and did a theatrical segment in the breakdown after the solo: a verbal back-and-forth with Mikey Davis' girlfriend Becky topped off by the heavy revving of a Camaro with a microphone on the tailpipe. It was the middle of one of those late nights when Mikey had snuck us into Pasha for an undercover recording session and we strung a bunch of microphone cables together, ran them out of the building into the parking lot and literally stuck a very expensive studio microphone damn near into the exhaust pipe of somebody's Camaro and recorded the engine revving and the car peeling out onto the street.

We used to videotape every concert and critique each small detail. Bryan's first KEEL show at The Roxy was a tape we watched only once; let's just say the lineup hadn't jelled yet and the other guys had a head start. I hadn't even officially given Bryan the position – he was on like a trial run – but I liked him, I trusted him, I knew he was a guitar hero waiting to happen, and so I turned to him one day and just said, "By the way – you're in the band."

I was coming through on my promise of results – along with Quiet Riot, Motley Crue, Great White, and RATT, KEEL was getting regular play on local radio just on the strength of our demo. We were consistently a Top 10 draw on the Music Connection Magazine "Live Action Chart," selling out everywhere, and with each show the money got better, the spotlight got brighter, the music got louder, the women got hotter, the piles of cocaine got higher, and the parties got wilder.

The hard rock and metal bands on the L.A. scene were no longer fighting an uphill battle – we were all steamrolling down the other side of that hill like a heavy metal avalanche, destroying everything in our path and gaining momentum with every new barricade we broke down. MTV was exposing the culture to millions daily, and the fever spread like a wildfire throughout the land, on every television and radio, and into every arena from coast to coast. And KEEL was right there at the forefront of the second wave; after those initial bands started scoring platinum hits, the record companies were scrambling to sign any act with a California address.

Within three months of our formation KEEL was at Prairie Sun recording our debut album "Lay Down The Law." Mike Varney trusted me to produce the album myself, and I brought my engineer Mikey Davis with us to record the project. Our manager Tim Heyne, feeling that he needed both physical and financial muscle to get us to the big time, took on a partner – a big sweet badass of a man named Ray Chambers, a top officer of the Hell's Angels and one of the scariest motherfuckers you'd ever cross. A mountain with tattoos, he wore a ball cap and carried a briefcase full of money and cocaine and he was fully prepared to do whatever it took to put KEEL on top. He was a striking contrast to Heyne, who was well dressed, tall, affable, trim, good looking, and great with people. Those in the industry whom Tim Heyne couldn't charm, Ray Chambers could intimidate – and with the Hell's Angels' money and muscle behind us, we had real power and potential.

In addition to Mikey D and the band, we were joined at the sessions by one of Ray's lieutenants, an Angel named Jerome. Jerome's task was to make sure we stayed safe and well supplied with drugs. He would arrive at the studio every day with as much coke as we needed to stay productive. Let me stress that not everyone in the band was on the powder all the time – Some of the guys dabbled, some abstained, I did neither. I snorted hard and heavy and kept the tape rolling the whole time.

My intention was to record the band live, with Marc, Bryan, Kenny and Bobby all tracking at the same time. We set up drums in the main studio and put the bass and guitar amps in various nearby rooms in the barn, the bathroom, wherever I could achieve some isolation, with each musician in the room with their respective amplifiers. Prairie Sun was not equipped at the time with any video gear for visual interaction, so everybody was flying blind, at the mercy of their headphone mix. First Mikey and I spent a few hours dialing in the big drum tones, blending close mics and room mics to get the desired ambiance to simulate the sound of a concert arena. Then one by one we adjusted the guitar tones and bass sound, getting individual sounds and levels on all the instruments. Finally when I liked what I heard, I asked the guys to just jam, play something together so I could get a blend of the instruments before we started recording.

Marc Ferrari launched into a powerful riff I hadn't heard before – huge chords separated by strategic spaces: A – C – D - C B A – C – D....suddenly the band joined in, Bobby laying down a groove and Kenny riding the A in eighth notes. My eyebrows rose, and my jaw dropped, and I yelled at Mikey "HIT RECORD! NOW" and the tape machine went red, with the guys hammering out the riff and following Ferrari without any visual cues, just playing along as he went to E for the pre-chorus and then back to the main riff with the chords held out for a natural chorus.

It was the first time anyone ever heard the music to what would become our signature song, "The Right To Rock." I had Mikey dub it off for me onto a cassette, tucked it away and got on with the business of recording the "Lay Down The Law" album.

The sessions went great, carving tracks all day and night, partying and putting the pieces together. We played a gig at The Stone in San Francisco during the recording process, opening up for Le Mans and a female band called Rude Girl. I hooked up with the bass player, a goddess with a huge rack named Eden, and she would come visit at the studio during the course of the recording sessions and fuck my brains out in the bandleader suite (a private upstairs loft in the band quarters). So I had great music, total control of everything that was going on, choice drugs at my disposal and amazing pussy when the day was done. Life was good. I thought of my pregnant married girlfriend at home from time to time, but felt justified that I was doing what I needed to do to get the job done.

Looming on the horizon were the lead vocal tracks. I had gotten comfortable in the studio when recording the demos back at Pasha but still the doubt lingered from the botched sessions with Lust and for the most part, Steeler. I was still deeply troubled by the vocals on the Steeler album, and to this day have a hard time listening to it, and now the band was called KEEL - there were no excuses, nowhere to hide, and nothing to do but deliver. I put it off as long as I could, and then with all of the music recorded, I sent the band home. Left at the studio were Mikey and I, and our supplier Jerome.

I had a hit of acid that a friend in Nashville had sent me a few months before. I hadn't dropped acid in a long time, and I haven't done it since, but the day I recorded the lead vocals for the "Lay Down The Law" album I ate that hit, snorted a big rail of cocaine, chugged the Jack and beer all day long, and laid down some of the most amazing metal screams I ever recorded.

I am not advocating drug use, just admitting to the truth. And the results are on tape. That was one of the most incredible sessions of my career; my voice had arrived and has stayed with me since although my drug years are long past. Throughout my career with KEEL, on into Fair Game, and even during all of "The Country Years," I was on cocaine for nearly every vocal track I ever recorded. (One exception was the Steeler album – no coke during that one, maybe that's why it's tough for me to listen to it). If I were to do cocaine now I would surely choke, but back then I had caught magic in a bottle, literally, with the vocal tracks on "Lay Down The Law" and I could proceed with confidence that at least on that album KEEL had a singer worthy of having a band named after him.

Before we could finish the mixes on the album, our management called me back to L.A. because the band was hot, there was a lot of interest from the major labels, and we had to showcase immediately. So I drove south and we prepared for two intense days of private showcases at S.I.R. Studios in Hollywood.

CBS Records was especially excited about signing the band, and requested their own private showcase, which ended up being Showcase Day One. These were full production events, with concert lighting and sound, smoke, full dress and all the bells and whistles, where a band plays a condensed 20 or 30 minute show, but about halfway through the first song at the CBS showcase we blew the circuits for the P.A. and lights. The amps on stage still had juice, so rather than just stop we kept going, in the dark, and I was screaming into the microphone as loud as I possibly could. I thought that was how you handled situations like that, just rock on. After about fifteen minutes, power was restored to the sound and lighting systems, and we resumed the showcase but the initial excitement had dissipated.

The next day was an open showcase to which a number of industry execs showed up. Normally the suits who attend these deals don't show any emotion or indicate their thoughts or intentions to the others in the room; smiling, nodding, tapping your foot, these are all prohibited because if you like the band, it might encourage others to like the band also and that could lead to a bidding war. So it was quite a surprise when Burt Stein, Vice President of Gold Mountain/A&M Records, stood up afterward and said "I want to sign this band!"

CBS offered KEEL a "development deal," which meant they would sign the band to a conditional agreement, give us a small sum of money, and we'd spend six months writing, working with producers and image consultants, and then at the end of the development period they'd decide if they wanted to proceed with a full recording contract. Gold Mountain/A&M made us a solid offer immediately; their enthusiasm about the band made the choice an easy one and suddenly I was a major label recording artist.

I remembered seeing the A&M Records logo on Sherleen's Herb Alpert and the Tijuana Brass albums when I was a kid. I'd seen it on "Frampton Comes Alive," Styx's "Grand Illusion," "Black Tiger" & "Mean Streak" by one of my favorite bands of the day Y&T, and overnight I began seeing it over my picture, in advertisements and promotions. I was 23 years old. I'd been chasing this dream for two decades already, I'd been in Los Angeles almost three years, and my band KEEL had been together less than six months.

"Yet another Los Angeles hard rock band signs the dotted line. KEEL, well known on the LA club circuit, have signed to Gold Mountain Records, which is marketed and distributed through A&M. The group is going into the studio with Kiss' Gene Simmons to produce an album which should be in the stores by February. In the meantime, their debut album "Lay Down The Law" comes out on Shrapnel Records this month."
BAM Magazine, September 1984

14

THE RIGHT TO ROCK

All my life I've been fighting for the right to make my stand
Scream my anthem to the night
And hold the power in my hand
I'm gonna do it my way, or not do it at all
Taking the world on my terms – I'll take it by the balls

I'm fighting for justice – for the American way
I believe in what I do, and I mean what I say

You've got it – the right to rock
We've got it – the right to rock

("The Right To Rock" – lyrics by RK 1984 – from the KEEL album "The Right To Rock" released 1985 – "The Right To Rock 25th Anniversary Edition" released 2010)

There was a holding period between the time Gold Mountain and KEEL made the commitment and the day we physically signed the papers. During this interim phase, creative wheels started turning but we couldn't make an official announcement. A&M wanted to move quickly to achieve the optimum release date of late January; Mikey and I were still mixing the Shrapnel album and the band did not have any new material to record for our major label debut. I came up with the title for an anthem called "The Right To Rock," and quickly wrote the lyrics to fit that jam we had recorded at the beginning of the "Lay Down The Law" sessions. I knew then we had our signature song, something strong enough to build a new album around, and in the excitement of the moment I stayed up the rest of the night and wrote "Back To The City" and "Electric Love."

The record company presented me with a list of potential producers for us to work with. It was like a "who's who" containing the names of guys who had the Midas touch of turning vinyl into gold, but one name stuck out to me larger and bolder than the rest.

"Gene Simmons," I told Burt Stein. "That's who I want. Hook it up."

They arranged for a meeting to take place at the Beverly Hills Hotel, where he was staying. Armed with all the confidence in the world and a cassette tape in my pocket, I strolled up the walkway toward the entrance.

"Ron?" said a big man with short hair, wearing a business suit and sunglasses, who was sitting on a bench outside the entrance. "Yes?" I answered, and he stood.

"I'm Gene Simmons."

I didn't recognize him - they had only recently shed their makeup, and this wasn't the Gene I'd envisioned - he'd cut his hair for a starring role in the movie "Runaway" with Tom Selleck, which had recently wrapped up filming – but just standing in his presence left no doubt as to his identity. I was walking with the giants now.

He invited me up to his room, which to my surprise was quite Spartan – not the penthouse suite I'd expected. He was very gracious and friendly, and I was trying to say and do all the right things, but I don't think I succeeded that day on the basis of the discussion; I think Gene was as hungry to embark on a new phase of his career as a record producer as I was to be a rock star, and the most powerful ammunition I had was in the pocket of my leather jacket, not in my sales pitch. Gene said he'd heard the "Lay Down The Law" mixes and liked what the band was all about, and asked if we had any new songs. I whipped that cassette tape out of my pocket; it was just the rough mix of the instruments, without any singing on it. I inserted it into the boom box on the table, cranked it up, and pushed PLAY.

Seven years prior, I had fought my way to the front row at my first concert to get splattered with his sweat, spit, and fake blood. Now, alone with him at the Beverly

Hills Hotel, I spit back, screaming "The Right To Rock" in full voice along with the music on the tape.

As soon as the first chorus was finished, he reached over and hit STOP.

"I'm going to produce this album," he said. "And we're going to start Tuesday."

A six month world tour to support the new KISS album "Animalize" was scheduled to kick off on September 30th, only six weeks away, and we had to be finished before the tour started.

Firing Bobby Marks was my next move, and one of the hardest things I've ever done. Bob was a truly nice guy and we never had a moment of conflict; he had been the musical bridge between the last incarnation of Steeler and the first lineup of KEEL, he'd worked tirelessly without ever questioning my policies or decisions. But upon listening to the "Lay Down The Law" tracks repeatedly during the mixdown process, I noticed an abundance of glaring tempo fluctuations and a total lack of consistency in the grooves. In musical terms, we refer to it as being "all over town." Instead of leading the other instruments, Bobby was being led - following the guitars and bass when it should have been the other way around. At the time, I blamed it on the mental beatdown he'd taken from Greg Chaisson during our last six months in Steeler; Greg had been a hard ass with Bobby, always yelling in anger, very intimidating, hammering on him incessantly, and it had shaken Bobby's psyche and robbed of him of the confidence to hit the drums with authority. Now, looking back, I share the blame for Bobby's shortcomings – I should have worked with him, had him rehearse with a metronome, and should have recorded the album with a click track. It was the last session I ever did without one. I didn't think Bobby had what it would take to make major label albums and tour arenas, so after he had given me his all for a year and helped us get KEEL to the point of being signed, I fired him from the band.

Of course we said nothing to the record company or to Gene, not wanting to raise any red flags or show the slightest instability after just getting the deal.

I had anticipated this drummer dillema and was prepared with a list of potential replacements in order of priority, so I called the dude at the top of the list: Fred Coury, who would go on to have a long successful career with Cinderella. Fred flew out from New York immediately and jumped right into rehearsal with us.

It had been decided that we would record the three new songs – "The Right To Rock," "Back To The City," and "Electric Love," along with three of Gene's songs left over from the "Animalize" sessions. He gave me a tape of a half-dozen tunes and I chose "Sooner Said Than Done," "So Many Girls (So Little Time)," and "Get Down." Rounding out the nine-song album would be new versions of three songs from the "Lay Down The Law" album: "Speed Demon," "Let's Spend The Night Together," and "Tonight You're Mine." Gene had us change the title of that last one to "You're The Victim (I'm The Crime)" which required switching those two phrases around; not to be outdone, I changed "Sooner Said Than Done" to "Easier Said Than Done" which involved changing that word in the lyric.

With Tuesday fast approaching, I was not afforded the luxury of easing our new drummer into the situation; I was more demanding than ever, and was very tough on Fred, making him pound the drums harder and harder until his wrists hurt. Bobby had been a very powerful drummer, and I didn't want to sacrifice that element for timing and precision – I wanted it all.

The next morning I showed up for rehearsal at the Mansion and Fred's luggage was gone. And so was Fred Coury. "He's gone," was all Kenny said. So I called the next guy on the list: former Angel drummer Barry Brandt. Barry had major label recording experience and had toured arenas with Angel, he was a cool guy, good looking, a real showman behind the kit, and we were all stoked to have him in the band.

He was a good player, but I was immediately concerned because he overplayed through all the songs, a lot of fills, changing up patterns and accents, almost playing like a drum solo during the songs when there should have been just a solid groove. Because of his track record, I cut him some slack, figuring that he was just getting comfortable with the tunes and working out his parts. When it carried over into the second day of practice, I still let it go, figuring that Gene would be able to settle him down in the studio. And then at the end of Day 2, I called out our starting time the next day. Barry got my attention.

"I can't rehearse tomorrow," he said. "I have to take a couple of days off." I looked at him, bewildered, as if he was speaking some foreign language. We were about to go into The Record Plant the following week to record our major label debut with Gene Simmons producing; taking time off was not an option. "Why? I asked.

"I have to paint my house."

"Cool," I responded. "Can you move your drums?" Now it was his turn to look bewildered.

"Why?" he inquired.

"So the new guy can set up." I'll never forget the look on Bryan Jay's face when I glanced at him over Barry's shoulder at that moment – the guys in the band either thought I was crazy, fearless, or both.

The new guy was Steven Riley, who subsequently spent time in W.A.S.P. and has spent a long time in LA Guns. Steve came in and learned all the songs the next day, and we were ready when a limousine brought Gene Simmons to the Mansion for a pre-production session that Sunday, two days before we were set to start recording. Gene fine-tuned some drum patterns, and had suggestions and input for all of the instruments, and we worked out arrangements, intros and endings. Normally the pre-production process consumes a few weeks, but we were now living life at the speed of rock & roll and everything was happening very fast.

We arrived at The Record Plant on Tuesday fired up and ready to rock, only to find that Barbra Streisand was finishing up a session in our room and was running behind. We got to meet her though, so we didn't mind hanging out in the lounge. I had managed to convince Gene to bring in my guy Mikey Davis to engineer the album, which meant that there would always be vials of cocaine on hand to enhance the experience and keep us awake. Gene was very anti-drug, so we had to be discreet; my idea of being discreet was singing in a completely dark room and snorting lines during playback so Gene wouldn't hear me in the control room.

We did all the drums, bass, rhythm guitars, and background vocals over the next few weeks. We did one gig during that time also, at the Orange Pavilion in San Bernardino, which was the only show Steven Riley ever played with us. We also finally officially signed our recording contract with Gold Mountain/A&M Records well into the actual recording process. Gene was great to work with, just one of the guys, and I don't recall any bad times or rough spots during those sessions until the day Riley came to me and told me he was quitting the band to join W.A.S.P. – I didn't take that well. Even though we were now "signed" we weren't making any money; the album budget was only $40,000.00 and that was all going towards recording expenses. Management was still in the process of negotiating merchandising and publishing deals, advances from which would keep the KEEL machine fueled but there was not much left for the guys in the band. The guys were all getting $100.00 a week; I was getting $150.00 a week because my last name was Keel. Nobody was complaining; Gene had explained to us how he and his bandmates in KISS were making $80.00 a week until "KISS: Alive" exploded and they became millionaires practically overnight. We were on our way, willing to pay our dues and hang in there for the payoff when we hit the big time. Blackie Lawless had offered Steve Riley $300.00 per week, three times what he was making in KEEL, and it was too good to turn down, so we paid him a $900.00

session fee as severance (his name was now on the recording contract) and I called the next guy on my list of drummers: Dwain Miller.

Dwain was an 18-year-old Phoenix kid who had auditioned for Steeler the previous year on recommendation from Greg Chaisson, and I really liked him but I think he was nervous at his audition and his playing was a little shaky. I can truly say that in our 30-year history, it was the only time I would ever characterize his playing as shaky – one of the nicest guys I've ever known, and the most underrated rock drummer in history if you ask me. Rock solid, a great showman, a naturally talented singer, and the consummate bandmate. Immediately upon getting my call, he piled his drums in his car (an old Pacer) and headed straight to L.A. and right into the studio with KEEL and Gene Simmons. We set up his toms and had him play the first tom accents on "The Right To Rock," just to be able to truthfully say he had played drums on the album. Dwain was credited with the drum tracks and he's in the band photo. Steven Riley was credited with "additional drums," but actually played the entire record.

It was time for Gene to return to New York to begin rehearsals for the "Animalize" tour, so Marc, Bryan and I went along to work on the album whenever Gene had a break. We would take turns laying down lead guitar solos and lead vocals. To save budget, we got Marc finished first and he went home, leaving Bryan and I to tag team the rest of the way. Bryan, Mikey and I shared a two room suite at the Gramercy Park Hotel, which would become my East Coast home over the next couple of years.

One day we were scheduled in the recording studio at ten A.M., and my only order of business that day was the final scream on "You're The Victim (I'm The Crime)." For some reason it hadn't recorded properly when I laid down the lead vocal, and thought no big deal, it's just one scream. Gene showed up that morning with some friends and business associates whom he's invited down, one of which was his songwriting partner Mitch Weissman.

Part of my rock star treatment was that every day, when I got to the studio, there was a six pack of Budweiser in the fridge, and a fifth of Jack Daniel's with a pack of Marlboro on the music stand by the microphone. It didn't matter if I was singing one line or three songs, there was my beer, my bottle, and my smokes, and that morning was no exception. I cracked the seal on the Jack and took a big swig, sat it back on the music stand but did not replace the cap. I told Mikey to go red at the spot of the scream, took a deep breath, and let it wail.

I held the note out for a long time. And then, wanting both to show off for Gene's people and also to capture the ultimate epic rock scream on tape, I held it out a little longer. And then I held it out too long and blacked out. As I fell, I knocked the open and damn near full bottle of Jack Daniel's off the music stand and whiskey went everywhere. Luckily I did not knock over the $3000.00 Neumann U-87 microphone which I was screaming into, however I did knock over the SM57 dummy mic on a boom which Mikey trained me to use as a shield between my pipes and the actual recording mic. I was twitching on the studio floor in an epileptic fit and came to slowly; the funny thing was that no one in the control room was alarmed; they thought that I was so pleased with my amazing killer scream that I was flopping around on the floor in some kind of gleeful victory dance.

Screaming so high, hard, and long that I deprive my brain of oxygen has happened a number of times since, but that's the only time I ever blacked out because of it.. Whether on stage or in the studio, I can tell when my brain begins to tingle and I start to see spots, and I go down on one knee and take a couple of deep breaths until it passes. Chances are if you've ever been to a KEEL concert and seen me kneel and bow my head, I'm not praying, and it is not one of my choreographed stage moves – I am just trying to maintain consciousness.

Once back in California, I met with Chuck Beeson, art director at A&M records, regarding the album cover. I supplied him with the KEEL logo, which as you may recall

I had designed myself as a variation on the Steeler logo. He asked for input about what I wanted to see on the cover of "The Right To Rock;" and back then the album cover was a really big deal – a 12"x12" piece of art which could make or break a rock release, where many fans judged the album and either bought it or not based on how cool the cover was. I was quick to admit that I was not an album cover designer (although it had been my idea to rip off the Van Halen 1 album cover concept for the Steeler album). I just had one stipulation for Chuck and the A&M Records art department: under no circumstances were they to fuck with my logo. Do whatever you want with the album cover; just do NOT change the logo.

A couple of weeks passed by, and Beeson summoned me back to his office to check out the album cover concept. I walked in and there was this art mockup, a little larger than actual album cover size, depicting the hilt of a sword with these angel wings on it, lightning in the background, and the KEEL logo had been totally scrapped in favor of an all new original logo design. And it was so fucking beautiful that I just said "O.K." Artist John Taylor DisMukes had created one of the all-time coolest album covers and the classic KEEL logo that we all know and love. The only difference in that original piece was that there was a devil at the top of the hilt crouched over the logo, with one hand at the top where the two "E's" meet. I asked that they replace the devil with a Flying V guitar and gave them a picture of my Charvel V for reference, and DisMukes did the rest.

A photo session was arranged for the back cover of the album and our new promo pics. I lobbied hard for some extra wardrobe money so we could get some new outfits for the photos, and we were allocated a budget of $100.00 per man to buy some new stage clothes. We went shopping together on Hollywood Boulevard, and we each bought a new pair of boots (I bought two pair, some red ones and a pair of leopard boots that looked awesome but were way too small for me). The photographer got all artsy on us, transforming his studio into a dark setting with mannequins wrapped in black plastic and then flooded the floor with dry ice fog so that all of our nice new boots were hidden from view.

"The Right To Rock has a lot of power and energy. It's real tough sounding to me, it sounds like a bunch of crazy kids in a bar making noise. They're hungry, and you can hear it. But, the album has some class and the attitude is right."
Gene Simmons

"KEEL's The Right To Rock is one of the best Top 10 heavy metal albums of 1985."
Rock Scene

"When it comes to red-hot metal, KEEL rocks and Gene produces."
Gerri Miller – Metal Edge

"Generously produced by KISS man Gene Simmons, who also contributes three songs, KEEL have undertaken their big time entrance with enough force and Metallic majesty to guarantee acceptance in a big way......Really I can't recommend this LP highly enough."
Derek Oliver - Kerrang

"KEEL is prepared to show everyone that L.A. has produced yet another top-notch metal attraction."
Andy Secher – Hit Parader

"KEEL has taken the country by storm with their no-nonsense AC/DC like rock 'n' roll and their hit anthem The Right To Rock."
Beth Nussbaum – Metal Mania

"The Right To Rock is a MUST for any rock 'n' roll fan."
Elianne Halbersberg - Faces

"With The Right To Rock KEEL have become yet another L.A. based metal act to successfully make the transition from independent label to the national spotlight."
Circus

"The Right To Rock puts emphasis on the guitar from start to finish."
Joanne Carnegie - Creem

"The Right To Rock is 1985's first entry in the category of anthem-rock-song and it's destined to be a top contender."
Dick Grimmit - The L.A. Rocker Magazine

15

NO PAIN NO GAIN

I've learned a lesson fools never learn
Play by your own rules or you'll get burned
I'll have the last laugh when I see the tables turn

But there's a high price you gotta pay
Just be a good boy and do everything they say
I say to hell with that, I'll do it my own way

Life's a game that has no rules
You play to win, or you play the fool – don't you know
No pain no gain

("No Pain No Gain" – lyrics by RK 1985 – from the KEEL album "The Final Frontier" released 1986)

My daughter Kelly Lee Keel was born in the calm before the storm, between the completion of "The Right To Rock" but before its release the following January. Of all the things I've experienced, the birth of my firstborn remains the most profound; the only thing that compares to it is the birth of my son Ryan a few years later. The birth of your children brings you closer to God and makes you feel like a God all at the same time, reinforces belief in miracles and gives us just a peek at the positive divine force of nature.

KEEL's debut album "Lay Down The Law" was also born that October but its release was lost in the hype of our major label deal, the fact that we were working with Gene, and the build up to the release of "The Right To Rock." It did, however, receive some rave reviews in the international press.

"Tough, mean & meaty, you won't find a better album of L.A. lunacy this side of Motley Crue's original "Too Fast For Love" LP.
Derek Oliver, Kerrang

"Apart from the abusive lead vocals, the set has some great melodic metal tunes. Possibility of radio interest here, with a range from amplified pounding to mellower acoustic songs."
Billboard Magazine

KEEL rode the wave of momentum well, performing to sell-out crowds at The Country Club and Pomona Valley Auditorium. On October 25th, the day Kelly was born, KEEL was listed as the #1 top drawing act in Southern California on the Music Connection Live Action Chart. Selling out one gig per night just didn't seem like enough, so we sold out two shows in one night at The Country Club on December 22nd with our first annual "KEEL Kristmas" concerts.

"Lay Down The Law" also debuted at #5 on the Japanese "Import Disks" chart.

We signed with Great Southern for merchandising – they were the #1 concert merchandising company in the world at the time. They advanced us $50,000 against future sales, and we received the same amount from our new music publishing company Famous Music (a division of Paramount, which was owned by Gulf Oil). There were also advances received from European and Japanese record deals as labels lined up to release our forthcoming album worldwide. We were told these funds were being used to finance our career and we were investing in our future; a full time crew was hired and put on retainer, including Mark Workman, our road manager Willie Korman, and our guitar tech Jim Quinn. I think those guys were getting $700.00 a week while the band was still getting $100.00 a week (remember, I got an extra $50.00 a week because I was the boss). Also on the payroll were attorneys, accountants, and the firm of Michael Levine Public Relations. We signed ICM for concert booking, one of the giants in the industry at the time, and were assigned to a young agent named Troy Blakely who would go on to become a giant in that field in his own right. More deals came across the table faster than we could read them, much less understand them – suddenly we were signed to JVC in Japan and Phonogram in Europe.

MTV was the primary selling and marketing tool of the day – the right video in heavy rotation could make a band platinum overnight. So while we'd spent $40,000.00 total recording the entire album, we spent $90,000.00 in two days making the video for the single, which was by unanimous choice the title track. We went through a number of detailed "treatments" as the most sought-after video directors vied for the job of producing our first clip; I chose one with a sci-fi theme, set in a future where rock & roll was against the law and we were outlaw rebels who had taken heavy metal underground. We enlisted our investors, the Hell's Angels, to appear in the video and the treatment made it seem like an episode of Star Trek; the final result was a cheesy comedic romp very reminiscent of what Twisted Sister was doing around the same time. I know a lot of people are fond of that video, and I'm thankful for what it did for my career, but it neither captured the true essence or the band nor stood the test of time and looks very dated today. Not as bad as Dokken's "Breaking The Chains" video, but close. The band had a lot of energy and killer choreography that was not captured in the clip; we were relegated to a supporting role as The Kid became the real star of the piece. The makeshift stage was a variety of stacked wood palettes so we could be lit from below, very shaky and fragile, so it was difficult to do any of our rehearsed moves, and whenever I would stomp my feet the slats on the wood palette beneath me would break and I would fall into the hole.

People would always ask "Who's that kid in The Right To Rock video?" He was a young aspiring actor named Marcello Krakoff, hired for the role. Everybody on the set loved him, and he became a cult hero; you may not believe this, but he's actually all grown up now. Marcello went on to do some TV and film work, and became a tattoo artist. Through the internet we reconnected and he joined us on stage for "The Right To Rock" at a show in Arizona a few years ago.

"I really loved 'The Right To Rock.' When your video came out, I was 14, and I would stand there and sing along and try to be as cool as you."
Sebastian Bach

Of course I had an affair with the make-up girl on the set. It started with the first coat of foundation; I was intoxicated with my first real taste of rock stardom, on location filming my first music video, and she was cute and flirtatious. I kept finding excuses for more make-up – every time I'd work up a sweat I'd go back to her for another coat of powder, and by the end of the day I had more makeup on than all four members of KISS and ended up in her bed. I got home very late smelling like perfume and pussy, and Dee Dee busted me immediately. In later years she would characterize me as a "serial adulterer" and while she has at times modified the facts when telling her side of the story, she was absolutely correct in that analysis. The make-up chick wasn't the first or last, just the first time I got caught.

"The Right To Rock" was released on January 21st 1985 and instantly became the fastest selling debut album in A&M Records' history. I give a lot of that credit to Gene's involvement – I know a lot of the KISS fans bought our album just because he had produced it. If KEEL was good enough for Gene Simmons, then it must be good enough for the KISS army and that was a very powerful endorsement.

"In the summer of 1985 I was just a 12 year old kid living in Auburn, Alabama. I was already into bands like KISS, Twisted Sister, Motley Crue and Quiet Riot, and one day I went to visit a friend that had just received a new shipment of 10 cassette tapes. This was part of the old program where you could get 10 albums for 1 penny as advertised in TV Guide.

"In this batch of 10 tapes was this cassette KEEL – "The Right To Rock" which was actually shipped by mistake. I remember thinking how cool the cover was with the angels and sword and read where it was produced Gene Simmons. I wasn't sure if this was the same Gene from KISS but the artwork on this cassette was cool enough for me to give it a listen. I guess my friend had already played through Side 1 because the first song I heard was "Electric Love" the lead track on side 2 and then it went immediately into "Speed Demon".

"I couldn't believe what I was hearing because each song was just as powerful as the last one. This was one of those stop-what-you're-doing, jaw-dropping moments. I had never heard anything like this before. This didn't even come close to the other bands I was listening to. The power of this singer and the amazing guitars just blew me away. At that point I made up my mind this cassette was going home with me that day. Obviously there was no internet back then and we didn't have MTV at home so I would

always go the grocery store with my mother just so I could stand at the magazine rack while she shopped and I would read as many metal magazines as I could before she finished. This was the only way for me get information on my favorite bands, and is where I got my first visual of the band KEEL because there was not a picture of the band on the cassette. This is also how I found out that this was the same Gene Simmons from KISS doing the producing."
Aaron Fischer

Our publicist Mitch Schneider was, and still is, one of the best in his field and he was very responsible for creating the illusion that KEEL was a platinum act when in reality we were not even gold. He secured major magazine features, television appearances, and arranged for me to be the host and guest-host of MTV's popular "Headbanger's Ball" program which spotlighted hard rock and heavy metal videos.

Mitch told me one day that we had gotten a short feature article in the new issue of CIRCUS magazine and to me that was a sign that I had really *made it*. That magazine had been my pipeline to rock & roll information and images for years; the first time I saw or heard about so many important bands and albums had been in the hallowed pages of CIRCUS and coverage in that magazine would expose you to millions of rock fans. So on the day it came out, I headed down to a newsstand on Hollywood Boulevard.

I eagerly picked up a copy and started flipping the pages. I found the KEEL article and was reading it when the guy who ran the newsstand came up behind me.

"You gotta buy it before you read it," he said. Then he looked at photo in the article, then he looked at me, then back at the article. I was wearing a sleeveless shirt, thus my first tattoo (my RK logo in red, outlined in black) was easily visible – and it was also visible in the magazine photo. "Hey, is that you?"

"Naw," said, whipping a five dollar bill out of my wallet. "But check it out." I pointed to my upper arm. "That son of a bitch stole my tattoo!" And he believed me.

I've done thousands of shows in my lifetime, but the first handful of gigs in 1985 are all noteworthy. It started with an opening slot for Dokken at the Palladium in Hollywood on February 15th, when KEEL delivered a triumphant hometown show just a couple of weeks after the album came out.

Then it was off to the Midwest for a series of performances; these were critical radio markets for us so we were catering to the local stations; if some of the key stations "added" your single to rotation, other secondary stations would follow their lead and if you got enough stations you would have a HIT. These gigs were extremely important, and since we were flying all we took were guitars and depended upon rental equipment at every show.

Nowadays we have a Tech Rider (a contract that states what equipment must be supplied for fly-in dates) – back then I guess we didn't, because when we got to Detroit for the first show, the drums and amps resembled Frankenstein's junkyard. Some of the drums were different colors, the amps were all acting up, there weren't even enough cables to hook everything up. Soundcheck was such a nightmare I was having a panic attack, because not only was this KEEL's first ever out-of-state-on-the-road-we're-finally-on-tour gig, the show was SOLD OUT and the big rock radio station in town WLLZ was broadcasting our performance live on the air. Hence the stress as the day wore on and stuff still didn't work. Eventually it got so late they *had* to open the doors and let the crowd in, and we hadn't even soundchecked yet, and we had no choice because they had to set levels for the live radio broadcast. The band had come straight to the venue from the airport and we were all in our sweat clothes with our hair pulled back, looking not at all like the rock stars the fans were expecting. So there we were, in sweats and street clothes, unshowered, soundchecking in front of a sold out audience at Harpo's in Detroit Michigan.

We eventually did get cleaned up and back just in time for the show, which was indeed broadcast live on WLLZ. We got through it OK, but it was one of those shows that was heavily bootlegged because the broadcast was easily recorded by a lot of people listening and by the radio station; I've listened to it a couple of times. You can hear Bryan launching into these shredding solos with a twangy clean tone because his amp or pedals were malfunctioning.

But that was our trial by fire – we felt like we'd withstood the road's initial body blows and we lived to fight another day, and subsequent concerts in Milwaukee and Boston went well. By the time we got to Toledo, we were fearless. The roads were covered in ice , and Ray Chambers was driving like a maniac, sliding all over the road with the fuel gauge on "E" – we were late for the show, and he kept saying "Ain't got time to stop for gas." He literally skidded into the parking lot of the venue and we ran out of the car and right onto the stage to the roar of the crowd.

"In less than one year, 23-year-old Ron Keel, vocalist, guitarist, songwriter and leader of the band that bears his name, has accomplished what it takes some musicians a lifetime to do.

"He formed KEEL in early 1984 after his first band Steeler (with guitar whiz Yngwie Malmsteen) decided to call it quits after four years of rotating personnel and minor success. Within the next twelve months, Keel secured a recording contract, recorded two albums and embarked on their first national tour. A whirlwind rise to prominence by any standard.

"On March 2, KEEL played the second show of their tour here, a free concert at Papagaio nightclub. Judging by the devastating performance turned in by this five-piece L.A. heavy metal troupe, their rapid ascent is no fluke.

"'The Right To Rock,' KEEL's first national release, produced by KISS bassist Gene Simmons, is a rampaging collection of metal anthems highlighted by "Easier Said Than Done" and "The Right To Rock." KEEL's ravaging three guitar attack, spearheaded by Ron keel's searing four-octave vocals, is something that should be experienced live to be fully appreciated. With Keel's every waking moment spent fighting for it, metal maniacs everywhere should soon have 'the right to rock.'"
Michael Pflughoeft – Milwaukee Sentinel

The Palladium with Dokken had been a big deal – 4,400 people, sold out – and the club gigs on that first Midwest swing had been cool because they were all packed and KEEL was the headliner. We came right back to SoCal from that trip for two nights opening for Triumph, the first of which was at the Orange Pavilion in San Bernardino where we had headlined only months before; I loved and respected Triumph and was thrilled to be their opening act. But I was hungry for the arenas, the 10-20,000 capacity auditoriums where rock was meant to be played, and the following day, March 8th 1985, I would finally get my chance at the Los Angeles Sports Arena.

Triumph were very professional and treated us well, making sure we had time for a soundcheck and generous use of the sound and lights. And they let us hang our brand new backdrop, a beautifully massive black fireproof canvas with the red-and-white KEEL logo carefully sewn on to it. Once our soundcheck was done, I went all the way up to the very back of the arena and sat in the uppermost seat, the one farthest away from the stage, and looked down upon it, fully lit in all its glory, with the huge KEEL banner suspended from the rigging, our wall of amplifiers, the KEEL logo on both bass drums, and just sat there enjoying the moment. The pace of my life was accelerating beyond my control, and in many ways has never slowed down, but there are moments in time when I've forced myself to stop and celebrate the victories along the way, and sitting there up in the cheap seats of the L.A. Sports Arena I made a promise to whoever had bought a ticket to sit in that spot later that night: I am going to fucking rock your ass off.

"There's something about Keel – the man and the band – that I haven't experienced in an American rock act for some time...and I'm talking 'Toys In The Attic' period Tyler. Firing his message straight from the hip and between gritted teeth is a lady-killing lad embracing nuthin' particularly fancy except an illuminated sign beaming star, star, star. Ron Keel is the heir to a throne whose other potential occupants are more or less a bunch of comic book comedians."
Derek Oliver – KERRANG

FRIDAY APRIL 5TH 1985: Loudness, Japan's premiere heavy metal rock group, begins their "Thunder In The East" tour here in Santa Barbara performing with KEEL and local band Cirith Ungol. It's an evening of rock n roll for hardy souls tonight at the Arlington Theater, 7 PM.

Our 58-date tour with Loudness would start a disturbing trend that would end up costing KEEL a large portion of the success we'd worked so hard for: we would become the perennial opening act for bands that really shouldn't have been headlining. Instead of playing arenas, we were playing 2000 seat theaters and clubs; on the Loudness tour, we even played a pizza parlor in Rochester, New York. In subsequent years this trend would continue with bands like Accept, Queensryche (before they broke big with "Mindcrime"), Krokus, and Quiet Riot when they were experiencing their dramatic decline in popularity. Make no mistake, I really liked (and still like) all those bands, I love being on tour (ANY tour), and appreciated those opportunities, but it's a simple matter of mathematics: if you are playing to smaller crowds, fewer people are going to see you, hence fewer people will buy your albums. Fewer people will buy your T-shirts and other merchandise, making it harder to recoup those large advances and pay your road expenses. We made good friends with those bands we toured with, had some great times, and our fans contributed considerably to ticket sales on those tours, but we were playing for 10,000 per week when we needed to be playing for that many every night.

We did some big shows – including the 1986 Texxas Jam at the Cotton Bowl in Dallas in front of 86,000 people – but we only ever did two legitimate arena tours: opening for Dio throughout Europe on the 1986 "Sacred Heart" tour, and 14 shows at the tail end of Bon Jovi's "Slippery When Wet" tour. On "The Right To Rock" tour, we opened for Joan Jett at the Astro Arena in Houston; that and the L.A. Sports Arena gig with Triumph were the ONLY arena gigs we did in 1985 as "The Right To Rock" spent 26 weeks on the Billboard charts.

To this day, I'm amazed by the amount of people that come up to me and say "I saw you on tour with KISS!" I hate to burst your bubble, but KEEL *never* did a show with KISS, although Gene was a huge supporter of the band and I begged him repeatedly to give us opening slots. He would just look at me and smirk, and say "Ron, I'm not stupid." I never knew what he meant by that, but I took it as a compliment. KISS was never afraid to take some ass-kicking bands out on the road with them, but we never got the chance. Gene did try to push some big buttons for us – I remember when we were in the studio recording "The Final Frontier" he was on the phone with Ozzy Osbourne, hammering on Ozzy to take us out on his 1986 tour. Ozzy ended up deciding upon Metallica instead. The good news for KEEL was that after the Ozzy tour, Metallica would achieve headline status with "Master Of Puppets" and begin their own arena tour, and KEEL was chosen to be the opening act; unfortunately the tour was postponed when James Hetfield broke his wrist skateboarding. By the time the dates got rescheduled we were already out with Accept, who were a kick ass metal band from Germany but were headlining much smaller venues.

I know at some point in 1985 or 1986 we were booked to open for Motley Crue on tour – I recall seeing the posters and advertisements, but none ever made it into my scrapbooks. I also know Nikki Sixx made a special trip to San Diego to see us opening for Queensryche, and the next day we were notified that we had gotten kicked off the Crue tour. We eventually did open the first two shows of their 1987 "Girls Girls Girls" tour because Whitesnake, the opener for the rest of the tour, was unavailable for the first two dates.

But in April of 1985, we were just excited to be ON TOUR and we believed the road would go on forever, that the stint with Loudness was just the beginning of one endless rock & roll party. The first single, "The Right To Rock," had run its course and it was time to consider a follow-up; the decision was made to do a special re-mix of the Gene Simmons song "Easier Said Than Done" and re-record the vocal in the process. The night before the Loudness tour began in full force (in Phoenix) Gene, Mikey Davis and I went into a Los Angeles recording studio to redo that lead vocal.

It was a long night – Gene was pushing me hard, I was pouring everything I had into each phrase, and it wasn't just one vocal, we were doubling as well. That was a fairly common procedure, to record an exact double of the lead vocal to add thickness and texture and to hide pitch errors. You can hear it on most of the KISS recordings, that's where Ozzy gets some of that effect, Stephen Pearcy on most of the RATT hits, Vince Neil, and I did it a lot as well. I haven't doubled a lead vocal since working with Gene, but back then we did it all the time and it's pretty easy to tell which songs were doubled. The "single version" of "Easier Said Than Done" was critical for us; album sales had stalled right above the 300,000 mark and if the next single was a hit, we just might have a gold record on our hands and on our walls.

The band and crew, in a rented RV, went on to Phoenix without me as I screamed my guts out all night long in the studio with Gene. We got a strong vocal and a great mix (this is the version that appears on the "25th Anniversary Edition" of the album, released in 2010 on Frontiers Records), and I got on a plane to Phoenix. I got off the plane, into a cab, and straight to the radio station for my first interview on KDKB – the radio station I had grown up listening to was now playing my music and I was on the air talking about it. My band KEEL was on tour and playing to a sold out crowd in my hometown - I was running on adrenaline and cocaine, with no sleep at all, when I showed up at the venue for soundcheck and continued screaming my heart out. And we had a good show that night, a proud start to our road trip and we'd delivered the goods in front of family, friends, ex-girlfriends, and a couple thousand rabid KEELaholics, as we were calling them.

We had done a package deal with La Quinta hotels for rooms on the Southwest leg of the tour; we had hotel rooms in Phoenix but little time to sleep in them – I think they let us take a nap for a few hours before heading off to Albuquerque, New Mexico for another show the next day. Nobody had stocked the RV with bedding before hitting the road, so we all stole the pillows from the Phoenix hotel and left town in the dead of the night.

There was no such thing as GPS or cell phones back in the day. All business was conducted by pay phones, which were everywhere then. Navigation was done by pay phone; we'd pull over at a truck stop in the middle of nowhere while our tour manager called our destination and asked for directions. In between hotel rooms, all business was done by pay phone, including the endless stream of interviews I was always doing. We would check into a hotel at seven A.M. after an all-night drive and Willie would give me my "to-do list" for the day – the local radio interviews would start early in the morning so we could catch listeners driving to work. Then there would be a list of new stations that were adding our single into rotation, and it would be my job to call them personally and thank them for playing our music. While the other guys slept, I talked. As Marc Ferrari is fond of saying, "Heavy is the head that wears the crown."

As we arrived in Albuquerque, the RV sputtered and died, broken down already at the outset of the tour. Exhausted, the guys in the band started out on foot for the La Quinta hotel, about a mile off the exit. We trudged into the lobby and before I even made it to the counter the clerk was shaking his head. "The La Quinta Hotel in Phoenix called and said you stole all the pillows out of your rooms last night," he said. "You're not staying here. And you've been banned from all La Quinta hotels in the future."

Over the next several months, whatever you think happened, happened. The miles, the shows, the interviews, the women, the drugs, the pleasure and the pain, all became a blur. One story often told is of the time we got the RV stuck under a low overpass in Pennsylvania, and could move neither forward or back until we let the air out of the tires. Of course we went forward (we were on our way to a gig), tearing the air conditioner off the roof in the process. We destroyed that RV to the tune of about $25,000.00 which entitled us to move up to an actual Silver Eagle tour bus. That was the bus that would take me back to Nashville.

One cool thing about having multiple home towns is you can have multiple triumphant homecoming gigs. I had left Music City four years earlier, and much had been made in the media and press about my history there and my status as the first major metal artist to break out of that market. This hype led to appearances at a couple of big events, the first of which was a headline slot at the biggest summer concert of 1985 in Nashville called "One For The Sun," an annual event held on the lake at Hermitage Landing. Opening the show were new acts like Autograph and Van Zant (a great melodic rock band featuring Skynyrd vocalist Johnny Van Zant), as well as the legendary Steppenwolf.

You can imagine I was feeling pretty good about life when my big tour bus pulled into the parking lot that day; looking out the window, as if in slow motion, I saw a group of faces I recognized. One of them was Ken Kennedy, my old bandmate in Lust; the guy who had intended to kick me out of the band because I would never be able to cut it in the recording studio, because I didn't have what it took to make it in this business. And there next to him was my ex-wife Kathy Wolfe, whom I hadn't seen since the divorce four years prior. I asked the driver to pull over, and when the hydraulic bus door opened, I was standing there in front of Ken Kennedy with a big smile on my face. I invited them on board, and reveled in watching him look around at the fixtures and features inside that mighty machine that carried us from town to town, living the dream. I was gracious and humble on the outside, but I thoroughly enjoyed sitting around the front lounge in that bus and hearing him admit, "Well, you really did it man. You made it."

"What's an essential part of a rock star's survival kit for life on the concert circuit? Go ahead and ask rowdy Ron Keel and the hard-rocking KEEL, back in L.A. following a seven month tour of 75 cities. To alleviate the problem of groupies handcuffing themselves to the group's tour bus, rented cars and hotel rooms, each member of KEEL, reveals Ron, now carries keys to unlock the handcuffs in emergencies. And you thought life was easy on the road."
Hollywood Press

Gene Simmons had personally introduced me to Dennis Berardi, the President of Kramer guitars, who gave me my first "artist endorsement." This is a situation where companies provide you with goods and services – in this case, free guitars – in exchange for you playing and promoting the instruments. Dennis was very generous and supportive and I had a few cool Kramers in the collection, as well my old Steeler Charvel and a couple of acoustics.

My Dad had come to visit and attend one of the Southern California gigs, and he was sleeping on the couch when I went into the living room the next morning to put away the previous night's guitars – I kept them stacked in their cases in a corner. He sat up and said, "Damn boy, you got enough guitars?" Always looking for an opportunity to impress the old man, I said to him, "No. I don't think I do." I went straight to the phone and called Kramer Guitars in New Jersey.

"Ron Keel, calling for Dennis Berardi. Sure, I'll hold. Hi Dennis, how are you? Great, man. Listen, I'd like to order a custom guitar; I want a Vanguard V, the Randy Rhoads body shape. I want the coolest leopard-skin paint job, matching headstock. Black Floyd Rose, black hardware. We're playing our first shows in New York in a few weeks, so I'd like to have it delivered to soundcheck at L'Amour East in Brooklyn on the 25th. OK? Cool, thank you Dennis. Take care – bye now."

Roy sat there on the couch, blown away and duly impressed.

I went about my business, back on the road and living life at the speed of rock & roll. On April 25th we rolled into New York, and I was hanging out at soundcheck that afternoon when some guy in a suit came in, carrying a guitar case. He walked up to me. "Ron Keel?" he asked. I said, yeah. He put the case down on a table and opened it up.

I swear I had forgotten all about the phone conversation with Dennis Berardi weeks before – hell, I didn't need any more guitars, I was just trying to impress my father – but there it was before me, the most beautiful leopard skin guitar in rock & roll history. It was to become the signature instrument for my entire career.

During a tour break in May, I went to Europe for the first time for a media tour. For this whirlwind round of interviews I was accompanied by Bennett Kaufman, an enterprising young record executive at Gold Mountain who was my handler for the journey. The media tour was coordinated by the promotional staff at Phonogram, our

European record company, and I was assigned a specific PR rep in each country that knew the local media and spoke the various languages. We landed in Paris on a gray morning and went straight from the plane to the car to a hotel room where I spent the day doing one interview after the other with members of the media until our French rep rushed us off to the airport to catch the next plane. As I got on the plane, I realized I hadn't even seen the Eiffel Tower, and thus actually had my doubts as to if I had really spent the day in Paris at all. There would be several more layovers and drive-throughs in Paris before I would be able to validate the existence of that historic monument.

The next stop was London, and there was more media in Great Britain than we could accommodate in a day, so we made base camp at a posh 5-star hotel and began an all-out media blitz. And when the first day was done, I managed to arrange a night on the town which included a visit to the legendary Marquee Club, London's equivalent to the Whisky A Go Go; and somehow very late that night we ended up at a very hip and historic London nightclub called the Hippodrome. I was really living it up, a rock star on my own traveling around Europe and the U.K. with my very own handlers and PR people and drivers to look out for me and satisfy my every appetite and whim. The only items not on the menu were pussy and cocaine, and I found the perfect mixture of both at the Hippodrome in the gorgeous form of a beautiful British blonde bombshell with a couple of vials of white powder tucked in between her spectacular breasts.

She had a couple of friends with her, and I had my posse, so we all went back to her place to keep the party going. I ended up in her bed around dawn, but made it to my first interview of the day just a few hours later. It turned out she was married to a very prominent rock star who just happened to be out on the road at the time; I do not condone affairs with married women, but I made an exception in her case because while I greatly admired her rock star husband I did not (at the time) know him personally. She was rich and resourceful and understood I was there to take care of business, and proceeded to orchestrate our affair throughout Europe over the next week – perfectly complimenting and supporting, never getting in the way, but always there on the next plane or waiting in my bed at the next hotel in whatever country was next on the itinerary.

When I got to Munich, Germany, the attendant at the front desk informed me that my wife had already checked in for us. Until I opened the door and saw Jane Doe in white lingerie, I seriously had no clue if it was my real wife come all the way from the states to surprise me or not.

I was scheduled to fly out of Heathrow at the conclusion of the media tour, and stayed just a few minutes too long in Jane Doe's bed. As I was running through the terminal, I saw the Pan Am 747 pulling away from the gate and knew I was in trouble. I begged the people at the gate to call the plane back, and they got on the radio while I literally pounded on the glass window pleading with them to come back for me. I was amazed when the jumbo jet reversed engines and actually returned to the gate; it seems my trusted handler Bennett Kaufman had poured the rock star juice on thick and strong and convinced them to come back for me. The plane was practically empty anyway, so it wasn't hard to see Bennett shaking his head at me in consternation; I just smiled at him and took a seat. We had practically the entire upper area - that bubble on top of a 747 - to ourselves. I proceeded to drink heavily, smoke cigarettes (you could smoke on a plane back then), and during the flight I wrote a song called "Just Another Girl."

I received my first royalty check from the Steeler album for a little over $800.00. I spent a cold day wandering the streets of Baltimore, looking in every jewelry store for a wedding ring. It seemed I was on my way to real success, our daughter Kelly would soon be one year old, and I thought – or at least I hoped – that taking the relationship to the next level may curb my adulterous tendencies. I really wanted to be a good man and do the right thing, so a few weeks later Dee Dee came out on the road for a visit and I ordered up a romantic dinner from room service.

The biscuits were hard as bricks, and we took turns throwing them against the wall. I had stuffed the box with the wedding ring down my pants, and at some opportune moment during dinner I reached over and put her hand on my crotch. Her eyes got real big, and she asked, "Is that a biscuit in your pants?"

Every Tuesday morning I'd have the bus pull over at the first pay phone and call the office in L.A. to find out our chart position for the week; "The Right To Rock" spent a total of 26 weeks on the Billboard charts, cracking the Hot 100 Albums to peak at #99. "Easier Said Than Done" was never given a legitimate shot at being the second single – there were some 12-inch singles sent to the primary radio stations but we were told it did not "test well." There was no second video, no second single to put the record over the top, but we had something almost as good: Tipper Gore and the PMRC.

When, in August of 1985, a group of Washington wives known as the "Parents Music Resource Center" declared war on freedom of lyrical expression, targeting hard rock and metal as "Porn Rock" with the goal of putting ratings and warning labels on albums containing explicit or content. Our album cover was declared "Satanic" because of a resemblance to the Ark Of The Covenant. Dee Snider, John Denver and Frank Zappa all went to testify at the Senate Hearings, while most of us thrust our fists into the air and screamed "Hallelujah!" Put a WARNING: EXPLICIT CONTENT label on something and sales go through the roof; some artists took to putting their own stickers on their albums to capitalize on the attention.

KEEL capitalized by re-releasing "The Right To Rock" single as a rallying cry for those who lobbied against the fascist establishment that sought to censor our work. The media machine was back in high gear, and suddenly

Gene Simmons and I were making the rounds on network TV talk shows and I was appearing alongside Donnie Osmond in "People" magazine, rejuvenating album sales and causing it to climb back up the charts. The numbers were hovering dangerously close to gold status when the plug was inexplicably pulled; Gold Mountain, ecstatic with a debut album that far exceeded expectations in terms of sales and international profile, decided to immediately exercise their option for another album and we were told to cease all touring activity and get a new batch of songs in order.

I don't find it strange at all that at 500,000 units sold – a "Gold" album – we would have been due a substantial financial bonus. Therefore, no matter how many copies we continued to sell in the years to come, official sales of "The Right To Rock" remain right around 499,999.

16

THE FINAL FRONTIER

The times are changing for you and I
We seek our future in the sky
On metal wings our race will fly
To conquer space and time

We'll face our destiny on the final frontier
Beyond this galaxy – out on the final frontier
We're the next pioneers on strange new worlds
Out on the final frontier

("The Final Frontier" – lyrics by RK 1985 – from the KEEL album "The Final Frontier" released 1986)

That summer, "Hit Parader" magazine published a fan letter that had a profound effect on me. It was from a young man who'd been through a hard time at home, his parents couldn't relate to him, he'd lost his job, lost his girl, and decided he couldn't take any more. Determined to end it all, he took a handgun and a boom box out into a field and sat down to listen to some rock and roll for the last time. The album he had chosen to go out listening to was "The Right To Rock."

In his letter, he said he found some inner strength in that song which convinced him to re-think his plan, and he was writing to thank us for saving his life.

When your music stops a bullet, that's powerful stuff, and that guy's story immediately made me re-think my entire lyrical and musical direction. I realized that there was more to this than banging your head and banging chicks, that I had some measure of power and with that came some measure of responsibility. "The Right To Rock" was a career phrase, a career lyric, a career riff, and an artist is lucky to get even one of those in a lifetime, so I didn't even try. Ferrari had written a great 'rock' anthem called "Rock & Roll Animal," for the new album; I set my sights on the stars, and wrote a song about hope for all humanity, built upon the belief that we would overcome our petty differences as well as the constraints of gravity – that we would be fruitful and multiply, and live long and prosper, throughout the universe and all eternity. That song became the title track to "The Final Frontier," our second major label release and the first one for MCA Records.

That concept, lifted from the cultural phenomenon known as "Star Trek," was the most positive and powerful message I could conceive of to build our new album around. I won't turn this chapter into a debate on "Trek" – which series or movies were better or worse – but people from my generation realize what an influence the original series had on almost every aspect of our society, from spiritual to racial to technological and philosophical aspects that we sometimes take for granted today. It was

John Lennon's "Imagine" with warp drive and phaser guns, and when so much heavy metal music was dark and destructive, I thought we could offer a positive alternative to the doom and gloom. We needed an identity to set us apart from all the other bands – Crue had the Devil, Stryper had God, and KEEL had Gene Roddenberry, the Great Bird of the Galaxy.

I thought it was brilliant – the KISS fans had helped make "The Right To Rock" a success, now all we had to do was sell our music to the millions of Star Trek fans around the world. We'd be the good guys, saving the day and doing the right thing. Instead of the cartoon characters that were lying about their age in their 20's, making up stories about their hedonistic lifestyles that were little more than PR stunts, KEEL would be REAL – the guys next door.

Of course we'd written our share of new metal anthems like "Rock & Roll Animal," "No Pain No Gain," and "Raised On Rock." We traded the wanton excess of "So Many Girls, So Little Time" for the sensitivity of "Tears Of Fire," but still gave the groupies their due with "Just Another Girl." I wanted to write a lyric about the heart of a professional boxer, and we came up with "Arm & A Leg." My Bad Co. influence came out in a song called "Here Today Gone Tomorrow," while Ferrari expressed a desire to show off his classical chops with an instrumental which I named "Nightfall," after the Isaac Asimov story and my old high school rock band. All that was left was to choose a cover song for the new album.

I'd strongly considered adopting a tradition of covering a different Rolling Stones tune on every record, and had worked up a metal version of "Satisfaction" that was pretty cool. Another one that was high on my list was the old Argent classic "Hold Your Head Up." But the blessing and the curse of "Because The Night" was cast upon me one afternoon when it came on the car radio while I was cruising through Laurel Canyon. It was dark yet strong, classy and sexy, and in my head I automatically heard the KEEL version come to life. I found a copy of the sheet music in a local music store and worked up a version in my home studio.

Portable multi-track recording had just become affordable and user-friendly and everybody had a TASCAM 4-track cassette multi-track unit. Before I got my first drum machine, I would record Dwain doing a variety of beats at a variety of tempos and use those to write riffs on top of. We wrote a lot on the road, Ferrari in his room with his 4-track and I with mine down the hall, each trying to out-do the other in a healthy songwriting competition that helped us both develop our craft.

Suddenly we were no longer with A&M Records; Gold Mountain had moved their entire roster to MCA for a sizable sum of money and KEEL was part of the deal. All the relationships we'd built with the staff at A&M were out the window and we had to start over as an adopted stepchild at the bottom of a very large artist roster; we just went with the flow, not realizing at the time how much this move may have cost us in terms of career success.

When the time came for my first production meeting with Gene, it was much more relaxed than that initial contact the previous year. We had become friends, Gene genuinely cared about the band and was excited to create an epic album that would really put KEEL on the map. He was so taken with the riff for "The Final Frontier" that he didn't even balk at the subject matter. When the topic turned to choosing a cover song, Gene suggested a KEEL-ized version of the old Sonny & Cher hit "And The Beat Goes On." Many people know that Gene was close with Cher once, and I believe he still carried a torch for her. He had cut the demo himself, in full Gene Simmons voice singing "And the beat goes on – and the beat goes on – drums keep pounding rhythm to the brain – la dee da dee dee, la dee da dee dah." To be honest, it was a good idea, a drum-driven anthem, all that, I thought it was pretty cool – but I whipped out my cassette of "Because The Night" and he popped it in the player.

And much like "The Right To Rock" the year before, he stopped the tape after the first chorus and said "OK – we're going to cut this song on the new album."

And much like 1984, our schedule was to be dictated by KISS' tour itinerary and we were under the gun to get as much done as possible before the Animalize tour began on November 29th. We did some pre-production rehearsals at S.I.R., weeded out some of the weaker songs and fine-tuned the stronger ones, and felt really confident headed into basic tracking at Village Recorders that we had a platinum album waiting to be made.

When we replaced Steve Riley with Dwain Miller, Gene took it in stride and had seen us live a number of times, so there were no concerns with Dwain's ability to lay it down in the studio, but he far exceeded our expectations and got the sessions off to an amazing start by cutting the album *twice* in *one day*. We did one set of tracks in a smaller, tighter room, then moved the drums upstairs to a big room with cathedral ceilings, and had Dwain record the songs again with that massive open sound. So we had our choice of drum takes to build on top of. Most of the time we ended up using the tracks from the big room, but it worked out great to have the tight sound on songs like "No Pain No Gain." At the end of the day, Gene and I were in the control room, listening to the fruits of Dwain's labors, when I leaned over to him and said, "It's his first album session. Ever." Gene looked at me, raised his eyebrows, and gave an approving nod.

Just like the previous year, we moved the sessions to New York once Gene's schedule demanded we do so. By then, we were into background vocals, solos, lead vocals, and these were to be done at legendary Electric Lady Studios on 8th Street in Greenwich Village. The cab let us off in front of an inauspicious metal door sandwiched in between two shops – you would have walked right on by without ever knowing that some of the most sacred ground in rock and roll history was behind that door. Hit the button, the receptionist sees you via the remote camera and buzzes you in. You walk down a flight of stairs to below street level into a place where some of the most important recordings in history were created; when Jimi Hendrix bought the property in 1968, producer Eddie Kramer convinced him to turn it into a recording studio and thus it became the first artist-owned studio in the business in a time long before any artists – even the Beatles – owned their own studio. The Stones, Led Zeppelin, Hendrix and many more since have laid down timeless tracks there and we felt right at home creating our magnum opus in that hallowed house of rock.

To keep expenses down (we were going over budget on this one, no doubt about it) the decision was made to finish background vocals and Marc's guitars first, leaving just Bryan and I to tag team lead vocals and solos like last time. Doing our best Queen impersonation, it took us three days to record the background vocals for "Because The Night" – all of us singing in various blends and configurations, at different distances from the microphone, stacking them, doubling them, adding multiple harmony lines. No technological tricks were used in the recording of those vocals, and no sections were sampled and flown in.

One of the last things to be recorded was "Nightfall," Marc Ferrari's classical piece. That happened to fall on a day when Danny Goldberg, the President of Gold Mountain Records, our label, decided to come down and check on our progress. Imagine his surprise when he walked in expecting a loud brash heavy metal album and heard those beautiful intertwined classical melodies deftly plucked on nylon strings. "What is this?" he asked, incredulous. "Segovia on drugs?" But I knew the piece was brilliant; it helped give the album an epic quality and the contrast coming out of that song into "No Pain No Gain" is one of the best slap-you-upside-the-head moments in metal history.

So Marc, Kenny and Dwain went home, leaving Bryan and I to finish up. Gene went on the road with KISS, leaving Bryan and I to get into all kinds of mischief in New York during his absences, which were sometimes up to three days at a time. The record company thought it would be cheaper keeping us in New York and working whenever Gene was available, rather than flying us back and forth; had they been able to predict the total of our room service bill, they may have thought otherwise. We started every day with breakfast and coffee, T-bones for dinner, and an endless stream of double Jack & Cokes. We were rock stars, and that's what rock stars do – they order room service. Not that we stayed in our room all the time: we had a few places we would hang, one of which was the Be Bop Café down the street from the studio, where we would chase women and drugs. We also did some cool tourist stuff; one thing I'm really glad we did was go to the top of the World Trade Center.

And on those off days, I was still very much on the clock doing publicity. All the rock magazines were announcing their "Best Of 1985" Reader's Poll results – and KEEL had swept the "Best New Band" category in all three major publications, Circus, Hit Parader, and Creem. So there were always interviews to be done, and we also took advantage of my time in New York by getting me back on MTV to guest host "Headbanger's Ball;" I co-hosted with Ronnie James Dio one time, with Dee Snider another time.

Gene was tireless in his work ethic – if he had a few hours in between KISS gigs, he would spend it with us carving tracks. Take by take, we chipped away at some pretty killer vocals and solos, we brought in guests like Joan Jett, Mitch Perry, Jaime St. James, Michael DesBarres and Gregg Giuffria to lend some luster to the album credits, we started to get a feel for the entire album conceptually and decided to use some sound effects to further enhance the dramatic aspects of the record. In search of the ultimate knockout punch, we went out and rented every boxing movie we could find; the bell sound and punch heard on "Arm & A Leg" came from the DeNiro classic "The Raging Bull." The weird space effect at the beginning of the album – which would become the classic live KEEL intro – was the sound of Luke Skywalker's lightsaber, recorded, sampled, played backwards and triggered by a keyboard synthesizer. Gene relaxed his iron-fisted grip on the band's sound and allowed me the creative latitude to use acoustic guitars and keyboards, which had been absent from the guitar driven "Right To Rock" recordings; he really seemed to trust me and share my vision for this album, letting me have my say and even letting me take the lead on important production decisions.

On the day we went over budget, Gene received a call in the control room from Danny Goldberg. Now, Danny and Gene go way back and that connection was the very reason Gene's name had appeared on that original list of producers presented to me when we got signed. I was on the other side of the glass that day, in front of the microphone cutting a vocal, but Gene kept the control room Talkback button pushed so I could hear the telephone conversation.

"Hello, Danny, this is Gene." Listening for response, nodding his head. "Hold on just a second." He put the phone on hold, and told me, "Danny's informed me we're now officially over budget." The recording budget allocated for "The Final Frontier" was $60,000.00. "Yes, Danny, I'm back."

Listening, nodding. Nodding, listening. "Okay, I'll tell you what I'll do. I'll write you a check right now for $60,000.00 and buy the album from you. Then I'll take it and sell it to another label for twice that. How does that sound?" Nodding, listening. "Okay, thank you. Bye now." Gene hung up the phone and looked at me through the glass. "Danny says to keep doing what we're doing."

I got to witness the great George Marino master the album. Mastering is the final process in the making of an album, basically adjusting levels and equalization to the master mixes, but back then the mastering artist also created a true master disc which was used to construct a mold from which all of the vinyl record albums were manufactured. It is truly a lost art, all done by computer these days, and then you just burn a CD. Not so back in the day, when a two-sided vinyl album had to be mastered one side at a time; the term "grooves" is misleading because on one side of an album there is only one long continuous groove, and if the mastering artist screws up at any time the entire process has to start over. George Marino is a legend in the business, having mastered some of the most important recordings of all time by artists ranging from John Lennon to Metallica, from Whitney Houston to Bon Jovi. Gene and I would bring in two final master tapes – Side 1 and Side 2, with the songs edited into the proper sequence with just the right amount of space between them. Back then, you could also do a crossfade, where one song fades in as the previous song fades out ("The Final Frontier" into "Rock & Roll Animal" is a prime example of an epic crossfade); these don't work so well anymore because of the digital markings required to separate songs when download of an album of individual MP3 files. Marino would listen down to an entire side of the album and take notes regarding what levels and frequencies had to be adjusted during the mastering and when he was satisfied, he'd put a smooth blank slab of vinyl on a huge lathe machine and start cutting the groove. If he made a mistake at any time during the cutting of one side, he'd stop, toss the vinyl and load another one, and start over. If he was satisfied with his work, about eighteen minutes later you'd have half of your album done. George passed away in 2012 but his legacy and work will live on as long as people are listening to the hundreds of classic albums he mastered.

With the album mastered, the only remaining business in New York for Bryan and I was checking out of the Gramercy Park Hotel and signing for the $6000.00 room service tab we'd rung up in a little over a month.

We commissioned John Taylor DisMukes, the artist who had created "The Right To Rock" cover, to create the artwork for "The Final Frontier." We discussed our vision of transforming the logo into a spacecraft and having it taking off out of the New York harbor with the skyline in the background. Instead of holding a torch, the Statue Of Liberty would be holding the KEEL logo sword. DisMukes was a master of detail, and before the days of computer-generated imagery he created these pieces of art with layers of airbrushing. In order to get the skyline and landmarks exact, we bought professional photos of New York taken from out on the water, along with slides of the Twin Towers and Lady Liberty, and John airbrushed over the top of those images to create the background for the piece. We took some geographical liberties and placed the Statue where we wanted it (it takes immense hubris to relocate national monuments to suit your own needs). DisMukes actually created a scale model of the spaceship which looked exactly like the final version, with hydraulics, propellers, cockpit, everything; using a camera/projector combination, he projected the model onto the master canvas and airbrushed it meticulously, one stroke at a time. The ocean waves were created with pieces of cutout plastic, which he would hold up to the master and spray in shades of blue and white. After the primary image was created, he surrounded it with the ornate border and re-created the KEEL sword logo top center – it was thought that having a band's name visible at the top of an album cover would help retail sales when people were filing through the bins at the record store.

We wanted live individual shots for the back cover, so we rented The Country Club in Reseda, our old stomping grounds, for the afternoon and hired Neil Zlozower to come in and take some faux concert shots. We set up the gear, fired up the lights, and piped some of the new music through the sound system to get a vibe going. But something was missing; what was it? Oh yeah – smoke. We needed smoke to enhance the beams of light, what's a concert without smoke? I asked Mark Workman, "Did you bring the smoke machine?" The look on his face said it all; Workman was a dead serious pro and absolutely hated to fuck up, and rarely did, but when you're shooting fake concert photos for the biggest album of your career and your LD forgets the smoke machine that just might be a fuckup. And he knew it.

He had quit smoking cigarettes cold turkey years before, but within minutes you could see him running around the stage, three or four lit cigarettes in his mouth at once, puffing away, blowing the smoke out and up and then puffing some more. He turned blue and nearly died but God damnit there was smoke on that stage and you can see it in the photos.

The bill for "The Final Frontier" album cover was a cool $15,000.00. We had been with MCA Records only a few months, and they were not known for extravagant expenditures when it came to album art, so I brought Gene to the unveiling meeting with me. Simmons actually carried the big 3-foot-square masterpiece, covered in cloth, into the MCA boardroom where the entire executive staff sat gathered at a huge round table where careers were made and broken. Gene calmly stood at the head of the table and unveiled "The Final Frontier."

"This is your album cover," he said. "It's going to cost you $15,000.00." The heavy hitters seated around the table just nodded and agreed with him.

Not only were we an adopted stepchild at MCA, we were turning into a very expensive stepchild at that. But the Executive Vice President of Marketing & Promotion, Richard Palmese, really got behind the band and would send out memos to the entire company that said "Kill for KEEL." He was our staunchest supporter at MCA and put his money where his memo was, spending exorbitant sums on promotion, marketing, publicity, and the video for a song he had pegged to be the first single: "Because The Night." He loved our version of the tune and believed beyond a shadow of a doubt that it would be our breakout hit.

I strongly disagreed, and immediately regretted my decision to record the song. Yes, I also thought it was a hit waiting to happen, but not as the first single from the new album, not the follow-up single to "The Right To Rock;" a soft radio-friendly cover song was not the best way to introduce an army of KEELaholics to our new music. Palmese was adamant, MCA was writing the checks, and we were instructed to have faith and given a guarantee that if it didn't work there would always be more singles.

Young hotshot director Peter Lippman was brought in to shoot the video, a two-day affair (this time, without the two day affair) at a cost of about $120,000.00. Damn near twice what the album had cost (not including the room service bill). Shot on location in Santa Monica, with the performance footage filmed on a soundstage. Some great creative use of lighting and choreography was combined with a new technology, a machine called the Da Vinci, which could go in during post production and cause things to change color. Nowadays this is child's play with even basic computer software, but in 1986 we became the first artist to ever use the effect in a music video.

Another first in that clip is the Kramer Ferrington thin-body acoustic guitar; once again, I'd called upon Dennis Berardi and asked for one of these new instruments they were developing so I could use it in the video. There were only a few of them made so far, Eddie Van Halen had one and there was a black one on its way to Eric Clapton; they could re-route Clapton's and loan it to me for the video shoot, which they did. I always thought it was pretty cool that I got to pop the cherry on one of Eric Clapton's guitars.

Since the Apollo missions in the 60's I had been tuning in on TV to watch our spacecraft lift off and I enjoyed following the missions on the evening news. Especially now that man's conquest of space was the theme of our new album, I felt that somehow I was a small part of that effort, musically supporting the choice to boldly go where no one had gone before; so it was with enthusiasm that I sat up in bed the morning of January 28th, 1986, loaded the bong and got ready to witness another historic launching of the space shuttle Challenger. That enthusiasm turned to horror as the world watched the vessel explode into bits 73 seconds into the flight, killing all seven crew members.

"The Final Frontier" album was already in manufacturing, but within a matter of hours, I was successful in getting MCA to change the liner notes to include a dedication to the astronauts who gave their lives that day, making the ultimate sacrifice for something that was not just important to me, I think it was important for mankind.

"I had read where KEEL's new album "The Final Frontier" was coming out, again being produced by Gene so I was pretty excited. Around this time my Boy Scout troop was set up outside a K-Mart where we were fingerprinting little kids. When it was time for lunch we went across the street to the mall which had the best music store in town. I didn't get to eat lunch that day because I ended up spending the lunch money my mother had given me to buy the new "The Final Frontier" album."
Aaron Fischer

Upon getting signed, we had vacated the Steeler Mansion, passing on the lease to another new band in town named Poison. From time to time I'd been back to check on them, just drop in and see how it was going, and they would tell me horror stories about what they'd been through, including entire gangs busting down the door and descending upon them. KEEL was now firmly attached to our new rehearsal digs – the main room at S.I.R., the same place where we had done the showcase that got us signed, so we felt like it was our chosen domain. To support "The Final Frontier" we had secured the opening slot on the European leg of Dio's "Sacred Heart" tour – 25 shows in 10 countries in one month – so it when it came time to put together the new show, we rented our room at S.I.R. at a cost of $1000.00 per day with full lights and sound, plus our crew on 24/7 retainer to be with us every day and make sure our guitars were freshly strung and fine-tuned. So it was 30K plus crew to practice for a month leading up to the tour.

We continued our boot camplike regimen and perfected it to a science. Rehearsal was a 12 hour block, from noon to midnight; it would start with Kenny and

Dwain doing the entire show by themselves on bass and drums and they got so fucking tight it was dangerous. Those two guys played with jackhammer precision and gave the rest of us the ultimate foundation to rock out on top of. Then we would warm up the voices, going through the exercises Sabine had taught me while creating vocal blends that duplicated what was on the album; just like we still do today with Bryan taking the lowest part, Dwain taking the highest part, and everybody filling the spots in between. The second run through was with full band, background vocals, and choreography - delivering the music and the backing vocals while flailing guitars in sinister synchronicity. After a break, we would dim the house lights and perform the entire show, with lead vocals, background vocals, choreography, light and sound cues, guitar changes, crew moves, everything. And if anyone made a mistake, we'd go back to the beginning and start the whole show over again. Once we'd executed the entire show to my satisfaction, we'd take some time to get loose and have fun – we'd switch instruments, I'd make each guy take a turn at lead vocals on the center mic, and we'd make up silly songs as we went along. It gave everybody an added appreciation for the difficulty of each other's positions while letting off some steam. After the goof-off set, it was band versus crew on the basketball court; yes, we had a full court inside the rehearsal room where we would expend the last of the day's energy.

This daily process turned us into the most formidable of well-oiled machines, so by the time the KEEL road crew packed up all the gear to have it shipped to Helsinki, Finland, we were truly prepared to show the world we were ready for the big time. We didn't really take into account the fact that it would take two weeks to ship the gear over there by boat; we flew into London and met our bus and driver for the tour there and proceeded en route to Finland, arriving there five days before the tour was set to begin – so nearly three weeks without hitting a note together. When we entered the 8000 capacity Icehall Arena, we realized the place really fit the name: it was indeed an ice hall, or rather, a hockey arena, and they intended to keep the ice on the floor and cover it up with plywood planks. Even though it was early April it was still snowing and bitter cold in Helsinki at that time; the arena was not even close to full when we went on, so we received neither applause nor body heat to fire us up. You could see our breath, our fingers were frozen, we could barely do our choreography for shivering in our boots, and we delivered an extremely mediocre performance that did nothing to justify over $30,000.00 in rehearsal costs.

When the band was paying our own hotel costs, we doubled up in the rooms. Ferrari and Dwain roomed together, Bryan and Mark Workman, and Kenny and I because we both smoked pot. On the way back to our room late after the Helsinki gig and after party, Kenny and I noticed the door to Marc & Dwain's room was cracked open and they were inside fast asleep. Slowly, quietly, we snuck in and took all their luggage, shoes, clothes, everything – we stashed it in our room and went to sleep. The next morning we were all having breakfast when they came down to report the robbery to Willie Korman (I don't remember what they were wearing) – eventually we copped to it and gave them their stuff back. Unlike some bands, KEEL weren't much for pranks on the road, but I was pretty proud of that one.

It didn't take us long to regain our musical steam and make no bones about it, we tore it up on that tour. Every date was sold out, Dio was at the top of his game and the top of the genre and for much of the tour – until the final three night stand at the Hammersmith Odeon in London – the name of our band did not appear on any advertising or tickets, it was just "Dio + special guest." We did get a mention on a bootleg T-shirt that I bought from a vendor in Germany, although they spelled the name of the band wrong ("Keele"). We shared the same European label, Phonogram; Ronnie and the record company did us a huge favor by having us on that tour and I'm still grateful, but a lot of the fans didn't even know who we were. From the first thunderous bass & drum beats of the opening song, you could hear the audiences chanting in unison, pounding their feet on the floor and thrusting their fists in the air in primal ecstasy – they loved the music and they loved the band everywhere we went. These were hardcore metalheads, greasy dudes in leather jackets bearing the patches of their favorite bands, and they may not have given a shit about our positive message or our new-found sensitivity but they could sure relate to the power and the precision of our music, the soaring guitars and screaming vocals bouncing off the walls of the arena and into the deepest recesses of their skulls.

From Finland to Norway, on to Sweden, Denmark, Germany, Belgium, to the Netherlands. Each day we received our expenses in the form of a per diem, and each night we'd end up with more coins and bills that we couldn't spend in the next country. Kroners or Deutsche marks or whatever, we took to calling foreign coins "shitters" – we'd walk into a bar, empty our pockets, hold out a handful of shitters and pray we had enough local shitters to buy a drink.

In Denmark there especially seemed to be a lot of anti-American sentiment, so we tried keep a low profile by speaking in fake British accents. On a bar-hopping expedition in Copenhagen, a guy walked up to me with a big smile and handshake and said "Ron Keel! Welcome to Denmark!" When he relaxed his grip on my hand, he left me holding the biggest most beautiful brick of hash I'd ever seen, so apparently I was exempt from the sentiment. It was on that day in Copenhagen that I found and purchased the most awesome pair of jeans ever, well made of blue stretch denim, long enough for the tallest guy, a perfect fit. It's those jeans I'm wearing in the classic Mark Weiss photo on the cover of this book, and no – that's not a sock.

One night after a gig in Sweden, we're hanging around backstage when Dio bassist Jimmy Bain comes into our dressing room. He had been very friendly with us, treating us well and sharing hash, and he asked me to go with him. I followed him into the maze of hallways beneath the arena, wondering where we were going, and after a lengthy obstacle course of twists and turns he opens a door into a huge empty room with nothing but a grand piano sitting in the middle of it. He said he wanted to play something for me, and sat down and began tinkling around with the ivory. I had in my pocket a small portable cassette recorder that I kept with me at all times, and I wasted no time in pulling it out to push RECORD while Jimmy went through the chord progression and I started to sing.

"In the calm before the storm, I'll be there to keep you warm, in the calm before the storm..."

That night, staring out the windows of the tour bus as the miles rolled on, I finished the lyrics to "Calm Before The Storm."

On April 26th we were getting ready for a show in Ludwigshafen, Germany with our eyes turned toward the sky. We were less than 2000 miles from what was, at the time, the greatest nuclear disaster of all time – Chernobyl. When the tour had started in Helsinki, we had looked across the water at the U.S.S.R., only miles away then; we were headed in the opposite direction now, but there's nothing like a nuclear explosion to put a damper on a rock tour. Then rumors began to circulate that due to violent civil unrest in Ireland our shows there would be cancelled; indeed the two shows scheduled for Dublin never happened, and we concluded the tour with three sold out nights at Hammersmith.

The wives had all come out to join us for the final leg of the Dio tour, and it was my 18-month-old daughter Kelly's first time overseas. She has always been a road kid, a great traveler. She would usually sleep through the gigs; I remember watching Dio's final show of the tour from the Hammersmith balcony with Kelly fast asleep in my arms through all the mayhem and pyro. After the show that night there was one hell of a party in the little

Hammersmith bar upstairs – Lemmy Kilmister locked the door, took over as bartender and sent us stateside with one hell of a buzz.

17

DRIFT AWAY

Sing to yourself the lyrics from Dobie Gray's "Drift Away" here...
I didn't write it, so we're not going to include them here...
Or else we'd have to pay a royalty and fee...
But there's a cool story about that song in this chapter.

(NOT "Drift Away" – from the album "Drift Away" by Dobie Gray, 1973)

Kenny Rogers reached across the elevator and shook hands with the members of KEEL. "Hey, thanks for being here, guys." The doors opened into the conference room at the Los Angeles Times and our publicist proceeded with a whirlwind round of introductions. When I was a kid, Barbara Eden was the star of a hit show called "I Dream Of Genie" and she was one of the hottest women on TV; now 20 years later she was still hot, but she was smiling up at me and saying "Nice to meet you!" And oh my God, I said to Kirstie Alley – I absolutely LOVED you in "Star Trek II: The Wrath Of Khan." And Dolly Parton, well, hello Dolly.

This was the press conference for a nationwide charity event called "Hands Across America," an ambitious undertaking to raise money for, and awareness of, poverty, hunger and homelessness. The plan was to create a chain of people holding hands over 4000 miles long, from coast to coast, and our PR firm had engineered a spot for us in the chain as celebrity participants. Once again, they put the media spin on my Nashville origin and fixed it so that we would be flown to Nashville and bussed to be in the exact center of the line, which was somewhere about four hours away from town.

On Saturday, May 24th 1986, KEEL arrived in Nashville with our road manager Willie Korman and we were given first class accommodations at the Radisson downtown. I hadn't been back since the big "One For The Sun" concert the previous summer, so it was of course time for a homecoming party; my good friend the Master Of Recreation Jon Rich picked me up at the hotel and we went out on the town. Jon and I had met in the Steeler days and we've been through a lot together the past three decades, and that wild Saturday in '86 was one of those nights – as the reigning rock star from Music City a lot was expected of me, and I delivered in magnificent fashion that night mixing cocaine, whiskey and rock & roll as we made the rounds at the local rock clubs. Jon got me back to the hotel and poured me into the bed at sunrise. I was basically unconscious when Willie made the rounds to roust us – I can tell from photos taken that day that I showered and did my hair, but I'll be damned if I remember doing it. We cabbed it to the departure point, where a caravan of busses waited to ferry participants to the location, and of course they put the Heavy Metal band on the Country bus. I was in no condition to care – the rest of the guys were apparently tired also, because as soon as our asses were in our seats we put our leather jackets over our heads and slept for the entire four hour ride.

The bus came to a stop in a field in the middle of nowhere, we all got off, held hands, took pictures, and got back on the bus. Now we were awake, and began to socialize with our fellow passengers, who were prominent artists like Pam Tillis and Dobie Gray, or big time songwriters and country music industry people. It didn't take long for somebody to whip out an acoustic guitar and start passing it around for what's known in the south as a "Guitar Pull" – sing a tune and pass the guitar. Everybody on that bus took a turn, and when they were all finished, the last person with the guitar in hand looked at me with fear and dread – they did NOT want to pass it to the wild bunch, but it would have been rude not to, so reluctantly the instrument found its way into my hands.

I wasn't sure what to play, and the brilliant songs and voices we'd just heard were a tough act to follow. Dobie Gray was seated across the aisle from me, and I don't know if it was cool or crazy, but I strummed an "A" chord and looked at him, and started singing "Drift Away." The look on his face was priceless, his eyes got real big and he smiled, and I don't know if it was relief or joy but I'll be damned if I didn't have that whole bus singing along.

Over six million people participated in "Hands Across America," including Ronald Reagan and Ron Keel. The event raised 34 million dollars.

"It's like a dream come true for me. Biggest crowd we've ever played for, and when I was growing up, the Texxas Jam was always one of the biggest events of the year in rock & roll."
Ron Keel – MTV News

"A lot of people must have agreed with Ron Keel, because over 72,000 fans sat in the Texas sun for 11 hours and 15 minutes. They were treated to high-powered sets by KEEL, Krokus, Dio, Loverboy, Van Halen, and Bachman-Turner Overdrive."
MTV News

"It's an event – it's like a Woodstock situation. I was there, at Texxas Jam #9- I survived it, and I enjoyed it."
Ronnie James Dio – MTV News

On the morning of July 19th, 1986, we rode to the stadium in not one, but two limousines, twin Dallas police cars leading the way with their lights flashing.

I had fought my way from the school concerts with Mr. Schmitt to the backyard parties, on to the bars and nightclubs and then the theaters and arenas, but none of that can prepare you for your first stadium show. The excitement and adrenaline was taken up a notch, and I hadn't slept the night before. It was unbelievable to me that Bachman-Turner Overdrive was before KEEL on the bill; ten years prior, I'd been playing "Taking Care Of Business" at those backyard parties, and now I was on the side of the stage watching BTO (with special guest Leslie West on lead guitar) opening for us. Looking back at the video clip now, the stage doesn't seem that big, but when I walked on for our opening song that day it took forever to get to center stage, and it felt like Marc on my right and Bryan on my left were in separate zip codes. We didn't yet have wireless guitar units so we were all on short leashes and had to modify the choreography accordingly.

The Texxas Jam was notorious for causing heatstroke, and in previous years performers like Ted Nugent and Joan Jett in had succumbed to it as well as hundreds of audience members. We went on at two PM when the temperature was 110 and humid as hell, made worse by a crew dousing the crowd with massive water hoses – this created a swamp in the pit in front of the stage, making it even harder to breathe and scream at the same time. By the end of the first song, I was barely able to do either; I'd come out with both barrels blazing, running around like crazy, fists in the air, screaming loud and long, and very soon I realized this was a different kind of situation and I'd better be careful or I'd wind up in the statistics of people who got heatstroke at the Texxas Jam. By the intro to the second song, "Rock & Roll Animal," I was on the side of the stage sucking oxygen. By the guitar solo, I was dunking my face into an ice bucket. It got to the point where the goal was just DON'T PASS OUT.

MTV reported the attendance at 72,000, but I have it from a credible source that the actual attendance was 86,000. It was truly amazing to be in front of such a sea of people, and by the time we got to the last song, and I knew I wasn't going to pass out or die, I could actually loosen up and enjoy hearing that sea of people shout "The Right To Rock!" back and forth with me.

Three days later, I was on my way to Tokyo for the first time for a week-long media tour. Accompanied by our manager Tim Heyne, the objective was to establish our media presence there and prime the market for our first Japanese tour dates, three months away.

Japan was in the full throes of metal mania and fully embraced the American and European bands; since Cheap Trick's "Live At Budokan" it had been a place of rock & roll mystery and magic where the stars could shine just a little brighter. I was coming straight off the road and had barely recovered from the Texxas Jam when Heyne-san and I took off over the Pacific; I hadn't had time to think about this promo trip other than buying a little "Japanese For Tourists" translation book. I would come to appreciate their culture, their work ethic, and their love of rock & roll, and how much the Japanese girls appreciated tall American rock stars.

We had a great business team there thanks to our Japanese record company JVC/Victor. Our upcoming tour was being promoted by Udo Artists, the all-time Japanese leader in concert production. In addition to meeting all of these people for the first time, I was introduced to some of our biggest supporters in the Japanese media such as Koh Sakai from Burrn! Magazine and Keiko "Ginger" Suzuki. On our first night in Tokyo, the executives from JVC took Tim and I to a very nice Japanese restaurant for dinner and lots of sake – there were vats of boiling water built into the tables where you would drop in meat, shrimp and veggies and then reach in with your chopsticks and retrieve whatever you wanted to eat. Thanks to my cousin Al Strickland, who served in Vietnam and taught me to use chopsticks at an early age, I was having no problem with this dining method and things were going along splendidly. They were teaching me basic Japanese, greetings and thanks and excuse me, we were all getting to know each other, it was all good until the gentleman seated across from me reached into the vat with his chopsticks, grabbed a shrimp, and held it out to me. "Try the shrimp," he said. I smiled and said "Arigato," and then used my chopsticks to take the shrimp from his chopsticks.

They all froze, then started turning back and forth to one another, mumbling Japanese in low tones, shaking their heads. "He doesn't know," was the first English I heard. "It's OK, he doesn't know. It's OK."

They explained to me that when Japanese are cremated, the remaining bone fragments are passed among the family members using chopsticks, and this is the ONLY time that "chopsticks-to-chopsticks" is acceptable. By plucking that shrimp I had violated an ancient Japanese funeral tradition and brought bad luck upon us all. And I had only been in the country for a few hours.

From then on, I was paranoid about doing something to offend everyone there which probably served me well during the interview phase of the trip, which involved a lot of speaking slowly to translators, being careful not to say or do the wrong thing. They set me up in a hotel suite, and they would shuffle interviewers and photographers in and out, and I did some fun TV appearances, many of which were taped on location at various local landmarks; I managed a televised visit to a Buddhist temple without incurring any wrath. I was interviewed on a boat trip in the harbor, shopping, eating, and not just sitting in some studio in front of static cameras. We rode the bullet train past Mount Fuji for a round of interviews in Osaka as well.

One evening I think the JVC staff was seeking revenge by treating me to "authentic" sushi. This was a small shop catering to locals, not a tourist sushi joint. Instead of a display case and a menu, there was a big fish tank with live animals swimming about. They ordered sea urchin for me, at which time the "chef" removed a spiky ball from the tank, set it on the bar long enough to beat it once with a hammer, and then put it on a plate and handed it to me as the creature's slimy insides oozed out of it. Deathly afraid of offending them again, I swallowed what amounted to cold fish snot and smiled the entire time.

"This time, KEEL's for real. So says the amiable and straight-talking leader of this particular pack, Ron Keel. With "Tears Of Fire," the latest video from his namesake band, the TV KEEL is finally the concert KEEL. 'Of all our videos so far,' he smiles, 'this is the one I'm most proud of. It's the one, when I'm 80 years old, I'll look back on and say yep, that was us.'"
FACES Magazine

I credit the choice of "Because The Night" as the first single from "The Final Frontier" with being the most damaging career move ever made on my behalf. Many fans turned away from us and never looked back; to this day, they treasure their "Right To Rock" and refused to buy the albums that followed. "The Final Frontier" was too diverse an album to be characterized by any one song, and MCA would have been wise to follow the three-single formula that many of our contemporaries were riding to platinum: the first single would establish your attitude, like "The

Right To Rock" had for us. I would have chosen "Rock & Roll Animal" accompanied by a powerful concert video for this, followed that up with the radio hit "Just Another Girl," and driven the album over the top with the power ballad "Tears Of Fire."

But when a big mega-corporation with millions of dollars says "trust me" you really don't have much of a choice, especially if they're dropping some of those millions trying to make you famous. Richard Palmese's gamble on "Because The Night" did not pay off and it was too late to go back and start the campaign over again. It's a great version of a great song, and is still an important part of my history and my shows, but in the context of a career it's difficult to explain how it was the first nail in our coffin back then.

Palmese made good on his promise of a second single of the band's choosing, but instead of the $120,000.00 budget we'd been given for "Because The Night," we were allocated a paltry $25,000.00 for the "Tears Of Fire" video. Much like "Easier Said Than Done" the previous year, "Raised On Rock" was "tested' at radio and it was decided if we had just one more shot on this album, it would be with "Tears Of Fire."

And there were times and places where we really had a hit song on our hands; in certain markets the single reached Top 5 on the charts and we had about 70 major radio stations on that release. We would drive into a major market like San Antonio or Chicago, listening for our song on the tour bus radio, and we'd hear Bruce Springsteen, Michael Jackson, Madonna...and then we'd hear "Tears Of Fire."

One day Tim called me and said he had good news and bad news. "The good news," he said, "is you're opening for Aerosmith in their home market, just outside of Boston, at Sullivan Stadium where the New England Patriots play football. The bad news is, you're third on the bill."

"Who's second on the bill?"

"Yngwie."

So Dee Dee and I spent our first wedding anniversary (August 31, 1986) in Foxboro, Massachusetts, and for an anniversary present, she got to take a shower in the Patriots' locker room. This was the grand finale concert on Aerosmith's "Done With Mirrors" tour, a stadium show with about 30,000 in attendance. We had learned a lot from the Texxas Jam experience a month earlier, and this time we were ready. The New England weather was much more hospitable, plus being first on the bill enabled us to get a proper set up and soundcheck. It's always cool meeting your heroes, and Steven Tyler and Joe Perry were very cool to us. After our gig, we were hanging out backstage while the crew set up for Yngwie's show; on his way to the stage, Yngwie walked right past Steven, Joe, and me with his head in the air, not a word said. He and his band were in place, and the announcement was made to "Please welcome – Yngwie J. Malmsteen's Rising Force!" The crowd went nuts, the intro started to play. I watched while Yngwie realized his wireless guitar unit was malfunctioning. His guitar tech was panicking, flipping switches and changing the battery, and the intro music was finished by then and the rest of the band keeping their distance, waiting in the wings. Yngwie refused to go on without his wireless, and as the minutes got longer the crowd grew restless, starting to throw garbage onto the stage and yell. Tyler and Perry made it known that Yngwie could have all the time he needed to remedy the situation and do his show. Eventually he had no choice but to forget the wireless and use a cord, but he spent the first part of his set with his back to the audience, fiddling with his knobs. I had the strangest urge to dance in the end zone.

Our headline tour of Japan in October-November 1986 was the height of KEELMania. All four shows, which took place in beautiful concert halls in Osaka, Nagoya, and Tokyo were sold out before we even arrived in the country; we were greeted at the airport by hundreds of fans in a frenzy, and after a solid six months on the road the band was in top form. JVC had released a special five-song album for the tour called "Tears Of Fire," kind of like a "greatest hits" package, which included the new single along with "The Right To Rock," the single remix of "Easier Said Than Done," "Because The Night," and "Raised On Rock." Mark Workman had free reign to design the light show, and he and I worked together to design our very own multi-level stage. On either side of the wall of amps, ramps led up to mid-level risers that had mic stands and monitors, and then additional ramps led up to a massive riser above and behind the drums and backline running the length of the stage. We added additional choreography that involved different guys singing and playing on the mid-level risers at certain points in the show, and then for the encore, "Nightfall," Bryan and I would appear on the high riser in back for the guitar harmony. We were to be using wireless guitar units for the first time, to enable us to navigate the stairs, ramps and risers. Every technical aspect of the sound system was provided according to specifics supplied by our long-time sound engineer, Tim "Quake" Mark. Quake, Workman, Willie Korman and our guitar tech Jim Quinn were augmented by an additional crack Japanese sound and stage crew, and we were assigned Udo Artists' premiere production manager, a man named Tak.

I had the most amazing surprise waiting for me in my hotel room, all laid out on the bed. No, not a beautiful Japanese girl – even better. An array of KEEL merchandise created exclusively for the tour: shirts, scarves, and the ultimate piece of memorabilia: a beautiful large tour program book, with a great collection of Mark Weiss photographs. I thought it was so cool, it didn't even bother me that I had had no say in the selection of the photos. On the dresser was a fruit basket from the promoter and a bottle of Jack Daniel's from JVC. Welcome to Japan, best of luck on tour.

The next morning we went to McDonald's for breakfast and for a walk around the area nearby the hotel. We got a lot of attention, both from people who knew who we were and those who didn't. We rounded a corner and were greeted by a huge KEEL billboard with our faces on it and Japanese text advertising the tour. You never forget your first billboard.

On the day of the first show, soundcheck was scheduled for two P.M. and thanks to the crew the massive stage set, musical gear and sound equipment were all ready to go like clockwork. The sound on the whole tour was incredible thanks to the state-of-the-art technology available to us, the skill and hard work of our sound guys, and the perfect acoustical architecture of those Japanese concert halls.

There was no opening act. About a half hour before showtime, the audience entered in a very orderly fashion and took their seats, one row at a time. Many of them brought gifts and set them on the stage – toys, flowers, cultural items, cards, hand-made banners, all kinds of stuff. Some were addressed to individual band members. At the top of the hour, the lights went down and the intro began. We came out killing it, while the sold out crowd sat there politely watching and listening. In between every song, they would stand up, applaud enthusiastically, and then sit back down. They weren't drunk, they weren't high, they weren't wild and rowdy – they were absolutely focused on every aspect of the show, the sound, the lights, the songs, and the show, tuned in to every detail. And it made us focus even harder on our precision and performance, a perfect dance between an audience and an artist. After "The Right To Rock" they would chant KEEL KEEL KEEL in perfect synchronicity and we'd come back on for the encore. After the show we'd get cleaned up and under heavy security pile into a car which would be surrounded by hundreds of screaming fans as we made our exit.

Later that first night while we were celebrating in the hotel bar I realized there were an unusually significant number of gorgeous Japanese women there. Not just the regular assortment of fans, these women were beautiful, classy, expensively dressed. We were drinking, acting like silly American rock stars, singing and tinkling around on the bar's piano. At some point I asked our road manager Tak about this. "What's with all these beautiful women?"

"They are here for you," he said. My response was the equivalent of "Yeah, right."

"Really," Tak said. "You choose which one you want." I really didn't believe him. So I picked out the most strikingly beautiful of them all, a tall large-breasted oriental goddess with perfect curves, dressed in a very expensive-looking white evening gown. "That one," I said.

"When you go to your room, she will come ten minutes later." Still doubting the seriousness of the situation, I had a couple more drinks. We all said goodnight and left the bar, and once back in my room I shook my head and laughed, and went to bed. In 10 minutes, to my surprise, there came a soft gentle knock upon my door.

I did not manage to get through that tour without offending many of our Japanese fans. It was innocent and unintentional, but a critical mistake nonetheless.

I started adding songs to the show. The gigs were going so well, this was the end of a world tour for us that had started in Helsinki seven months earlier, and we didn't want it to be over. So the shows got longer and longer, and by the last night in Tokyo we were doing a 2 ½ hour gig that included several Steeler songs, several songs from "Lay Down The Law," and "Just Another Girl" (the only time we ever did that one live). Post-tour feedback made it clear that the fans that saw us in Osaka, Nagoya, and at the first Tokyo show were upset because we gave the fans at the final gig a little something extra. My motivation was pure selfishness; I just wanted that last concert to go on forever. At the end of that performance, Dwain, Marc, Kenny, Bryan & I took a bow among a stage full of gifts and presents, flowers everywhere, banners draped over all the monitors, and I thanked our Japanese fans who had made this dream come true. "Domo Arigato," I said. "We'll see you next year!"

Next year never came. I would return to Japan for a very special rock & roll project ten years later, but I would never again step onto a stage in that country.

Of course there was an epic end-of-tour party, where I was granted an exquisite full-body massage by eight beautiful Japanese women at one time, after which I called down to the front desk and had them send up some large boxes and tape. Over the course of the week, I had accumulated such a wealth of gifts and memorabilia that the only way to get it home was to box it all up, tape it tight, and check the boxes on the plane.

The next morning at the airport, hundreds of wonderful fans were there to send us off. They crowded around us, taking photos, asking for autographs, it was awesome – until I was asked to show my passport. I realized that my passport was heavily taped up inside one of a half dozen big cardboard boxes containing hundreds of cards, gifts, trinkets, souvenirs, and other stuff, and I wasn't getting on the plane without it. So I sat there on the airport sidewalk, ripping off tape, rifling through boxes in a panic, looking for a passport in a haystack, while hundreds of Japanese KEELaholics photographed the entire debacle.

KEEL – Shibuya Kokaido – November 2nd, 1986 – final show of the "Earth Exploration 1986/Final Frontier Tour:"

The Final Frontier
Rock & Roll Animal
Arm & A Leg
Just Another Girl
Back To The City
Because The Night
Here Today, Gone Tomorrow
Raised On Rock
Till Hell Freezes Over
Lay Down The Law
Princess Of Illusion
Electric Love
You're The Victim (I'm The Crime)
Drum Solo
Tears Of Fire
The Right To Rock
Bryan's Guitar Solo
Speed Demon
        Encores:
Nightfall
No Pain No Gain
Cold Day In Hell
Hot On Your Heels

18

DIE FIGHTING

Life is a gamble – so make your move
Get ready when it's time to choose
Yeah there's a lot at stake – and so much to lose
Meet your maker – pay your dues

I'm rockin' hard just to stay alive
When times are hard the tough survive
Or die fighting

("Die Fighting" – lyrics by RK 1982 – from the KEEL album
"Larger Than Live" released 1989)

When we walked into rehearsal that day, we were truly living on a prayer.

Our third major label album, simply titled "KEEL," far exceeded the first three albums in terms of songwriting, production, vocals, musicianship, everything. We'd shoved all our chips on the table with this make-it-or-break-it effort; MCA had spared no expense with the production, promotion, and a huge big-budget video for the single "Somebody's Waiting." We were poised for platinum but needed a strong combination of airplay, video play on MTV, and a major arena tour. An extensive opening slot on Bon Jovi's marathon "Slippery When Wet" tour had broken Cinderella big time, to the point where as the tour was winding down they had achieved headline status of their own, and we were being considered for the final leg of that tour which would take Jon, Richie, and hopefully KEEL throughout the northeastern United States to sold out arenas in Maryland, Pennsylvania, Massachusetts, New York, and New Jersey.

When the smoke cleared after "The Final Frontier," we had to face some hard facts: despite strong reviews and six months of touring, the album peaked at #54 on the charts and failed to go platinum as expected. I still attribute this to the wrong choice of "Because The Night" as the album's first single, but the damage had been done. We lost our European record deal with Phonogram and that was a bigger red flag that I realized at the time.

Now on our second album for MCA, we had shed some of the stepchild stigma and they still seemed committed to the act, but I would come to realize that our margin for error had now diminished considerably. Gene Simmons was interested in producing the next album, and we certainly wanted to carry on with him at the helm, but he had some stipulations. On "The Final Frontier" he had given me a lot of creative freedom to fulfill my vision; since that hadn't worked from a sales standpoint, he again wanted to assume total control and one of his requirements was that the lyrics on the new album contain 90% sexual content. Unable to come to an agreement, we parted ways and KEEL went to work with one of the premiere rock & metal producers in history: Michael Wagener. Everything Wagener ever did sounded sonically amazing, he'd worked with Crue, Metallica, Dokken, Ozzy, Great White, and we were all excited about the project, feeling like all the pieces were finally in place. We had some real hit songs in our arsenal, like "I Said The Wrong Thing To The Right Girl," "Somebody's Waiting," Don't Say You Love Me" and "Cherry Lane." I had written an anthem called "United Nations" with the theme that rock & roll was a common language that could unite the youth of the world in a common bond without prejudice or barriers. We had a great power ballad, the piece I'd written with Jimmy Bain on the European tour "Calm Before The Storm." There were some great metal songs as well, like "If Love Is A Crime," "King Of The Rock," and "It's A Jungle Out There." Before entering Amigo Studios for the actual sessions, we went into Baby-O (another favorite Hollywood studio of mine) and recorded demos of all the songs in contention. This helped us evaluate the material and make the final decision on what songs would make the cut; some of those demos, like "Proud To Be Loud," "Reach Out And Rock Somebody," "Friday Every Night," and "Hold Your Head Up" would end up providing the bulk of the material for our 1998 compilation "KEEL VI: Back In Action."

Wagener's recording methods were very modern and scientific compared to the old school methods employed on our previous albums. It was our first experience with digital tape and we had no limitations on tracks – we would stack rhythm guitars on top of each other, sometimes doubling a part six times with six different amps and six different guitars to make the sound as fat as possible. And for the background vocals on "United Nations," we set some kind of Guinness World Record by inviting 75 rocks stars, media, industry, friends and fans to sing on the chorus and then we proceeded to double it, triple it, stack it, multiply it, until there were thousands of voices singing "We are United Nations" in the massive chorus, which was then flown in to the necessary spots throughout the song.

MCA also opened the checkbook to the tune of $15,000.00 to buy us a complete wardrobe make-over, courtesy of Hollywood fashion designer Ray Brown. Each band member got to work with Ray on custom clothing designs that fit our personality and stage needs. Ray was making clothes for everybody from Motley Crue to Judas Priest and so many other bands of the day, and they all were starting to look the same. And now, KEEL was dressed just like them. To further blur our individuality, they brought in the latest stock rock video director for "Somebody's Waiting" who proceeded to put together our stock rock video complete with pyro, Van Halen's light rig, and 3:09 of generic quick clips that did nothing to capture what was cool about KEEL.

The video shoot took place at Perkins Palace in Pasadena, the site of our very first show three years before. A few radio announcements inviting fans to be in the video was all it took to pack the place again, and we dressed up in our fancy new outfits and went through the song 65 times during the 18-hour shoot. For the top of the song, after the pyro, I had choreographed a jump off the triple-stacked speaker cabinets (about 9'), catching the mic stand in mid-air and arriving center stage for the opening line of the first verse. I did that jump dozens of times, and was so disappointed that the director hadn't used it in the final clip that I walked out of the screening. Apparently MTV agreed with me; they aired the video a few times and featured it on "Headbanger's Ball," but declined to put it into heavy rotation, which was critical for us.

So when we assembled in our old rehearsal room at S.I.R., waiting for word about the Bon Jovi tour, it was literally do-or-die.

Ferrari had paved the way for the Bon Jovi tour over a lunch with Jon. Gulf Western, the oil company that owned our publisher (Famous Music) as well as Madison

Square Garden, had sweetened the pot by offering the New York concert promoter a deal on the show costs at the Garden. Finally came the day that our management would be speaking with Doc McGhee, their manager, and finalizing the deal. It was out of our hands, and all we could do was play, so we went about our day as usual – starting with the rhythm section rehearsal, background vocals, and choreography. At some point, one of the guys at the front desk came and got me and said my manager was on the phone.

"Well," Tim said, "Queensryche got those tour dates with Bon Jovi. I'm sorry."

It was a long walk back down that hallway to the rehearsal room to break the news to the guys. We had some shows booked with Quiet Riot that summer, but they were experiencing a dizzying decline in popularity and that tour would not expose us to nearly enough people to make a dent in album sales; radio was lukewarm to "Somebody's Waiting," and the video was not going to get enough TV play to attain "hit" status. So I told the guys we weren't going to be going on tour with Bon Jovi.

We sat there in silence, heads hung for a few minutes, and then I said, "Let's go to work."

And we played our hearts out for nothing and for no one. We channeled all of our anger and frustration into the music, rehearsing for the tour we'd lost. We bent strings farther, screamed louder, pounded drums harder, and rocked with a vengeance like there was no tomorrow. Because there really wasn't. And when it was over, we felt just a little better.

Then, the guy from the desk peeked his head in the door, looked at me, and put his fist up beside his face to signal I had another phone call. Exhausted and drenched in sweat, I trudged back down the hall to the phone.

"Change of plans," it was Tim Heyne on the other end. "You got the last 14 shows on the Bon Jovi tour. And, Doc McGhee gave us the first two shows on the Motley tour also." Our fortunes had changed and, for the time being, we still had a shot.

The second show on Motley's Crue's "Girls Girls Girls" tour appropriately took place at Veteran's Memorial Coliseum in Phoenix, Arizona, that same hallowed building where I had attended all those concerts as a teenager. Where I had fought my way to the front row and then spent the entire show with my back to the stage so I could get used to singing to a sold out arena. Twelve years prior, I had played in the parking lot with Blue Steel and puzzled at why the crew had been putting microphones on my drums. Every kid who aspires to be a rock star has one of those buildings, where they saw concerts as a kid and made a promise to themselves that "someday I'm gonna play here." One of my favorite accomplishments was making good on that promise at the Coliseum on June 2nd 1987, in front of Mom & Dad, my sister Sherleen and her family, so many old friends (and doubters) from my younger days, and the band was simply on fire. No lag time between rehearsal and the beginning of the tour this year, and the night before in Tucson with Crue had been the perfect warm up date before putting the hammer down on the hometown crowd.

We never got to grind it out on a real arena tour, two hundred one-nighters from town to town, but somehow the Gods of rock & roll found it in their heart to make a lot of my dreams come true. That headline gig in Nashville, the Coliseum in Phoenix with Crue, the sold out tours of Europe & Japan. And then the Bon Jovi run.

Bon Jovi began their "Slippery When Wet" tour opening for .38 Special and finished it headlining multiple nights at the biggest arenas in the country. The week after selling out three nights at Madison Square Garden, they went across town and sold out the final two gigs at Nassau Coliseum. It was one of the biggest mega-tours of the decade and we were excited to get a piece of it. Even though a large percentage of the audiences were young females, they had a lot of energy and responded quite well to KEEL; we didn't get a whole lot of advertising (Bon Jovi didn't need to put us on the promo to sell tickets) and when we joined the tour in Landover, Maryland on July 21st many people even thought we were Cinderella.

KEEL was given a 35 minute set, and with the pressure on to sell the new album, that was the material we were pushing - the only "old" song in the show was "The Right To Rock." The second day of the tour Jon Bon Jovi came up to me backstage.

"Hey man," he said, "why aren't you doing that "Because The Night" song?" I explained to him that we only had 35 minutes and were trying to feature the new album. "Put "Because The Night" in the show or you're off the tour," was his response. That evening, and every night thereafter, we played "Because The Night." But overall Jon was really cool to us – he would come in and give us clothes out of his wardrobe case that he was tired of wearing, he would hang out in our dressing room and shoot the breeze with us. On the final night of the tour, after their show was over, he and Richie made it a point to come get the guys in KEEL and take us into their dressing room for an end of-of-tour toast and celebration, just the five guys in Bon Jovi and the five guys in KEEL, no crew, no family, just the ten of us.

Every night, they would walk right off the stage and into waiting cars that would take them to their private jet and they'd be home in their own beds, leaving us to contend with thousands of crazed female fans. By the second night in Landover, it seemed everybody who'd been at the show ended up at the hotel and the place was crawling with people, outside in the parking lot, on every floor, it was out of control. Some girls who didn't like the way they'd been treated took to setting off the fire alarms. Kenny and I actually steered clear of the mayhem, remaining behind our locked door; we'd rolled the very last of our dope into one joint and smoked it and we were kicking back watching TV when something thumped against the door. Thump, thump. I got up and opened the door, and there was Dwain in his room across the hall, sitting in a chair heaving fruit at our door. I went out in the hallway yelling at him to stop, and then realized that at one end of the hall there were a number of police officers gathered, observing. Looking to the other end of the hall, I saw the same thing. Cops converging from both sides of the building.

Moments after I shut and locked the door, the thumping began again; this time it wasn't fruit, but nightsticks and cops demanding that we open up. "Which one is Bon Jovi?" the officer in charge asked me. When I informed him we were just the opening act, they got really pissed – they thought they were getting to bust Bon Jovi. The room reeked of pot, and they put it through a very thorough search but luckily we had none left. After the search, we were told to pack up and move out immediately – we were not only being kicked out of the hotel, we were being kicked out of town. I went down to Willie's room to tell him, but he knew and was already in the shower. We rounded up the entourage and gave everybody ten minutes to meet in the parking lot.

Bryan Jay was not at the hotel, but off on a "personal errand" – we'd taken up a collection and sent him on a mission to get some blow. He was off in the night being driven by some fan in search of drugs, and all I could do was leave him a note at the front desk. We packed up all his stuff and by the time he got back we were halfway to Pennsylvania.

We did not have a bus on that tour – all of the shows were within a short distance of each other, and there were multiple nights in almost every town, precluding the need for an expensive tour bus that would just sit in the parking lot. So we were traveling in a 15 passenger van, and that night we were sleeping in a 15 passenger van, hoping that Bryan would be able to get to Hershey in time for the show the next evening. He did, through a combination of resourcefulness, luck, and relentless demands upon the fan that gave him a ride, and we went on with the tour.

Doc McGhee commented to Tim Heyne that they all loved KEEL, great band, but maybe the show was a little heavy for Bon Jovi – would we consider putting a ballad in the set? We added "Calm Before The Storm" to the show and immediately saw a spike in album sales, but it was too little too late.

Playing Madison Square Garden is a milestone in the career of any performer. On the day I first set foot in that legendary arena, I had no idea that back in Los Angeles, the plug was being pulled on my career. Executives at MCA and Gold Mountain had determined that "Somebody's Waiting" would not achieve enough momentum as a single and video, and that a meager 14 dates on the Bon Jovi tour would not be enough to justify further investment in the album. There would be no second single and the promotional budget would be terminated. All of this was being discussed 2700 miles away in Burbank while I'm on stage in New York at the Garden, holding 20,000 people in the palm of my hand, feeling like the king of the world.

I was pretty nervous that first night at the Garden but that's to be expected; despite some technical problems we had a strong show (the bass rig went out on stage, but we still had bass in the P.A.). The second night it felt natural, and by the third night I was skateboarding down the aisles high-fiving the security guards. In three nights we played for almost 60,000 people and sold over 25,000 albums in the northeastern U.S. that week, causing a rise in chart position but for a band that needed to reach the million-sales mark, it was a Band-Aid on a bullet wound.

Sometime that summer we found out that Dee Dee was pregnant again. On March 2nd, 1988 – coincidentally Jon Bon Jovi's birthday – Ryan Kristopher Keel was born. He came into the world breaking his collarbone on the way out because he was a Keel boy and thus of large stature, while his mother was a petite thing. I've never had a broken bone in my life, and my son broke one being born.

Grown now, Ryan has become the man I most admire in this life – no parent could be prouder than I am of him.

Due to MCA's decision to withdraw support of the album, we left a few hit singles on the table. To this day, fans won't stop talking about songs like "I Said The Wrong Thing To The Right Girl," "Cherry Lane," and "Don't Say You Love Me." MCA offered an alternative when film director Penelope Spheeris selected KEEL to record the signature song for her new movie, a punk western called "Dudes;" the song was a cover of "Rock & Roll Outlaw," originally done by the Australian band Rose Tattoo.

Production on the track was handled by Kevin Beamish, who had made his mark with the multi-platinum REO Speedwagon hits. The video combined the best action scenes from the film with performance footage filmed at Paramount Ranch, and we got to dress up in cowboy gear and act like badasses with guns which was a lot of fun and provided for our most entertaining video. The soundtrack album also featured W.A.S.P., Steve Vai, Megadeth, and Jane's Addiction but with all those heavyweights on board MCA still managed to drop the ball and the project faded into obscurity. It is a very fun movie starring Jon Cryer, Daniel Roebuck, and Flea (Red Hot Chili Peppers) – unfortunately it has never even been released on DVD. I'm glad we got to see it in the theater.

We weren't sure what was going to happen next, but I was certain that nothing was going to happen without music, so we went right back into writing and rehearsing. After three strikes we didn't even think about counting ourselves out; like all of the rock stars of the 80's, we thought it was going to last forever. New bands were coming out of nowhere and going platinum overnight, as long as we were still in the game we had a fighting chance. But there was now a fair amount of finger pointing and placing of blame for our failure to breakout big; MCA Records was an easy scapegoat because of the decisions to release the wrong singles, throw a ton of money at those singles, and fail to follow them up. It was logical to blame the lack of a long-term major U.S. arena tour. Then within the band, we started to blame the music. Some felt we needed to be heavier, while Marc and I competed with each other to write hit singles when we should have worked harder at writing together. We went into an intense writing phase where everything we wrote was the song that was going to break us, while nothing we created was good enough. There were no fights, just everybody voicing the friction and frustration we all felt. It was a dark time and we grew further apart until Marc decided to quit the band and go out on his own.

And then Atlantic Records signed us to a half million dollar recording contract.

Marc's departure did not set well with Jason Flom, the Atlantic Records A&R man who signed us (through Gold Mountain – Goldberg still retained our rights); he was a Ferrari fan and was not happy about the personnel change. We brought in a keyboard player, Philip Wolfe, with Bryan assuming all the lead guitar duties and I started playing a little more guitar. I was coming up with some strong material like "Evil Wicked Mean & Nasty," "Private Lies," and "Dreams Are Not Enough," one of the best songs of my career, and it felt like we might have one more shot with Atlantic behind us. Gene Simmons even gave us a new song to work up called "Burning Up With Fever."

The time came for us to present our fresh batch of songs to our new record company, and Jason Flom and his assistant arranged to come down to rehearsal and see a showcase. Tim Heyne was there to greet them when they arrived an hour late, and then they wanted to eat. They ordered take out at the Mexican restaurant next door, brought their dinner in and sat down on road cases in front of the stage. I provided them with a list of the songs we were about to play, they picked up their forks and we picked up guitars and drumsticks.

We opened with "Private Lies." We hadn't even gotten to the chorus yet when Flom, pausing only momentarily and not looking up from his Styrofoam container, took his pen and aggressively crossed that song of the songlist right in front of us. Shocked but determined, we launched into "Evil Wicked Mean &

Nasty." Halfway through the first verse, Jason Flom took a bite, took his pen, and with a broad swipe of the pen crossed that one off the list. And so on it went, bite after bite, crossing out song after song, until nothing was left. Even the Gene Simmons song was a casualty that day.

After that, Atlantic kept feeding us outside material and telling us to work up this song or that; sometimes it seemed like a joke, because they were demanding we work up songs that had already failed for other acts like Dirty Looks. One song they wanted us to cover was "Fool For A Pretty Face," a Humble Pie song that I fell in love with and really enjoyed singing, so it wasn't all bad.

We replaced Phil Wolfe with Scott Warren on keyboards, and Scott brought in some new enthusiasm and was a lot of fun to work with as well as bringing great hands and sounds to the band. Going stir crazy in rehearsal, we booked a show at our old stomping grounds The Country Club and did one of the best shows of my entire career – years later my bandmates in IronHorse had gotten into my video collection and were watching that KEEL gig and I walked through the room and did a double take, realizing that whatever else we were going through in 1988 we were still delivering a blistering high energy rock show.

Atlantic Records eventually let us off the hook, meaning they dropped us before ever recording or releasing an album. All of the business relationships began to crumble as the house of cards fell and we no longer had our foreign deals either; the booking agency dropped us, the accountants left us with a massive tax bill, and eventually we cut ties with a man who had been like a sixth member, our manager Tim Heyne. He is still a friend and supporter, and will always be an honorary member of KEEL.

We negotiated out of our deal with Gold Mountain by giving them one last album – 1989's "Larger Than Live." I was given the chance to produce the album myself because they didn't want to cough up the budget for another big name producer; I decided to do a half-live half studio album because they wouldn't cough up the budget to record a proper full album, plus I thought it would help give the project a unique identity. There were a couple of songs on the studio side with real radio potential – "So Many Good Ways To Be Bad" and "Dreams are Not Enough" especially – and they deserved studio production treatment, while I was hoping the concert recordings would convey the magic the band still possessed on stage.

The writing sessions with Steve Diamond for "So Many Good Ways To Be Bad" also yielded a song that became "Rev It Up," the title track to Vixen's sophomore album. Even though it went through quite an evolution, the embryo of the tune was mine, and it was the first time one of my songs had been recorded by another artist and I'm still very proud to have been a part of it.

The live portion of "Larger Than Live" was recorded during two sold out shows at the Roxy which would be Bryan's last with the band until our 25th Anniversary Reunion in 2009. During overdubs for the studio portion I brought in Tony "The Kid" Palmucci to finish the guitar solos. We had a show booked in Phoenix over Thanksgiving weekend 1988 which we were unable to do because Bryan was no longer with us; I went to Phoenix on my own and did a short set with a local band to curb the fans' disappointment and that was the last straw with Kenny, who used it as an excuse to quit the band. I found a guy who looked just like him, and I apologize for not even remembering the dude's name, but it's him in the "Dreams Are Not Enough" video, not Kenny.

That video was the last KEEL band activity in the 80's. As I had felt during the final months of Steeler, change was inevitable and the band that bore my name no longer felt like mine. None of us could have predicted the extent of that change, and everybody expected the Decade Of Decadence to go on forever but the 90's loomed on the horizon, and the music of Pearl Jam and Nirvana would be the soundtrack of rock's next generation.

"Larger Than Live" came out in September 1989. To fulfill 65,000 orders, Gold Mountain released 25,000 units and effectively the disc was out of print immediately. By the time we filmed the "Dreams Are Not Enough" video, I had assembled musicians for my new project and was ready to move on to the next challenge when a traumatic tragedy struck at the very heart of my family and threatened everything I held dear.

19

STREET OF BROKEN DREAMS

They come to California looking for the promised land
Trying to hit the big time like a million other bands
Some get rich and famous – some are blinded by the light
Some just keep on trying – but most give up the fight

But shooting stars will come and go
They crash and burn on the street below
You can find them down on Sunset Strip
Where the fallen angels go

("Street Of Broken Dreams" – lyrics by RK 1990 – recorded by Fair Game)

I was excited and energized by the challenge of becoming the first rock frontman with an all-female backing band. I was going to have to start over anyway, no matter what I called it, so I thought the female lineup was a great marketing angle and would be extremely entertaining to audiences. I had been a big fan of The Runaways, Vixen, and other female rock bands, I'd co-written a song on the last Vixen album and was really impressed with the level of musicianship, and that was really the vision that gave me the confidence to build this new project.

I signed on with Joe Gottfried for artist management; Joe had made Rick Springfield a star and was looking for a new artist. He provided me with a huge rehearsal room at Sound City where I could have 24/7 access, and he offered to let me cut demos in the studio whenever there were no paying clients. Grammy-winning producer Keith Olsen's studio, Goodnight L.A., was right next door, and during that time he was producing Ozzy and Scorpions and they all loved to hang out with me because I had the band with the hot girls. One day I was jamming "Sweet Home Alabama" with Zakk Wylde, the next I was playing softball in the parking lot with Scorpions.

I auditioned every available female musician in the Los Angeles area while wrestling with the family drama at home. Please understand this is a family matter and we don't need to go into details: Dee Dee's father was an evil motherfucker who committed some heinous crimes which affected us all, I rigged a recording device to the phone which captured a conversation which got him arrested, and a long painful trial ensued as I was trying to keep my family together and resurrect my career. All sources of revenue had evaporated, and we sold the beach house and moved to a smaller home in Chatsworth. We took a mortgage on that house to survive and help finance the new band. A few years later I was pleased to hear that Dee Dee's father had died in prison.

After months of auditions and assembling various configurations of musicians, I chose the girls I wanted in the band and brought them together to let them know my decision. As soon as I got home from that first band meeting, the bass player, Janna James, called on behalf of the band and told me they all quit.

Turns out this girl didn't want to play in a band without her old friend, and that girl didn't want to be in a band with so-and-so, she wanted this girl in the band and not that girl. And thus began three years of drama and personnel changes that made Steeler look like a pillar of stability. I gave in to guitarist Tina Listo and brought in her friend, drummer Stephanie Leigh. Steph was a great drummer, a hard living rock star and sexy as hell but I knew she'd want to steer the band in a heavier direction and I was determined to maintain a commercial hard rock sound. Steph and Tina had major label experience in a band together called No Shame, signed to CBS, and that was a big plus.

I was writing all of the material and finally starting to develop that skill in a direction I was comfortable with. My melodies started to sing instead of scream, my lyrics became more natural and less contrived. I took the band into the studio to record a four song demo, and arranged a photo session with Neil Zlozower. I hired Motley Crue's attorney David Rudich, and enlisted the services of KEEL's former publicist, Mitch Schneider at Michael Levine PR. We were almost ready to begin making pitches, but I did not yet have a name for the band.

My original name for the band was "Ron Keel's Electric Playmates," but the girls weren't too keen on that. They wanted to be "taken seriously." I invited Gene Simmons to a rehearsal, and he loved the idea and he loved the girls, but he kept insisting that I call it KEEL. "Ron," he said, "it's your name. It's your band. Whatever band you have, you should call it KEEL."

I was still heading over to Arizona every chance I got to go camping and roaming the mountains with my father. One day I was wandering the ruins of an old mining town when I came across a concrete column, and inscribed in the pillar with a chisel were scrawled the words "Fair Game." That was it; as soon as we got back to town I called everyone and told them the name of the band was Fair Game.

By the time the band showcased for several major labels – including my old friend Bennett Kaufman, now head of A&R at RCA Records – Fair Game had an album's worth of great commercial rock songs, a strong live show with the customary Keel choreography, twin guitars harmonizing and swapping solos, sweet female harmonies behind my lead vocals, and an impressive international profile that included a centerfold in Kerrang! Magazine and major press in the local media.

Then my manager Joe Gottfried suffered a heart attack behind the wheel of his car and died.

Joe had believed in me and supported me; after his passing, Fair Game never recovered. Janna James and guitarist Eva Marie stuck it out with me until the end, with a number of drummers and lead guitarists making the rounds through the revolving doors. We landed two songs and a brief role in "Bad Channels," a sci-fi B-movie, but that did little to recoup the three years and mortgaged home we'd invested.

After 11 years, it was starting to feel like neither rock & roll nor California were home to me anymore. The business had embraced grunge and turned its back on the bands that had turned 80's hard rock and metal into a multi-billion dollar industry; although many bands like KEEL would reunite in later years, few could weather the storm that smelled like angst and teen spirit. It wasn't just me - our entire rock & roll culture had experienced an unprecedented backlash and was suddenly considered uncool overnight.

I grew a beard, put on a cowboy hat, went into a local bar with my acoustic guitar, introduced myself as Ronnie Lee from Tennessee, and asked if I could play for tips. At first it was because I really needed the money, but it was also very liberating. I would play my Bad Co. and Bob Seger and that's all that was expected of me, every dollar in the tip jar was a bonus, and I didn't care if anybody even listened. There's something about singing while guys are playing pool yelling "Eight ball, corner pocket," that'll keep you grounded.

The rock stations that used to play Quiet Riot, Crue, Great White and KEEL were no longer broadcasting on my frequency, so I started hitting the "seek" button on the car radio. One day during a drive to Arizona for a camping trip, I listened to a countdown of the top country songs and really enjoyed it. New artists like Brooks & Dunn and Garth Brooks really resonated with me, the production was reminiscent of 80's commercial rock, and the songs were good time party songs about drinking and chasing women. Even though I am a creator of music, I'm also a fan, and I need to be entertained, I need to hear music that speaks to my heart. I guess after hitting rock bottom and playing for tips again, I was getting the message of country music loud and clear.

On April 29th 1992, Los Angeles became a war zone during the Rodney King riots in which 53 people were killed. I stayed up all night by the door with my .357 Magnum and kept watch. Two months later, the 7.3 Landers earthquake shook us to the bone and left cracks in the walls of the house. I'd had enough - we sold that house, took what equity we had and moved to Arizona.

20

MY HORSE IS A HARLEY

I was born a hundred years too late
I wasted thirty years trying to compensate
I'll just accept my fate – it's ain't fair but that's the breaks
I'll be a 20th century man if that's what it takes

My horse is a Harley – my gun's a guitar
Just a space age cowboy with a Stone Age heart
All I need is a redneck girl and a honky tonk bar
My horse is a Harley – my gun's a guitar

("My Horse Is A Harley" – lyrics by RK 1994 – from the
Ronnie Lee Keel album "Western Country" released 1995)

Country can come from a lot of places. It can come from having a father who was a construction worker listening to Haggard and Jones, from a mama that would shake you in the middle of the night and say "Wake up – we're moving." It can come from being homeless on the streets of Nashville. It can come from having it all and losing it almost overnight.

Country can come from a lot of places – but first and foremost, it's gotta come from the heart.

I was listening to so much country music on the radio that I knew the words to every song, I was starting to identify the artists by the sound of their voice, and I became more and more interested in the way the different instruments worked together. There was the sweet sound of pedal steel guitars crying and screaming, there were the fiddle and the honky tonk piano swapping solos, dobro and harmonica, and also limitless guitar tones from twang to overdrive. I really wanted to try my hand at writing music like that, painting the canvas with all those colors. In the early 90's, if you were looking for rock stars, you found them in country music with artists like Garth Brooks, Travis Tritt, Dwight Yoakam – these guys were dressing up, rocking out, putting on larger-than-life concert shows and selling millions of albums. I saw Garth Brooks in concert at the Forum in L.A. right before we left town and it was a spectacle to rival any KISS or Bon Jovi show I'd seen, and I said OK – country music has decided to meet me halfway, I'm going to do the same.

I had no misconceptions this was going to be easy or quick; I knew there would be an extensive development process and I had a lot of work to do. I also knew that I had it in my heart and in my genes, and that was the most important part – skills can be learned, but the real magic has to come from within. I decided I wanted the freedom to develop those skills in anonymity, without the benefit or burden of being the "ex rock star," so I had business cards made that said "Ronnie Lee" and contained my new Arizona phone number.

I called my old friend Jon Rich in Nashville, who was working at one of the big country music publishing houses, Buddy Killen Music, and I asked him to find me some songs in the Killen catalog that I could work up. I bought a collection of country CD's, half classic like the stuff my Dad used to listen to, and half hot current releases by the stars of the day. I immersed myself in the art form, learning songs at a furious pace, and I started to go out to jam nights at the various country bars around Phoenix, first just watching and then I'd sign up and sit it with the bands, getting some stage experience and making friends.

I bought a 1979 black Ford Ranger 4x4 with KC lights and a four inch lift kit, and I had the truck, the hat, the guitar, and the attitude.

I used to run into this pedal steel guitar player named Ralph Borchert, and I would sit by the stage and just listen to the sounds he would caress out of that thing. He got me a fill-in job as a guitarist with his band, and my first country gig was as a sideman at the Squaw Peak Steakhouse in Black Canyon City, Arizona. Ralph and I put a band together and started rehearsing out at his place and booked our first gig at a place in Phoenix called Barwinkles. None of these guys knew anything about my history or my real last name – I wanted to learn the craft and earn respect on the basis of who I was now, not who I had been.

I still had my long hair, I was wearing leather and fringe, and rocking out with my wireless headset, running around the bar and standing on tables, acting like Garth junior. We kept getting requests for this song called "Neon Moon," by Brooks & Dunn; I'd heard it on the radio but hadn't learned it yet, so when we took a break I went out to our guitarist's car and listened to it; the cassette package had the lyrics on it, so I taped those to the top of my acoustic guitar and sang "Neon Moon" for the first time.

I ran into my old bass player Beaver Brown, who I'd played with back in my teens in my last Arizona rock band during the Jim Daley days. He knew a drummer that knew a bar owner that was looking for a country group, and Ralph and I teamed up with them and went into the Dodge City Saloon on 16th Avenue for a Friday-Saturday night and managed to keep the job. It was my first house gig – a small but effective platform from which to grow into my goals. And of course I had set my sights on superstardom; I am never going to be content to dream small. The short range goal was a house gig where I could build a band while working on my songwriting skills, and once I had enough songs for an album to get it recorded somehow and take it to Nashville to pitch the majors.

The first thing I did was fire the drummer who got me the job in the first place. He was an egotistical slob who had no respect for the music; I gambled that the bar owner would side with the fun loving energetic lead singer who would bend over backwards to draw a crowd and entertain them. I brought in "Slamming" Steve Fagiano on drums, an Italian from Chicago who specialized in marching drum music, not exactly country but a sweet guy who really cared about the music. I did my first country photo session, carefully choosing a shot where my face was hidden by the cowboy hat so I wouldn't get recognized as Ron Keel. I renamed the group "The Ronnie Lee Band" and started handing out flyers everywhere, just like in the old days.

We were making $37.50 a man as a four piece, even less once Hal Michael Monti walked into the Dodge City Saloon carrying a Stratocaster, because I hired him on the spot. He was a world class guitarist who had it all – experience, chops, work ethic, and the desire to build something with me and not just collect a paycheck. He would remain at my side for the next seven years. Beaver's health was failing him and he gave me two weeks' notice; bassist Gary "Clem" Clemmons came in with a country heart and a fire burning out of control. Gary was fearless and knew every song in the book, and started teaching me how to work a dance floor according to the steps. "Mix it up," he'd say. "Follow a two-step with a shuffle. Slow it down every fourth song for a buckle-rubber, and mix in a couple of waltzes here and there." Working the dance floor is an art that really paid dividends for a country band whose job was to get 'em dancing and keep 'em drinking and it was obvious from the crowds that what we were doing was working and that we'd reached our peak potential in that little saloon. One night Clem and I were out in the parking lot smoking a joint when he looked at me and said, "I want a new job." I thought, what a great name for a country song, something every working class stiff can relate to, so while I was off writing "I Want A New Job" Gary was plotting our exit strategy from Dodge City.

I was starting to come up with some songs I could believe in; "Say No More," "Living Well Is The Best Revenge," and "I Want A New Job," and we worked them up and started playing them on stage and people just kept on dancing.

The way you got a new job was to dress up, go out to the other bars, and make your pitch to the bar owner. So we went out to Cave Creek, to a honky tonk called the Buffalo Chip Saloon, and there were just a few couples in there dancing to Randy Wade's band. Clem made the pitch and we got the job on Fridays and Saturdays. It wasn't long after that the bar was sold to Marla McGhee, whose father Max had played on the old Green Bay Packers championship teams; one of her stipulations was, she would buy the bar if she could keep the band. She really loved us and was committed to making the Buffalo Chip a real attraction. The place had the greatest vibe – dirt for a parking lot, a real hitching post out front where local cowboys could tie up their horses, wood and log décor and rows of cowboy boots lining the ceiling inside. This was the real west, and our high energy honky tonk style was the perfect complement to the rough and rowdy lifestyle of the patrons. They drank hard and they danced hard, and the crowds started to get bigger as we expanded the gig into a Thursday-Sunday job and kept jacking the money up until we were making a decent living, plus we secured a regular Tuesday gig in Phoenix so we were playing five nights a week, four hours a night.

During this time I wrote my signature country song, "My Horse Is A Harley," and we went into a small local studio and cut a four song demo. For $75.00 we filmed three videos out behind the Buffalo Chip, with the drums and pedal steel in the beds of our trucks and hay bales all around, no edits or cuts, one take, and then it was into the bar to go to work. We were starting to get some local press and media attention as well, and weekends at the Buffalo Chip were off the hook. This was every bit as wild as the heyday of the Sunset Strip I'd experienced a decade earlier, and just like heavy metal had taken the world by storm in the 80's country music was doing the same thing in the 90's and I was in the eye of that storm.

My Mom and Dad loved country music, and even though they had enjoyed my heavy metal heyday, they were ecstatic I had embraced country music and they would always come out to the Chip and see the gigs, often bringing their little portable video recorder.

Every now and then some cowboy would walk up to the front of the stage and ask, "Are you Ron Keel?" and I would say, nope, never heard of him.

NEW TIMES MAGAZINE – BEST OF PHOENIX 1994
BEST COUNTRY SALOON: THE BUFFALO CHIP

"Here's the deal. It's Saturday night, and you're standing near the edge of the dance floor listening to a great house band rip through the latest country hits.

"There's a card game going on in one corner, and two pool games in another. Right next to you, an evocative blonde in jeans is showing her friends how to drink an entire longneck without using her hands.

"This, ladies and gentlemen, is saloon utopia. It's rowdy, the music is loud, there's no pretension, and this isn't a fake country place. The crowd is here to honor the country traditions – beer, music and shameless self-indulgence."

There was an old cowboy named DJ who was a fixture at the Chip, a real Lost Dutchman type, big curly white beard and overalls, trusty dog always at his side. He was Santa Claus to the kids, everybody loved him. One night he was right in front of us on the dance floor twirling around with one of the cute local girls when his eyes got real big, and he clutched at his chest and collapsed. Everybody was in shock, and they called 911 and the police cleared the bar while the paramedics tried to save him, to no avail. While DJ was dying on that dance floor, I was out in my truck writing a song about it entitled "Last Call." Rather than sadness, I chose to think about the joy of a full life and the ability to go out having a good time, in a place where everybody loves you.

Well I've waltzed across Texas
And I've walked down the aisle
Rode through the badlands never counting the miles
Sailed 'cross the ocean, and sung in the rain
Enjoying life's pleasures, and enduring life's pain

But when my time has come – when it's all said and done
I want to go having fun

Let me die on the dance floor, wrapped up in your arms
Sing me back home with an old steel guitar
When it's last call for romance, save me a slow dance
And hang up my boots in the bar

Well I've flown like an eagle, seen fire in the sky
Climbed many a mountain – there ain't much I ain't tried
Made children smile, and made pretty girls cry
And I ain't afraid to say my last goodbye

To make some extra money on the side, I had placed an ad in the local music magazine giving "Songwriting Lessons." For $20.00 an hour, I would coach people through the songwriting process – tools of the trade like recorders and notebooks, compiling lists of titles and phrases, understanding rhyme schemes and song structures, tricks like modulations and Acapella breaks. John Segin and Keith Gaertner were two guys going through their mid-life crisis together – they had played and written together in their younger days but spent most of their adult lives succeeding in business and were now interested in getting back into music. After their first session with me, Segin pressed a $100.00 bill into my hand and said "Buddy, you are undercharging for your services." After submitting some forgettable song ideas, one day they came into a lesson fresh from a writing session on the beach in Mexico, with a song aptly titled "Down In Mexico." It was absolutely brilliant, paying homage to Buffet and pre-dating the beach craze that would later become Kenny Chesney's trademark sound. I told John and Keith that not only was this a great song, but that I was planning on cutting an album and wanted to record "Down In Mexico." They became interested not only in the creative aspect of what I was doing but also the business end of things, and as our friendship grew we formed a production company called Working Class Entertainment to be the umbrella under which Ronnie Lee the recording artist would operate.

I was devastated when Gary Clemmons quit the band on the eve of the "Western Country" sessions to pursue a lucrative construction opportunity in the Pacific Northwest. He had been a friend and mentor, a true country spirit and an inspiration, but his decision was made; 16 years later we'd get back together and relive those times on stage but in 1995 I had no choice but to go on without him, replacing Steve on drums at the same time.

A couple of Hal Monti's ex-bandmates were brought in to fill those positions – bassist Mike "Junkyard" Wood, and drummer Joe Morris. Both incredible musicians, almost overnight we were on a competitive level with any up and coming national act, although Mike was a loose cannon and brought a new drug – crystal meth – into the picture. He came up to me at his first gig and said "Let's go, I wanna pack your nose" and we went out to the parking lot. Mike claimed that "cocaine is for kids" and much preferred meth, which would keep you up for days. The fact that Junkyard did such an incredible job on the bass tracks for the "Western Country" album and he hadn't slept in weeks was a true testament to the guy's talent.

I was determined to do the album in Arizona, with my own band - as opposed to Nashville session players. There were a lot of parallels between the 90's Arizona country scene and the 80's Hollywood rock scene, and I had aspirations of spearheading a "western country" movement based on the Southwestern cowboy culture.

"Western Country" in my opinion is a masterpiece of traditional 90's country music. A collection of songs that literally saved my life – when many 80's rockers had fallen from grace and had nowhere to turn, I found solace, sanctuary, and a means of expression in country music as well as a way to make a living. I was making more at the Buffalo Chip than I'd made at any point during my career with KEEL, the beer was colder, the whiskey was hotter, and the country girls in their tight jeans and boots were even wilder than the rock chicks. As a first time producer on a country music album, I got very lucky with "WC" – the core band was very well rehearsed and Ralph's pedal steel work fit perfectly between my voice and Hal's lead guitar work, but we also had a couple of session guys, Wayne Holland on piano and Craig Delphia on fiddle, that were playing the songs for the first time and just played all the right stuff in all the right spots. In fact, Wayne Holland's piano instantly became such an immediately important part of the music that we expanded to a six piece band and made room for his keyboards on the crowded Buffalo Chip stage.

I was faced with the tough decision of releasing the album as "Ronnie Lee," or re-assuming my last name Keel. I had learned the craft and mastered the art form, taking my act from the Dodge City Saloon to become one of the most talked-about top drawing country acts in the Southwest, and drawing upon the credibility of my previous accomplishments may help launch this new career. Plus, it was my name, and my family's name, and pride played a part in that decision as well.

An album release party was scheduled at the Buffalo Chip for March 22nd, 1995. I hired a video company to produce a 15-minute presentation which mixed classic KEEL video clips with the now-famous "tailgate" footage where I'm sitting on the tailgate of the Ranger with my guitar proclaiming my dedication to country music. I hired television news anchor Ron Hoon to host the event; Hoon had come out to New York during the recording of "The Final Frontier" to do a "hometown boy makes good" feature for Phoenix TV, and we cut in a few shots of him interviewing me on the streets of Manhattan.

The night of the album release party there was a red carpet, a TV news crew, family, friends and fans, many of whom had no idea what they were about to witness. They were impressed when Ron Hoon, a local celebrity of some import, got on stage and began talking about how he had met me in New York during my rock career a decade prior...and that's when they started looking at each other asking "What? What rock career?" Hoon introduced the video clip, and the lights dimmed as my 15-minute video opened with the pyro from "Somebody's Waiting." I watched from a distance in a room off to the side and felt really good to be alive and back in the game.

"Keel always seemed in transition, a story not ready to be told. He repositioned himself as Ronnie Lee Keel (formerly Ronnie Lee). His bio says he embraced country music a few years ago as 'the next step on the road to my true destiny' after my personal life was devastated by tragedy and dreams shot down in flames.' If ever there was a wait-and-see act, it was this one.

"Now comes the CD, WESTERN COUNTRY, an all-Arizona project, recorded at Apache Tracks. Almost everything on it is written or co-written by Keel. There are songs of alienation, remorse, defiance, and a whisper of vulnerability. This is good stuff, intelligent and real. The man can write a song and pick a guitar, and he has an emotional well he knows how to tap."
Sandy Lovejoy – KNIX Country Spirit Magazine, April 1995

We quickly outgrew the Buffalo Chip, but it was with regret that I left that place behind. After a year and a half, that bar had become one of us, a friend, a home, a partner. On our last night, I ended the show with "Last Call," and asked the band to loop the refrain. I walked off the stage for the last time and nailed my cowboy boots to the ceiling, where they hang still.

That summer we opened shows for Chris LeDoux, Diamond Rio, Jo Dee Messina, and Mark Wills. A treasured memory is sitting at a picnic table with Chris LeDoux when we shared the bill at the Payson rodeo, and we sat there, just the two of us, changing strings on our guitars together.

It was time to take it to Nashville, and with the help of my partners and Jon Rich we set up a round of meetings in Music City. Here I was again, pounding the streets, walking down Music Row pushing my music. I met with Bert Stein, now based in Nashville and managing Vince Neil's solo career as well as Brady Seals from Little Texas; and Jon introduced me to mega-mogul Buddy Killen at that time and numerous others. It was a good start and the response to the music was very enthusiastic, but I was surprised to get hit with the fact that my age (33) was a issue; I had assumed country music would be a safe place to mature and grow old like the legends.

Marc Ferrari was just getting his MasterSource Music Library off the ground and needed country music for his catalog. Ever since our song "Back To The City" from "The Right To Rock" had landed in a theatrical film called "D.A.R.Y.L." he recognized the opportunities for placing songs in TV shows and he was now collecting music for that specific purpose. He submitted a collection of material of all styles to TV and film music supervisors in the form of a boxed set, and selected some of the "Western Country" songs as the premiere tracks on his "country" CD. As a result, songs like "My Horse Is A Harley" ended up in a great deal of TV and film projects, including TV shows like "X-Files," "Desperate Housewives," "The Guiding Light," sporting events, a lot of CMT music programming, literall y hundreds of placements. Makes you feel good to hear your music on the big screen, see your name in the credits of films like "1000 Acres," "Chill Factor," "The Messengers," and many others, and cash those royalty checks.

21

TO HELL & BACK

Please don't say that you'll wait for me forever
You will forget in time
Somewhere where the cold wind blows
In a world that will make you my girl
Now the wasteland is calling me
Bring an end to my new beginning
On the road to where nowhere is – between here and hell

("Ride Like The Wind" – lyrics by RK 1996 – from the
Saber Tiger album "Project One" released 1997)

A year had passed since the release of my album and I was still slugging it out in the honky tonks. The quest for success once again became a fight for survival; after high paying house gigs at several Arizona venues we ended up at the Cheyenne Saloon on Bell Road for three hundred dollars a night, five hours a night, five nights a week. For a six piece band, that's fifty bucks a man. Enough to just about break even after gas, guitar strings, batteries and a bottle.

One night I came home from the Cheyenne as usual, checked in on the kids asleep in their beds, and when I looked in on Dee Dee I noticed a message coming out of the combination phone/fax on the dresser. I picked up the printed sheet and went downstairs to the garage which I had converted to my studio, grabbing a beer on my way.

```
DEAR MR. RON KEEL -
WE ARE FANDANGO RECORDS, BASED IN SAPPORO,
JAPAN. WE HAVE JUST SIGNED GUITAR STAR
AKIHITO KINOSHITA TO A MAJOR RECORDING
CONTRACT - MR. KINOSHITA IS BIG POPULAR
GUITARIST WITH BAND SABER TIGER, WHO HAS
ALREADY RELEASED MANY ALBUMS IN JAPAN
INCLUDING GREATEST HITS COMPILATIONS. HE
IS REFERRED TO AS YNGWIE MALMSTEEN OF
JAPAN. WE ARE SEARCHING FOR AN AMERICAN
ROCK SINGER FOR THIS PROJECT TO RELEASE
WORLDWIDE. YOU HAVE GOOD NAME AND HISTORY
IN JAPAN, AND WE WANT TO KNOW HOW MUCH IT
WILL COST TO MAKE CONTRACT WITH YOU TO
SING ON THIS ALBUM. PLEASE CALL US TO
DISCUSS THIS. REGARDS, TOSH SAKABE -
FANDANGO RECORDS
```

At first I thought it might be some kind of a joke, but after a fifty dollar gig at the Cheyenne I didn't have a lot to lose, so I called the number at the bottom of the fax. The person who answered didn't speak any English, but seemed pretty excited when I told them my name, so maybe it wasn't a joke after all. Eventually, Tosh Sakabe, the only English-speaking person on the staff at Fandango Records, was on the other end of the line basically re-iterating the message of the fax: how much would I charge to come to Japan and sing on the new Saber Tiger album.

"I'll do it for $75,000.00," I said.

"I call you right back," replied Mr. Sakabe. I hung up the phone and smiled, lighting a smoke. Within five minutes the phone rang again. "We give you $30,000.00."

"I'm there," I said.

I was going back to Japan. And I was going there to rock.

Not all the communication leading up to the session was that clear; there was some confusion about the lyrics and the melodies, and apparently Kinoshita, who had written all the songs and melodies and was producing the album, was very particular about having everything conform to his vision. I came to grips with sticking exactly to his melodies, and convinced them that if they wanted to market the album to Europe and the U.S., they needed me to write the lyrics. I did some sample vocals over the top of the instrumental tracks and flew to LAX to meet Tosh Sakabe and Mr. Hirabayashi, the President of Fandango Records, at LAX when they were there for a layover during a transcontinental business trip. Hirabayashi put the headphones on and listened to a few tracks, and we signed the deal. I was to be paid half up front and half upon completion, and I had a couple of months to write all the lyrics and get my full rock voice back.

Wanting to make sure my band kept our job, I hired a local country singer to come in and sub for me at the Cheyenne a couple of nights a week so he'd be ready when I left. I went and checked him out a few times; it was kind of weird to see another singer fronting the Ronnie Lee Keel band. I went to see Phoenix-area voice coach Sharon Stewart and explained to her what I had to do: recover the rock voice I'd left behind over four years ago. I combined her technique with my old Sabine training and started boosting my range. I hadn't hit one of those piercing Ron Keel screams since the last Fair Game rehearsal, and I wasn't even sure if I still could – four years of pushing air through my pipes singing country music five nights a week in smoky bars was only part of the problem: the question was, did I still have that rock voice in my heart?

The lyrics had to be crafted to exactly match the melodies, so I created "syllable charts" to map out the phrases:

XXXX – XXXXXXXXX became:
You're in control – now that you've got my full attention

I filled notebooks with phrases, titles, clichés and lyrical ideas. After working so hard to adopt a country-based writing style, it was challenging but fun to adopt this approach and get away with lyrics that were more abstract than country music might allow. To get myself mentally prepared I took to wearing a kimono around the house, eating sushi and drinking nothing but Japanese beer. I recorded demos in my garage studio, trying to get comfortable with the material in the limited time left before the session. Just before departing for Japan, I started to hit some of my trademark Ron Keel screams again and was feeling good about the task at hand.

Dee Dee, Kelly and Ryan were to accompany me for the first few days and then leave me to the business of the sessions, which would take place in Sapporo, on the island of Hokkaido off the northern coast of the Japanese mainland. It took us a couple of days to get there, with an overnight stop in Tokyo, and the first order of business was to take us up the side of a mountain on a chair lift. They were trying to be gracious, but I really just wanted to get to the hotel and sleep. The next day was the "Welcome Ron Keel To Hokkaido" party at the home of the record company President; a lavish affair with catered sushi which I just couldn't eat.

"I need to maintain my regular diet," I told Tosh. "I can't eat this stuff. Can I get a hamburger? Pizza?" Thirty minutes later, a half dozen pizzas showed up. The boxes said "Pizza California – I Feel Delicious!" but when I opened those boxes I was disgusted to see whole miniature octopus carcasses decorating the pizzas. Eventually Tosh Sakabe found a place called Moss Burger near the studio, and that was pretty much what I lived on the whole time.

The first day of the recording session I went in at 11 AM while Mr. Hirabayashi took my family to a local amusement park. I had created a "communication sheet" containing the Japanese versions of phrases I would need during the course of the recording: "A little more vocal in the headphones, please;" "Can I try that again, please." Neither Kinoshita nor any of the recording engineers spoke English, so Tosh Sakabe sat in a chair beside me while I was tracking and acted as the interpreter. I chose to start with "Give Me All Your Love" tonight, the most conventional (KEEL-like) track on the album, and after the first verse, I consulted my sheet and asked in Japanese "Can I hear that back, please;" everyone in the control room was laughing their asses off. "What did you say?" asked Sakabe; I showed him my "communication sheet" which he insisted was all wrong. So I guess it was a good thing I had an interpreter.

Kinoshita let me spend about six hours creating what I considered a master vocal. We listened back to it, and I was satisfied. After the playback, Kinoshita and Sakabe exchanged some words in Japanese. Eventually Tosh looked up at me form his chair and said, "Now he wants you to sing it again. And this time, do it *his* way." I was devastated, not only because he wasn't happy with my work but my throat was trashed and I was in no shape to start all over after six hours of belting it out. But I sucked it up, smiled, and said "Let's do it."

Over the next six hours, I executed the vocal that ended up on the album. In my opinion it was nowhere near as good as the vocal I produced when I was fresh, but

I'd been hired to do a job and it's only a take when the producer says it's a take.

But I was absolutely traumatized. It had been a tough first day, and that had been the "easy" song. Physical exhaustion coupled with panic, and upon returning to the hotel I started running a fever, experiencing hot-and-cold sweats, and throwing up. Physically I felt like shit, and mentally I was afraid I'd bitten off more than I could chew. How in hell was I going to be able to finish this album? I spent the night puking and sweating and not sleeping at all. At about 8:30 in the morning, I called Tosh Sakabe.

"I am ill," I said. "I have a high fever; I have been throwing up all night. I need some rest and I would like to delay starting the session until later this evening."

"It's OK," he replied. "We will come by at 11:00, and pick up your family to take them shopping so you can rest." But I didn't rest, I just rolled around in between puking and panicking.

11:00 came and the phone rang. I was sitting on the edge of the bed, drenched in sweat, smelling and feeling like death, but I knew in my heart what I had to do. I picked up the phone.

"I'll be right down."

I didn't shower. I didn't change out of my sweat pants, just threw on some tennis shoes, wrapped a towel around my head, grabbed my lyric book and went to the elevator. I'm sure I looked like hell when I walked into the hotel lobby.

"Let's go," I said.

Sakabe shook his head. "Go where?"

"Let's go to the studio."

"You are...OK?"

"I'm OK. Let's go to the studio." So he drove me to the studio. I don't think anyone there expected much from me, and the mood was dark as the entire project hung upon what was about to happen. They asked me which song I wanted to do.

"Ride Like The Wind." Eyes got big. I had chosen one of most challenging, high-screaming songs on the album.

I can't explain what happened that day. I don't know who was in front of that microphone, but it couldn't have been me. I assumed the stance and opened my mouth and MUSIC came out – the first verse flowed effortlessly out of me, then the second, and then when I went up high for the chorus, I hit it the first time. After the first chorus was down, I asked Tosh Sakabe to do me a favor, because I knew the President of the record company must be very concerned.

"Call Mr. Hirabayashi," I asked, "and please tell him that Ron Keel is here singing his ass off."

In the days that followed, I chipped away at the vocals one song, one verse, one chorus at a time. I had overcome the worst, and the song I cut that second day, "Ride Like The Wind," ended up being my favorite not only because of the adverse circumstance under which it was recorded but there's just an amazing tone to that vocal. After a couple of days, Dee Dee, Kelly and Ryan went back to the states and I was on my own. Immediately I was offered the services of a prostitute, but I declined. Each day I would start tracking at 11:00 A.M. and after stopping at Moss Burger I'd get back to the hotel around 8:00. There was no English television and no one at the hotel spoke my language, but I could order easily enough at the hotel bar. One night while sitting at the bar drinking sake, the bartender reach under the counter and pulled forth copies of "The Right To Rock," "The Final Frontier," and "KEEL" and handed me a Sharpie, smiling. I smiled and nodded.

About 75% of the way through the vocal work, Akihito Kinoshita's father died. The session was put on hold, and Sakabe-san looked after me while Kinoshita grieved and took care of making his father's funeral arrangements. There wasn't really much to do if you were an American rock singer in Sapporo; we went to the spa to enjoy natural hot springs, and we went shopping. Tosh surprised me one evening by telling me he had found a country bar, and I got all excited until we got there – it was no bigger than a large walk-in closet, with two small tables with two seats each and four stools at the bar. There was nobody else in there, but it felt good to hear American country music. They were playing some of the same songs my band was doing over 5000 miles away.

I was the only Westerner invited to attend the elder Kinoshita's funeral, and judging from the size of the affair he must have been quite a prominent man. It was a fascinating experience and I was honored to participate, taking great care to follow along with the correct procedure so as not to offend.

Eventually we got back to work on the vocal sessions, and Akihito was much easier to work with. The death of his father had softened his hard ass, and he was much more tolerant of me taking some vocal liberties with the material. Finally, the last line of the last take of the last song was done, and when I heard him say "OK" through the headphones I collapsed on the carpet, my body shaking, my ears ringing, my throat raw. Right in the middle of "the country years" I had returned to Japan to record the hardest and heaviest album of my career.

22

SINGERS, HOOKERS & THIEVES

I sold my soul to the music when I was thirteen
Dropped out of school and went chasing that rock & roll
dream
Now I don't regret all the choices I made as a kid
And I won't say I'm sorry for living the life that I lived

Singers, hookers & thieves – we're all one of a kind
Sellin' or stealin' – we're all just trying to get by
You use what you got to get what you need
May the good lord have mercy on singers, hookers & thieves

("Singers, Hookers & Thieves" – lyrics by RK 2013 – from
the Ron Keel album "Metal Cowboy" released 2014)

THE RAT'LERS

Dee Dee and I had begun to fight more and more during those years, in a vicious cycle of co-dependence where we would have these violent fights, and I would move out. While I was moved out I would get laid, then I would eventually come back home because I loved my kids only to be reviled as an adulterer. I came to the logical conclusion that if your wife tells you she doesn't love you anymore, and tells you to get the fuck out, and if you move out and you are separated, you are free to pursue pussy. Invariably we would miss each other and make up, and I'd come home to start the cycle all over again.

In 1997, my father suffered a mild stroke and ended up in the hospital. He seemed OK when I went to see him that evening, but later that night there was another stroke, this time a big one. He went from healthy to incapacitated in the blink of an eye, his right side completely paralyzed.

He was a proud guy and I know it killed him to be helpless and bedridden. I was singing at the Rockin' Horse is Scottsdale at the time, and John C. Lincoln Hospital provided me with a room where I could stay the night and be close to Pop, which put even more strains on my already strained marriage. I was trying to teach him how to talk out of the left side of his mouth and write with his left hand. I wheeled him around in his chair, taking him outside for air. I suspended all of my out of town gigs to be with him, but we had a six-nighter booked for the week before Christmas at a place in Flagstaff called The Museum Club that was a great gig, everybody loved it, the venue was cool and the money was good. Before we left town, I sat at Roy's bedside.

"We got a gig at the Zoo, Pop," which was the nickname for that club. "It's just six nights, and I'll be back, OK?" He raised his left hand and gave me a thumbs up and a grunt.

We made it through the week until Sunday, which was the last night of the gig. Snow was falling as we made our way inside, grabbed a drink, and went to tune up when a note taped to my microphone stand informed me that my father had passed away.

I walked through the desert for three days scattering his ashes in the Superstition Mountains crying and feeling his teeth and bone fragments slip through my fingers.

The Ronnie Lee Keel band had continued to be a top draw at rodeos, casinos, honky tonks, roadhouses and nightclubs throughout the Southwest and I'd finally come to terms with the fact that I would not get another shot at a major recording career.

And then The Rat'lers called.

"The Rat'lers, a rockin' country act who are currently creating a big buzz in the Nashville community with their 'Dwight Yoakam meets The Stones' approach, have added lead vocalist Ronnie Lee Keel, formerly of the rock group KEEL, to the lineup. The band, which was formed by the group's songwriter and bassist Ric Kipp, has also signed on for a 28-date tour of Europe, which will take the group to Germany, Spain, Greece and Italy, through July."

Music Connection Magazine – June 5, 1998

Ric Kipp had found my old promo kit in a file at Buddy Killen's office in Nashville, left behind after the "Western Country" visit several years before. He was working on a publishing deal with Buddy Killen Music and looking for the right voice for his project The Rat'lers – they had recorded an entire album with a singer the Nashville establishment deemed too rude and raspy sounding, and apparently all they had to do was find a country singer with a radio-friendly voice who could rock. The album was in the can, and they wanted me to come to Nashville, re-do the vocals, participate in the video for the title track, do the promotional photo session, and do a 28-date tour of U.S. military bases throughout Europe and the Mediterranean. They had management, financial backing, major interest, and the tour was already booked. I told Hal Monti, who had been with me over four years, that it was too good for me to pass up, and he understood and wished me well.

Once again, I was Nashville bound.

Jon Rich made hotel arrangements for me for a month, and drove me back and forth to the sessions, rehearsals, video and photo shoots. The songs were all hits as far as I was concerned, great writing and production and my voice fit the material perfectly. The image was good looking, long haired modern day outlaws with attitudes several years before this look became commonplace in country music.

Everything was going along great until the morning we were to depart for the European tour. I was a hired gun, pretty much doing what was required of me and just glad to be fronting a hot new Nashville outfit that was getting a lot of attention and had a real shot, so I wasn't privy to all the history, or why weren't any of the guys who'd played on the album still in the band. Apparently Ric Kipp wasn't big on stability, the concept of the group was more important that the individual players, but I felt secure because I was the voice. Anyway, we'd all gathered at the Nashville airport and I noticed Ric and Kevin "Casey" Compton, our manager, involved in what appeared to be a very serious discussion and our lead guitarist Chris Morrison was nowhere to be found. Casey came up to me.

"Chris isn't gonna make it," he said. "We're gonna have to do this tour as a three piece, and you're going to have to play guitar." I was blindsided, and reminded him that because of luggage restrictions, I hadn't even been allowed to bring an electric guitar on the tour with me (even though we had 28 boxes of merchandise). All I had was an acoustic.

We got on the plane to Detroit in shock, and I never did get a straight answer about what happened with the guitarist. Probably a money thing, it usually is. Or maybe he didn't even have a passport, I didn't know and Kipp didn't seem to care. Up until that point it had been an awesome situation full of promise and potential, but the blaring blunders were starting to become apparent.

The first thing I did when we landed in Detroit was call Hal.

"The lead guitarist is a no-show," I told him. "Get a passport. Get your ass to Frankfurt Germany." Then we got on a plane to Frankfurt.

Technically, we were working for the Department Of Defense, provided with a two-man military sound and stage crew and gear. We were based out of Wiesbaden, and would drive sometimes twelve hours round trip to the gigs on the first leg of the tour. Hal had gone over to Los Angeles to go through the rush procedure to get his passport, but we were going to have to get through the first five shows as a trio with me on guitar.

One of the crew guys had an electric guitar I borrowed, and I practiced and improvised and by the fourth and fifth shows we were actually starting to get this cool country power trio groove going on.

In the days it had been taking to process his passport and make his travel arrangements, Hal had done his homework and we hit the stage on fire every night after he arrived. The crowd response to that act was rabid – U.S. military are some of the best people, and audiences, you'll ever entertain but the working class outlaw element of the Rat'lers image and music struck a very powerful chord in everyone who heard it. Songs like "Caroline," Honky Tonk Highway" and "Thick As Thieves" resonated loud and clear and the more it became apparent that the band and the songs were really special, the more obvious it was that Kipp seemed hell bent on making every wrong move possible to de-fang the Rat'lers. He would get drunk late at night after the gigs and call the people back in Nashville at Killen's company that were behind the band; they offered him a solid deal and he turned it down out of fear of losing control of his material.

I got to experience some beautiful places on that tour. We rented a Zodiac boat and snorkeling gear in La Maddalena, Sardinia, we drove over the Alps a couple times, it was my first time in Italy and despite the best efforts of the locals we found the leaning tower of Pisa anyway. We were scheduled to play on the deck of the aircraft carrier U.S.S. Eisenhower docked in Naples, and the stage was set with a massive American flag behind it, the jets all lined up on the deck in formation, but the seas ended up being too choppy and the gig was canceled.

Near the end of the tour, we received a shipment of 1000 CD's of the Rat'lers "Thick As Thieves" album. In another one of Ric Kipp's brilliant marketing moves, there was no CD booklet or cover, just a plain red disc in a jewel box. We still sold out of them within a few shows, that's how enthusiastic the response was. Before heading home, a return tour later that year was already confirmed.

Upon returning to the States, we headlined The Georgia Games, an amateur Olympic-type event at the Georgia Dome in Atlanta where the Falcons play football. It had been 12 years since my last stadium gig - at least this time I got a photo in the end zone.

Once I got back to Arizona and paid a few bills with the money I'd made touring with the Rat'lers, I was broke again and scrambling for gigs. Just like metal and hard rock had in the mid-80's, country music had peaked in the mid-90's and in the wake of the decline a lot of country nightclubs on the once-thriving Arizona scene were changing format, cutting down the number of nights they had entertainment, or shutting down altogether. Jobs were getting hard to find, and good jobs were getting even harder to find. Pat James had taken our place at the Buffalo Chip and he ended up staying there for 17 years. I put a band together with a very talented singer, Vikki Rae Jordan, called Western Heart, and we co-fronted the band in local clubs in between the tours of Europe with the Rat'lers in '98. One night I was working at the Silver Spur when I saw a guy all decked out in leather and fringe, long dark hair, tough looking dude with a nice friendly smile and charisma from his cowboy hat down to his shiny boots. I walked up to him

"Hey," I said. "You play bass." I don't know if I was just being hopeful or taking a wild guess.

"Yep, I sure do," he replied.

"We need to talk."

His name was Geno Arce, and he's pretty much been with me off and on ever since.

Western Heart was hosting a jam night on Sundays at a joint in Apache Junction, and I invited Geno to come out and sit in with us. He was a rocker too, who had just decided to make the switch to playing country music, and though he had a lot to learn he was a quick study and his simple precise finger style was strong in the pocket. We became fast friends and I decided to build a new band with him when I got back from the next European tour; the plan was to put together my own Arizona version of the Rat'lers, using good looking long-haired outlaw musicians with rock star attitudes. Before I left for the tour, I gave Geno 30 songs and 30 days to be ready for our new job, at a little hole in the wall bar in Casa Grande called Mel's.

Hal and I spent another month in Europe with Ric Kipp that October – same response from the audiences, and the same results in terms of career equity: zero. I had made a good connection with the agent, Fred Woods, who swore he was done with Ric Kipp but promised me a return trip to Europe the following summer.

Our guitar player at Mel's was a sweet dude and a good player named Joey Carter; he was another rock guy trying to make the transition to country and he was always loud and distorted but he looked cool and we were friends. But Joey was a skinny man, and four beers would put him down. One night he'd had six, and was sitting on his amp shitfaced during the gig. Now, I'm as tolerant (probably more so) than anybody when it comes to drinking on the job, but I'll draw the line at sitting down drunk on your amp. So after the show, I told him he was fired and gave him his two weeks' notice.

Well, the next night he comes in all smiling and acting like everything's great. He had a good attitude, and in the next week and a half he wasn't acting like somebody who'd been fired, he was talking about the good times to come and all. Finally it dawned on me that he'd been so drunk when I fired him that he hadn't remembered getting fired for being drunk.

Somewhere around then Dee Dee and I had our final fight. I don't remember what it was about – it usually was just anger out of the blue, but it had been a tough year for us, after my father died and I was spending months away from home in Nashville and Europe. What had once been love or something like it had been chipped away at by both of us for so long there just wasn't enough left to live on. I moved out for the last time, determined to stay close to Kelly and Ryan, who would come over and stay the night at the new place with Geno and I, and go camping and take trips out to Tortilla Flat where we did a day show.

That Tortilla Flat gig saved our ass a lot during those times because the bar scene was dying. Tortilla Flat is an old stagecoach stop/tourist trap up on the Apache Trail about 18 miles from Apache Junction. When my Dad and I used to go exploring in the mountains, we'd often stop there for a beer. During the season (Christmas through Easter) they have a little three piece country combo out on the patio, and even when I was a kid I'd ask to sit in on the drums and play Creedence tunes; by 1998 I was a full time member of the Tortilla Flat Band. There were about seven guys who rotated in the three positions seven days a week, weather permitting; on days when you were scheduled, you'd call in to see what the weather was like and if the show was a go, you'd head up the trail and get set up for an 11:00 A.M. start. Sometimes I'd head out straight from my night gig, get there around 2:00 in the morning and pitch camp, and roll out of the tent and onto the stage. The idea was to look as rough and trail-weary as possible to fit in with the cowboy atmosphere. There was (and probably still is) a big milk can for a tip jar, and in addition to the $75.00 a day pay sometimes we would leave with hundreds per man in just tips; the gig was over at three, giving you plenty of time to get to your night job.

There was this decent club we used to play in Yuma called Johnny's, and more and more often they would call me whenever they had a cancellation. The money was good and it was nice to get out of town for a week at a time, but it was a ball buster, long nights and they ran the shifts like clockwork. It was one of those gigs where you actually had to watch the second hand on your watch.

Johnny's was a great place to watch sports, screens everywhere but you couldn't see any of them from the stage. One night during the show everybody was pointing to the screens and then pointing at me on stage, then pointing back and forth from me to the screens. They were playing the VH1 "Where Are They Now" special, where Ron Keel "goes country," containin that tailgate footage I'd filmed for the "Western Country" CD release party. One young lady was particularly impressed by seeing me on TV, and before the next break was over she was dancing in my arms, and within a couple of days I was in her bed. She was a featured dancer at the local strip club, owned by the same guy who owned Johnny's, and in her living room she had her framed spread from Playboy and a copy of the check she'd received from the magazine.

After all my rock star exploits and world travels, it took playing country music at a roadhouse in Yuma for me to finally tag my first centerfold.

I lost Geno when he joined a full-time band right down the road from our apartment in Mesa; he deserved it and I was happy for him, and due to child support issues and passport restrictions he wasn't going to be able to go with me on the next European tour anyway, which was nine weeks away.

I called the owner of Johnny's in Yuma.

"Mike, we leave for Europe in a couple months," I told him. "You know you're going to have more no-shows than shows during that time, because you work your bands to death six nights a week and nobody wants to play there. I'll come down there and do the next nine weeks solid – you won't have to worry about cancellations, and I won't have to be worried about my next gig."

I spent some time with my centerfold during that nine week run, but also spent a lot of time writing during the long hot days. Some of the songs that would become the foundation for IronHorse were born during that time – "In My Wildest Dreams," "Redneck Rock & Roll," "You Can Have What's Left Of Me." We didn't play any of those songs, we didn't even learn them or work them up, I just held on to them like spare dreams for a rainy day that might never come. I knew the band I had that was headed for Europe with me was a decent cover band, nothing more. Good guys, and I especially loved the drummer Mark Allen who had done a lot of work with me during the country years, but I'd been pounding it out in the honky tonks for six years and I was starting to get burned out and wondered where I'd end up after this next tour.

I had a pet tarantula named Dog who was a lot of fun, I used to let him crawl around on me and we'd let him wander the table top during late night games of cards after the Yuma shows. He always seemed to know when the bars closed, because about 1:15 we'd get back to the band house and he'd be up on his hind legs wanting out.

Dee Dee had taken the kids and left for California, which was probably best I guess, although I regret not being a part of their lives during the years that followed. Before I left for that tour I put all my stuff in storage and told Geno to take care of my tarantula. I filed for divorce and went to Europe.

23

THE SHOW MUST GO ON

No matter where I go I'm always leaving
There's another town somewhere down the road
One more song and I'll be gone
Tear it down and move along
The show must go on

I've seen places most people only dream of
10,000 friends I'll never see again
The highway is my home
There's no one place that I belong
Don't you know – the show must go on

("The Show Must Go On" – lyrics by RK 1999 – from the
IronHorse album "IronHorse" released 2001)

IronHorse: L-R Gaetano Nicolosi, Geno Arce, RK, Jay Rusnak, Dean Lehman

After a big 4th of July festival show a Naval Air Station 1, Sigonella, Sicily, and the round of local bar-hopping that followed, I was wrapped up on a dance floor in some club with a hot Navy girl who had been our DOD handler for the day. I had already sealed the deal to spend the night with her; me and the boys were just hanging out for a couple more drinks when I spotted the blond at the bar. She'd had her eye on me since we'd been on stage, and had followed along as we made the rounds to Mama Elio's pub across from the Navy base, and here she was again, playing it cool while I stood next to her ordering another round.

"You gonna go home with her?" she asked me. I nodded and said "Yeah."

"You should come home with me."

"Okay." And I did. I had just met my next ex-wife.

She was career Navy, almost done with a 20-year tour of duty, and had no problem arranging leave and flights to come out and visit a couple of more times during that otherwise miserable tour. It was only miserable because of the attitude of the guys in the band; we were getting flown around on Navy C9 jets, performing for enthusiastic military audiences, seeing Europe – hell, at one gig in Crete we got to visit a lighthouse built by the Egyptians, for Christ's sake - and all they could do was bitch about the food, bitch about the hotel, bitch about having to fly to the middle of nowhere to play for 20 people because some of the bases were remote and there were only 20 people stationed there. And I was giving them an equal split of the money, $900.00 per man per week tax free which was good money back then (or even now, for that matter).

After 20 years in the military, surrounded by jarheads, Lindsey was turned on by the long-haired guy in leather with the cowboy hat. Our first date was in Venice, Italy, and it doesn't get much more romantic than that. We fell in love hard and fast, she with my nomadic outlaw spirit and I with her discipline and stability. Those same qualities in each of us would lead to the disintegration of the marriage six years later; turns out she didn't want a nomadic outlaw musician after all.

After the tour was over, the band went back to Arizona for two shows at the Oxbow in Payson and went our separate ways for the last time. The next morning after the second gig, I went to the pay phone and called her in Italy and told her I was coming back.

While I was making arrangements to do that, I heard from my old friend Casey Compton, former manager of the Rat'lers, who was now in charge of merchandising for Lynyrd Skynyrd. He asked what I was doing and I said not much, and he offered me a two week job working with him on Skynyrd's "Edge Of Forever" tour. I love Casey and thought it would be a blast, plus the money was great, and I would get to go on tour with Lynyrd Skynyrd, so I hopped on a Greyhound and met him in Vegas.

And it was a blast – until after the show, when 5000 people would descend upon the merchandise table and order one of these, two of those, a double X shirt, a fishing lure and an autographed CD and I would have to do the math. I developed a deep respect for the T-Shirt Guys – the first to arrive, counting in all the sizes and varieties of items for sale, and the last to leave, counting out and settling up with the venues and promoters. But I went back to Italy with an "Edge Of Forever" CD, a brain full of great southern rock, and a few thousand dollars in my pocket. Maybe not enough to retire, but enough to take a little time to figure out what was next. I had no desire to play music, no desire to step on stage, I just wanted to eat Italian food, drink a lot of wine, and fuck my new girlfriend.

It was fun, it was comfortable, we lived on the military base across from where I had done the 4th of July gig, she would go to work at the air terminal and I would stay home and work on my book. Not this book, but a fictional modern day western adventure which I'd always intended to write. Of course I brought my musical gear with me but I didn't touch it.

That lasted about three weeks, when I started to get the itch to play.

Lee Wilkerson was a career Navy husband - his wife Cindy was an officer at the Naval hospital, and he was a guitar player, and of course we struck up a friendship. Then we started plucking around on guitars on the back porch while drinking beer and watching Mt. Etna, Europe's largest active volcano, erupt from our vantage point in the backyard. We started doing little acoustic duo gigs in the area.

Mama Elio's Days Inn Pub was a nice club across from the base that held about 500 people. They'd get a mix of locals and Navy patrons, and one Sunday after Lee and I did an acoustic gig there Mama came up to us, this tiny old Italian lady, and spoke to us in her broken English.

"I want you play here," she said. "You play Thursday, Friday, Saturday with band. Sunday this," (meaning the acoustic duo on Sundays). "I pay you one million Lira!" I thought fucking A, a million a week! Sign me up! I think that ended up being about $200.00 per man. Lee and I said, OK, but we don't have a band. I told Lee we'd do it three piece, he could play guitar, I'd play bass and sing, but we'd need a drummer. One of the waiters at the bar said, "I know drummer." He got on the phone, and literally 15 minutes later Gaetano Nicolosi walked in with a pair of drumsticks.

Gaetano was young but very accomplished, already teaching at the local music academy. He didn't speak any English, so we had to have an interpreter for our first band meeting.

"Tell him we play every Thursday, Friday, and Saturday. We start when we want, we quit when we want. Tell him we rehearse every Tuesday and we split one million Lira a week."

I put together a set list of classic rock, some country – hell, we played led Zeppelin and Brooks & Dunn and everything in between in that band. I went to a music store in nearby Catania and bought a cheap red bass guitar, Lee had a great P.A. system, and suddenly people were driving from miles around to see the crazy American with the wireless headset microphone running around the bar, dancing on the tables. The coolest thing was, the Italian members of our audience had no idea what I was singing half the time – they'd certainly never heard of Brooks & Dunn – but they appreciated the voice, and they enjoyed the show. We'd end every gig with "Stairway To Heaven" and then afterward the audience would line up in front of the stage and wait their turn to kiss me on either cheek in the tradition of their people, it was very touching.

We called the band KEEL III, because there were three of us.

Right behind the stage was a doorway to a huge domed building where they stored all their junk and old furniture, we called it the Thunderdome, and I set up my little four track recording unit and drum machine there and started to work up some of the songs I had written the previous year. Wilkerson and I sat one day and co-wrote a song called "The Show Must Go On." We started to work up some of those songs like "In My Wildest Dreams" and "Redneck Rock & Roll" and play them live.

We used to drink like fiends at that gig. As we would enter through the front doors, the bartenders would see us coming and by the time we got to the bar there would be a double shot of vodka for Lee and a double shot of Jack for me, and it would not stop. There were a lot of times when we'd drink six doubles each before we even started the first set. There was a triangular space between the mixer rack and the PA speakers maybe four feet high, and we'd set our beers and shots on the bass bin, only to see them vibrate off during a song and land in that hole. Every now and then we'd look in there and see the broken glasses piling up, and eventually it became a game – we'd finish a shot or a beer and throw the shot glass or bottle into the hole, which we nicknamed The Graveyard. Enentually the pile of bottles and shot glasses was a foot tall, then two feet, three feet. One day the bar must have run out of shot glasses, because I came in to the gig and the speakers had been moved, the area was cleaned up, and they were tearing Lee a new asshole. They never said shit to me.

I was on stage at Mama Elio's on New Year's Eve 1999; I wanted the last song that I played in the previous millennium to be special, something with a profound meaning, but before I could catch him Lee launched into "Play That Funky Music White Boy." We took a break and added a bottle of champagne to our list of libations for the evening, and that was all Lee could handle. Before the first song of 2000 could begin, he was staggering out of the bar – he'd brace himself up against a beam with his left hand, take a few steps, brace himself against a table with his right hand, take a few more steps. He ended up passed out in his front yard in the freezing cold and we finished the night as a two piece band. I love that guy.

Lindsey had done her 20 years in the Navy and was closing in on retirement at the age of 40, so we started to think about going back to the states together, her transition to civilian life, what I was going to do with my life. She had a young son whom I'd grown very close with as well – he'd spent his entire life on military bases throughout Europe and the Mediterranean. Her family had a house on some property near Columbus, Ohio, in a little town called Plain City, and they were offering to let us stay there for a year to get our feet on the ground.

I wanted to go into a local studio in Catania and record a few original songs, kind of as a souvenir of my time in Italy and the reminder of the good times at Mama Elio's with Lee and Gaetano, so we found a studio and spent a couple of days laying down "Wildest Dreams," "Show Must Go On," and "Redneck."

When we finished the session I stopped in at Mama's with a copy of the CD and they put it on over the speakers. I was sitting there drinking, listening to what we'd done, in between a couple of Navy guys.

"Man, that's some good sounding country music," said the guy on my right. I thanked him. The reaction of the guy on my left was totally different. "Dude – that rocks!" So I started a discussion with the two of them, to try to determine if it was country or rock & roll, and when they couldn't reach a conclusion, I knew I had something special.

Later that night, it hit me suddenly, like a ton of bricks and I woke up out of bed shouting the word IronHorse. I called Geno and I told him we were moving to Ohio and forming a band called IronHorse. The next day, I told Gaetano he was coming to America with me to play in a band called IronHorse. And I responded to an email I'd received from a young Swedish guitarist – I know, here we go again – whose name was Rob Marcello, and he said if I ever needed a guitar player to let him know. So I let him know.

My goal was to create a perfect hybrid – country songs approached from a rock perspective, with screaming guitars and big drums. An international lineup of guys creating a unique brand of music somewhere south of KEEL and north of the Rat'lers.

Although Lindsey still had a couple of months before her Navy career was officially over, I flew back to the states and Geno and I loaded up all our gear and personal belongings in a Penske truck, towing my car behind it, and set out from Phoenix for Plain City, Ohio. Barely north of Phoenix, in Black Canyon City where I'd done my first country gig so long ago, we ran into my old bass player from that gig, a guy named Doc Holliday (no shit). We'd stopped at the Laundromat to take a piss, and there was Doc doing his wash. He turned us on to enough white powder to get us halfway to Ohio.

We built a little sleeping area right behind the cab and took turns driving. Geno didn't have a driver's license, so we agreed that if he got pulled over we'd switch real quick. Sure enough, in Memphis he was driving and got pulled over for speeding, and when we saw the red and blue lights we looked at each other and yelled "Switch!" When the cop came up to the driver's side window he did a double take, and I showed him my license.

We got to Plain City, Ohio just after sundown, ready to get our drink on after 1800 miles, and pulled in at the first bar we saw, the Plain City Pub. Now these folks hadn't seen guys like Geno and me, and there was a rough and tough contingent of corn fed farm boys at the bar that night. I started ordering up shots of Jack, and a very large fellow a couple of barstools down finally turned to me and said in a voice made of pure gravel, "You ain't gonna just come into town and drink all my whiskey, now are you?"

"Hell no," I replied, and asked the bartender to pour that man a shot.

He ended up being friendly enough. In fact, he ended up being George Dolphin, one of the best friends I've ever had.

And that little Ohio town and the people in it became my family, my friends, and shared one of the most special times of my life and career with me, as IronHorse became their dream as well as mine. They were our people, and we were their band.

It started out simple enough, probably just the way it should have, by getting the old farmhouse livable and setting up the barn for rehearsal. For emotional inspiration as much as to soak up the sound, we hung the KEEL banner in back and the Steeler banner in front. On the other walls, on the ceiling, anywhere we could, we hung all those banners given to me by the fans from throughout my career, the banner from the "Tears Of Fire" video and the banners from Japan and Europe.

After all I'd been through by that time, you might think my confidence shaken, my resolve tested to the max, but I had no doubt that at that point in my life and career a wonderful opportunity was before me, and I was finally figuring out the combination to a very complex lock that would open to prosperity and fulfillment. I believed in IronHorse every bit as much as I had believed in or Steeler, KEEL, or any of my other projects. The minute I stop believing in something, it's over.

And like those bands, IronHorse probably deserves its own book. I know there are a hard core group of friends and fans who would buy it and read it. Over six years, two albums, and seven hundred shows, there are more stories to tell than these pages can hold; the tales I could include of that magical time would only insult the tales untold. We held the dreams of an entire community in our hands, a town that embraced us and loved us and loves us still. Much like the magic of Hollywood in the 80's, and the western country in the 90's, during the IronHorse years I was able to live that dream once again and create a band whose music touched so many lives in so many special ways.

From the very first rehearsal in the living room of that farmhouse, with Gaetano banging on phone books because his drums were being shipped from Italy and hadn't arrived yet, working up a song I had written called "Don't Stop."

Rehearsing in the barn all day every day, when our neighbor and friend Doug Tuller would pull up on his tractor yelling "Play some AC/DC, God dammit!" And we played "Sin City," changing the words to "Plain City."

Playing every dive and bar in Central Ohio, bringing the big show just like I had done when Steeler first moved to Los Angeles. On the back wall we'd hang the Swedish flag, the Italian flag, the American flag, and the Confederate flag, each one of us flying our colors and our music was the anthem of those who believed. We'd unload the trailer, set up all the P.A., all the lights, the smoke, the gear, do our show, tear it down and load it up and do it all over again the next day at another bar, sometimes in the snow, sometimes in the sweltering summer heat.

Learning hundreds of songs from country to metal – searching for and striking the nerve that touched fans of both styles.

Taking to the road in a 32 foot motor home and notching 100,000 glorious miles from New York to Daytona to L.A. and back again; from recording our debut album in a Connecticut blizzard to Arizona filming our first three videos on a summer day so hot that the drums were melting.

Having our song "Run For The Border" hold on to the #1 spot on the Soundclick Southern Rock chart for six months straight.

Dealing with the immigration laws and lawyers just so Gaetano and Rob could stay in the country – putting Gaetano on a Greyhound to Philly to catch a plane to Rome just to get his passport stamped to he could get back on a plane to the U.S. and back on a Greyhound to get back to Ohio in time for the next show.

Jamming a set of KEEL songs with Bryan Jay and Marc Ferrari at our first Los Angeles show.

Playing the Thursday night fish fry at Lee's Sports & Spirits, and then opening shows for .38 Special, Marshall

Tucker, and The Outlaws, headlining events from the Lone Star Biker Bash at Texas Motor Speedway to Freedom Fest in San Diego. Fighting and loving, loving and fighting, losing Rob Marcello and gaining Jay "SnakkDaddy" Rusnak with a few Matt LaPorte shows in between.

Falling down the basement stairs at Stop 42 in Delaware, Ohio and sustaining a concussion that left me unable to sing, speak or spell.

Creating an amazing album entitled "Bring It On" in Nashville which reunited me with "Rock & Roll Outlaw" producer Kevin Beamish and enabled us to collaborate with southern rock legend Henry Paul.

Getting so close to a major record deal that I could taste it and feeling it all fall through my hands once again, shattering not only my dreams but the hopes of all who believed in us.

You think I crammed a lot of shit into 1978, or 1986, you should have been there during the six years I fronted IronHorse. Some of you *were* there. Some of you still are.

We got back together for the last time in 2012 to help raise $27,000.00 for a young man named Parker Headings who needed some medical treatment to get him out of his wheelchair for the for time in his 10-year existence. Seeing the photos a year later of Parker taking his first steps tells me all I need to know about the power of love, the power of music, and the power of IronHorse.

To all of those that shared those times and that dream: You're our people. And we're you're fucking band.

But like the man said...the show must go on.

"In October 2004, IronHorse was putting together a two day record release weekend in Ohio for 'Bring It On.' Bob Casalez and I pooled our money and decided to surprise the guys with our appearance. We were greeted with smiles and hugs at the Friday night show. The next night we made it to Big George's Bar in Plain City, Ohio.

"After playing two full sets of IronHorse tunes, Ron took the stage once again in front of a packed house.

Stepping up the microphone he said 'I don't know what time it is in New York City, and I don't know what time it is in Los Angeles (with a glance in my direction, he continued) and I don't know what time it is in Winnemucca, Nevada, but I do know that in Plain City Ohio, it's Keel fuckin' thirty.'

"With that, Jay broke into the opening chords of 'The Right to Rock."'
Sheldon Bergenheier

24

WHEN LOVE GOES DOWN

You can stand your ground with a heart of stone
Think you're better off – when you're all alone
Say you're not afraid to draw the line
Build another wall just to hide behind
You can play the field – like it's all a game
Fill your little black book with another name

Then you find someone who makes your life complete
Out of nowhere – you get what you need

Oh when love goes down - it comes on strong
Like a tidal wave or a hit song
When love goes down it's a wild thing
Makes you wanna rock – makes you wanna scream
When love goes down

("When Love Goes Down" – lyrics by RK 2013 – from the
Ron Keel album "Metal Cowboy" released 2014)

As Ronnie Dunn

A few years after my father died, my Mom's health started to fail. IronHorse was in Arizona filming our first music videos and doing a show at Alice Cooper'stown in downtown Phoenix, and we'd parked the RV out on the street by her apartment; we'd use the shower and swim in her pool and she loved having the company. She had never lived a healthy lifestyle – she was still on the toxic diet she'd raised me on, still a day-and-night chain smoker into her mid-70's – and it was taking its toll. She'd pretty much stopped eating and her internal organs were on their way to a complete shutdown.

As we showered and started prepping for the show downtown, I noticed Lucille had come out of her room with a nice dress on and makeup on her face. "What are you doing?" I asked.

"I'm going to see your show," she said. And she did. I got her a VIP booth where she sat with Sherleen's daughter Marcia, and it felt so good to look out from the stage and see her smiling, thrusting her fist in the air and singing along during "The Right To Rock." After the gig we had to hit the road, but the next morning I turned around and went back to Phoenix when I found out my Mom had fallen coming home the night before and broken her hip.

At the hospital, she seemed bright-eyed and in good spirits. They were going to keep her for a few days and build her stamina enough to perform surgery on her hip. I stayed as long as I could and left her in Sherleen's care because IronHorse had a big show in Columbus the next night opening up for Marshall Tucker and .38 Special and it was a 27 hour drive.

I was just about to go on stage when my sister called my mobile phone and said I should come home, that mama wasn't going to make it and I needed to say goodbye. I thought maybe she was being dramatic, I'd just seen my Mom yesterday and she seemed OK, and after the show the next day I would get the first flight out.

I shouldn't have waited. Lucille Keel died the next day and I never did get to say goodbye.

I think when we look back on our lives we all have things we'd do differently. I've often been asked if I have any regrets, and without hesitation the answer is always, two. Not being there when my father died. And not being there when my mother died. I realized too late that there are times when the show must NOT go on.

After a year in Ohio developing IronHorse, much of it spent on the road, I convinced Lindsey I needed to be near Nashville to get the project to the next level and we moved to Columbia, Tennessee, a small town about 60 miles south of Music City. We rented a house with a big basement where the band could rehearse and stay when they were in town, but they had put down solid roots in Ohio, falling in love and that's where they remain. They would make the trek down to Nashville for shows, recording sessions, business meetings and other band activities, and I would go back and forth from Nashville to Ohio for gigs because we'd built such a strong and loyal following there.

Marcello quit the band just as we were getting some traction in Music City. I'd offered him a band of brothers with a real shot at success, but we weren't broadcasting on the same frequency at the time. He was much younger, and I was the authority he needed to rebel against; he'd only wanted to play with me because of what I'd been and done in the 80's, and he rejected the southern style cowboy metal I was trying to market with this new project and left IronHorse. The band, our mission, Jay Rusnak (the guy who ultimately replaced Marcello) and the support group of people that believed in us were all so strong that we survived that blow and got another shot with the "Bring It On" album; but ultimately we could not sustain a concerted effort to seal any type of substantial deals in Nashville and once again I had to come to terms with the death of a dream and what was probably my last and best chance to really make it.

We still performed as IronHorse, but I started branching out and doing other projects in Nashville. I wrote a lot of songs with my good friend John Edwards, an incredible songwriter from Arizona who had moved to Nashville to pursue that dream; I did a duo project, kind of like a heavy metal Brooks & Dunn, called Keel & Wayne. We cut a song I wrote called "I Gave It All To You" and did a music video for the track, supported with some tour dates across the country, and we got some serious industry interest but that train wrecked pretty quickly. I went back to my first instrument, the drums, and started doing pickup gigs on the weekends just for the love of playing, local country bands, southern rock and classic rock. I did a couple of all-star acoustic tours, a package I called the "Acoustic Outcasts" – Terry Ilous from XYZ (more recently with Great White), Kelly Keeling, a few other guys. We had an extensive tour booked with Don Dokken joining us but Hurricane Katrina had other plans.

I'd had an idea in the back of my mind for a few years at this point about trying my hand in the tribute industry. I'd seen a few tribute bands in our travels with IronHorse – a ZZ Top tribute here, an AC/DC tribute there, a Lynyrd Skynyrd tribute in Cleveland that packed the house and made twice as much money as we did. On some level all entertainers are actors playing a role anyway, and it looked like fun, dressing up and pretending you're somebody else. Problem was, I didn't look or sound like anyone else.

Unless...I thought back to the country years, performing in the roadhouses and the honky tonks with the Ronnie Lee Keel Band. Whenever I would sing Brooks & Dunn songs, people would say "Wow, you sound just like him!" I sure loved their music – starting with their second album, I'd bought every Brooks & Dunn disc the day it was released, and worked up every hit single they ever had, performing them at my cover gigs. The Rat'lers had even included a few B&D classics in the set when we toured Europe. Ronnie Dunn and I were the same height, same build. But when I looked in the mirror, I just didn't see it. Besides, Brooks & Dunn were the biggest selling country duo of all time, duo being the operative word – who was I going to get to play Kix Brooks?

So I started to let my beard grow. On the long drives to Ohio for IronHorse gigs, I would sing the Brooks & Dunn catalog for nine hours straight and fell in love with that music all over again. In Tennessee, I was playing drums behind a friend of mine named Joey Hart, and one night he walked into the gig wearing a Kix Brooks flame shirt and the light bulb went off over my head. I started playing with some graphic designs; I blacked out a photo of Brooks & Dunn to make it appear like a silhouette – you could see Kix's hat and Ronnie's spiky hair and the guitars, but you couldn't see the faces – and I put at the top BORDERLINE: A TRIBUTE TO BROOKS & DUNN. I printed out a copy and carried it around in my truck.

After a particularly taxing gig where Joey and I worked our asses off all day and night for fifty bucks, the band had bailed and left us to wind all the cables and load out the gear. I enjoyed playing drums, and I enjoyed being in a band, playing in the honky tonks, but I wasn't getting any younger, IronHorse was going nowhere, and I was hungry for a new challenge. So I went out to the truck and got the printed flyer I'd made with the Brooks & Dunn silhouette and showed it to Joey. "This could be us," I said.

And it was fun. I chopped off my hair and let the goatee grow big; I watched videos and practiced Dunn's facial expressions in the mirror. I copied the way he stroked his guitar and lifted his eyebrows when he sang. In my home studio, I recorded my voice over karaoke versions of the B&D songs – one line at a time, copying every phrasing, every breath. I didn't just focus on the hits, I learned every song from every album, every TV and movie soundtrack, obscure stuff they'd done on a tribute album or for the Olympics. I spent six months immersing myself in the character before I felt like I was ready to walk onto a stage and make people believe I was him.

I told no one in the business – not the IronHorse fans, certainly not the KEEL fans. With my new haircut and big goatee/beard, I did an IronHorse gig in Ohio and in the corner of the club was a life-size promotional cardboard cutout of Brooks & Dunn advertising some product, Coors Light or Toyota Trucks or something. During the show I noticed people looking at the cardboard cutout and pointing back and forth to me on stage, so I knew they were seeing the resemblance.

Joey and I would dress up in costume and walk down Broadway in Nashville and stop traffic. People asked to take photos with us and wanted our autographs. We would tell them that we were just a tribute act, not the real thing, but they didn't care.

And it was fun.

I did my first Brooks & Dunn Tribute show at the County Fair in Columbia on September 4th, 2004, and it worked. It continued working at bars and clubs throughout central Tennessee; we'd go into a 300-seat beer joint, and I'd make the pitch: "We want to play here, and you don't even have to pay us. We'll give you 300 tickets to sell behind the bar for $10.00 each – you let us hang one of these posters at the doorway. Whatever the ticket sales are that will be our pay, you make your money off the bar." And we would pack the place, make a few grand, and get some stage experience for the act.

I saw a show on CMT that really opened my eyes to the possibilities: "CMT Most Shocking: Impostors – The Life Of A Celebrity Impersonator." It had been filmed in Las Vegas during a celebrity impersonator convention, so I told Joey we were going to Vegas.

Over Memorial Day weekend in 2005, we rented a car and drove to Las Vegas for the convention. When it was all said and done, it cost us about $1500.00 for the car, gas, hotel, and the performance fee (they charged us double because there were two of us) – you got three minutes on stage at the Imperial Palace to showcase for booking agents and talent buyers, and we did a little three minute Brooks & Dunn medley.

And again, it was fun. During that event, I really enjoyed meeting and getting to know some of the people behind the characters in the impersonator industry, how it was this small close-knit circle of people that were really serious about their characters, and about their place in the entertainment industry. Of course we gravitated to the "country table" – socializing with Willie Nelsons and Garths and Kenny and Dolly, and I met the cutest Shania Twain impersonator who looked just like – well, you know who. Outside the showroom there was a table where all of the acts had piled business cards, promo photos, video demos, and whatever marketing tools they had in hopes that they would get discovered. I added my Brooks & Dunn Tribute promos to the stack.

Once back in Nashville, Joey and I had a big falling out. He crossed a couple of lines friends and business partners don't cross, and I was looking for another Kix when I got a call from a show producer in Las Vegas. He had a show called "Country Music USA" and was looking for someone to play the role of Ronnie Dunn.

I started a 17-month run as Ronnie Dunn at the Ramada Express (now the Tropicana Express) in Laughlin, Nevada on October 15th, 2005. I was on stage for a total of fifteen minutes and I was making more money than I ever had in my life. We were doing a couple of weeks on, a couple of weeks off, and at first I would fly back and forth to Nashville. My marriage to Lindsey and my commitment to IronHorse were both hanging on by the thinnest of threads, both having run their course as some things must.

Lindsey and I had each changed and fallen out of love. Neither one of us cared enough to fight for the marriage so we just let it die. One time, instead of flying back to Las Vegas for the next run of shows, I packed up what I could in my pickup truck and just drove away. We never even said goodbye.

IronHorse died harder - bringing that project to an end was very tough to do; it was better to do a gig every now and then, see the guys and enjoy our time together with our friends and fans, than to lose that altogether. But time and distance took its toll on our bond and our music, and the magic quality of our shows suffered because we just didn't play together often enough, and in 2006 I passed the microphone to someone else. They kept going for a while, and even made another album without me. We did a couple of one-off reunion shows for charity, the final one on May 13th, 2012 when we helped raised that 27K for Parker Headings. There were a lot of tears in Plain City that night as a powerful dream drew its last breath. I still try to go back there once a year or so and sing, see my friends, talk about those times and feel just a little bit of that magic in the air one more time.

I'd fought with Los Angeles and wrestled with Nashville, and I was itching to go 12 rounds with Sin City – Las Vegas – the Entertainment Capital of The World. During my stint with "Country Music USA" in Laughlin, I started exploring the other opportunities. I had released a solo acoustic album entitled "Alone At Last" and was very interested in pursuing solo acoustic shows. I read that my old friends Y&T had a show coming up in Las Vegas and I talked them into letting me open the show with my solo acoustic act. It went great, and they started inviting me to do the acoustic opening slot in other cities like Chicago; my acoustic guitar and I also did some tour dates with bands like Quiet Riot and Jackyl around that time. 2009 found me once again on tour with Y&T, this time as their opening act on their entire UK tour throughout England, Scotland, and Wales.

At a charity event in New York in 2004 I had met Vegas rock entrepreneur Sam McCaslin from Retrospect Records, and we started working together, doings gigs like crazy. We would do a country show as the Ronnie Lee Keel Band at Sam's Town Casino & Hotel from 5-10 and then go do a Ron Keel rock concert at midnight, playing all the KEEL stuff. Las Vegas seemed to provide an unlimited array of options from the tribute gigs to the solo acoustic shows to the country bars and rock clubs. Some other former L.A. rockers had started to migrate to Las Vegas also – still close to L.A., with all of the nightlife and entertainment opportunities without the smog, earthquakes, and the high cost of living. My old friend Kevin DuBrow had been one of the first, and when I moved to town I called him up; we were going to get together but he ended up dying before we got the chance. Brent Muscat from Faster Pussycat was now in Vegas and had put together a band called Sin City Sinners, and I did some special guest appearances with them. Paul Shortino, from the band Rough Cutt, had also made the move right around the same time I did and we started doing acoustic gigs together under the name KEEL SHORTINO.

And of course there was a girl there. The cute little Shania Twain impersonator that I fell head over heels for.

When the producer of "Country Music USA" came to me and told me our contract was up in Laughlin, but not to worry – the longest the show had ever been down was seven months – I decided I wanted to produce my own country tribute show and bring it to Las Vegas. A man could starve in seven months. Besides, that producer guy was younger than me, not as experienced as me in the business, and if he could put thousands of dollars a week into his pockets owning and producing a country tribute, then so could I.

I'd worked with a video editor in Arizona on the first three IronHorse clips back in 2001 named Leonard Quenneville who was now living and working in Las Vegas and we'd kept in touch. He was always working show biz angles, producing various local and internet TV shows and similar projects, and we met to discuss working together to produce a Las Vegas production show which ended up being "Country Superstars Tribute." We managed to secure a showroom at Fitzgerald's casino and the show debuted there on June 28th, 2007, built around my Brooks & Dunn act and featuring tributes to Tim McGraw, Toby Keith, and the Shania Twain impersonator that broke my heart. Twice.

I was hungry to succeed and believed in the potential of the show, but in many ways I built it for her. She wanted to star in a Las Vegas show and I wanted to make that happen for her, and I did. We all worked really hard getting the show off the ground, Leonard and his wife Shawna sacrificed a lot and I was married to the gig from the moment I woke up until the moment I passed out every night 18 hours later. We printed our own color-coded tickets, manned the ticket booth ourselves, I'd go up and down in the hotel elevators trying to sell tickets. We'd do the accounting and the numbers and the taxes and the marketing and promotion. The web site and the videos and the posters and the PR. After each show, the band would break down the equipment and store it behind the curtain on stage while the performers were out front doing the meet & greet; every morning I would get up, go down to the showroom and rebuild the entire stage from scratch. We had risers for the keyboards and pedal steel guitar, I'd set up the drums, run every cable and make sure the stage was ready every night at seven. I had rented a condo a couple of miles away, but there was never time to go home; the hotel provided a room for us to use for storage, production, and as an on-property office, and I ended up just moving in. I lived there for a year.

Shania broke up with me for the second time right before Christmas 2007. I'd never been on the receiving end of a heartbreak before (except the first time she broke up with me) and I was pretty messed up emotionally. I'd finally experienced that all-consuming love that fills you up and tears you apart when it ends, the kind that makes you feel alive and then you cry until you just want to die. I went through a rapid succession of transitional relationships with a number of women and tried to drink myself to death. I spent Christmas alone that year, on foot in the Valley Of Fire, with Jack Daniel's, God and Don Henley in my headphones, and somehow I survived, but the whiskey and women couldn't fill the emptiness in my heart.

Only rock & roll could do that. So I joined a band.

My buddy Sam McCaslin was playing in a local cover band named Highwire, and when they parted ways with their singer I talked my way into the gig. I needed to scream and sweat again, to test my limits, to revisit that place inside me where rock & roll was waiting for me like an old friend. They were playing Vegas bars trying to break into the casinos and thought maybe having someone with my name and track record might help. So on Tuesday, February 19th, 2008, I was again back on stage at Sam's Town, this time with "There's Only One Way To Rock" on the tip of my tongue.

Always thinking about marketing, I had brought a camera with me to the gig with the intention of grabbing a full band shot before we went on stage. I handed Sam's brother the camera and we went around the corner, snapping a few band shots, when Renée came around that same corner with a much better camera.

I'd seen her here and there, from the corner of my eye. Long red hair, dressed in black, sophisticated and classy but with a wild streak. And a really nice girl, therefore not at all what I was looking for.

She invited me out the next night, and I avoided her, but like two runaway trains we were bound to crash into each other. After exchanging a few messages and connecting on an intellectual level, I found myself falling again so I put up my guard – my heart was still in pieces and I intended to keep it that way. I told her I was seeing a number of other women and had no intention of making any commitments.

The more I learned about her, the more I liked about her. I'm still learning, and falling more in love with her every day.

We hadn't been dating long when she gave me the ultimatum: If you choose to see others, see others. If you choose to see me, see only me. I'm not going to compete for your affection.

I said yes without hesitation, and we've shared everything together since then. All that has happened – the KEEL Reunion, my Metal Cowboy project, and everything to come – is because of her. If she hadn't come along, I'd be out in the desert with a guitar, a bottle of whiskey, and a truck. Because of Renée, I'm out in the desert with a guitar, a bottle of whiskey, a truck, and the woman I was born to love.

R&R – M3 Festival 2009

24

BROTHERS IN BLOOD

It's been a long rough ride – hard luck and foolish pride
But the road goes on, and some things never change
Some die, some disappear – lost on the last frontier
And some survive to claim what still remains

("Brothers In Blood" – lyrics by RK 2009 – from the KEEL
album "Streets Of Rock & Roll" released 2010)

"STREETS OF ROCK & ROLL is a great release...this is a must have for fans of the genre whether you're familiar with KEEL or not. Already we have a strong contender for one of 2010's best releases."
MetalExcess.com

"KEEL's biggest song back in the day was 'The Right To Rock.' The majority of material on this album blows that song out of sight."
RockRealms.com

"Stunning...superb...rock-solid old-school with driving guitars and a stomping rhythm section. The album really is worthy of the KEEL name, a band that never got the real recognition they deserved outside the hard rock scene, but

now they are going to set the record straight with this release."
Mayfair Mall Zine

"This is the type of record 80's hard rock fans have been waiting for. We have been waiting for a 1980's band to come along and release something that could have been released 20 years ago but still sounds good today, and THIS IS IT."
HardRockNights

"KEEL has decided to stay true to the brash rockin' style that made their name in the first place. Ron still possesses a gravelly rasp, however in the passing years the surprising thing is, if anything his attack and register seem to have improved."
SeaOfTranquility.org

Hollywood. Sunset Boulevard, the street of broken dreams. After 20 years away, there was just enough of that old mythical status to make you think that maybe – just maybe – one more dream could come true.

When I moved there from Nashville with Steeler in 1981, it was a place where all things were possible; when I left twelve years later, I saw it as a polluted, over-priced, gang-ridden shithole where bands had to pay the clubs to play a gig. If the Rodney King riots and the brush fires and the earthquakes had never happened, bands like Nirvana would probably still have come along and choked the musical life out of one of the most amazing rock & roll revolutions in history – the L.A. 80's Metal phenomenon.

Being back on the streets of Hollywood, and back on stage with KEEL for the first time in 20 years, was a completely surreal experience. It was very satisfying to realize that what we created and accomplished still mattered, that our music and our memory had survived against all odds. It was the most pressure I've ever felt before walking on stage; I've done thousands of shows, and that one really was different. The fans had waited as long as we had; some had come from as far away as Japan and Australia to attend the 1st KEEL Reunion show on January 31st, 2009. Close friends, family, loved ones, people who love us and believe in us, some who have worked hard alongside us to make the Reunion a reality.

They were all out there, just beyond the curtain.

And then the curtain opened.

KEEL Reunion Show Review – January 31 2009
By Paul Gargano

Keel weren't the biggest band to emerge from the '80s hard rock scene, but that's the difference twenty years can make.

The band blew out of the gates in 1984 and had as strong a five year stretch as a band could ask for, touring the world with the likes of Van Halen, Bon Jovi and Aerosmith, and being hailed as the best new band by some of the biggest magazines of the era. They released four albums in four years, had hit singles on radio and MTV, and sold more than two million records. Then they splintered into separate directions in 1989 and weren't heard from again.

Until last night, when a reunited Keel - frontman Ron Keel, guitarists Marc Ferrari and Bryan Jay and drummer Dwain Miller - performed for the first time in 20 years, delivering a 75-minute set at the Knitting Factory that reminded Hollywood, CA, just how good the '80s felt.

The set wasn't an exercise in cerebral fitness, but the best hard rock seldom is. Songs like 'Reason to Rock,' 'Rock and Roll Outlaw,' 'Raised on Rock' and the band's hit anthem 'Right to Rock' didn't shake things up thematically, but what the songs lacked in diversity the band made up for in delivery. Every song was a fist-pumping, feel-good, guitar-driven rocker

that promised little more than a few minutes of escapism, and delivered true to its word.

At the helm, Ron Keel looked great. He's aged gracefully, and while Keel is every bit a rock and roll band - and the music doesn't stray from the safe confines of '80s rock for even a moment - the band's namesake isn't trying to hide from the more country-inspired path he explored over the past decade. While the rest of his band was in black, he wore blue jeans with ripped knees, tan boots and a tan button-up shirt. He looked like he could be as comfortable at Stagecoach as he was in front of the faded clothes and frayed ends that filled the Knitting Factory to capacity.

There was no bitterness or surly banter demeaning modern music, just big smiles, a lot of thank yous to the crowd for coming out, and a palpable energy that was contagious.

'Here Today, Gone Tomorrow' featured Keel - who performed with a headset mic for much of the set - Ferrari and bassist Geno Arce (a six-year veteran of Keel's more recent band IronHorse) rocking their guitars in synchronized form across the front of the stage. Ferrari handled his lead guitar duties with ease, missing his long locks from days gone by but never coming up short with his licks, and Arce and Miller forged a rock-solid bottom end, also providing much melodic depth with their backing vocals.

As a band, Keel had a lot working in their favor, most notably a twenty year absence that has heightened their legacy as many of their peers have toured themselves to oblivion and back. But to their credit, they also took nothing for granted, delivering a well-rehearsed set that not only justifies their 25th

Anniversary reunion, but also gives it a pair of legs to stand on and run with.

Covers of Bruce Springsteen's 'Because the Night' and the Rolling Stones' 'Let's Spend the Night Together' were crowd favorites, as were Keel classics 'Somebody's Waiting,' 'I Said the Wrong Thing to the Right Girl' and 'Tears of Fire.'

It was a late night - the show didn't end till shortly after 2am - but the encore was worth the wait, Cinderella drummer Fred Coury, Quiet Riot bassist Chuck Wright and former Black 'N Blue and Warrant frontman Jaime St. James joining Keel, Ferrari and Jay for a jaw-dropping run through the Thin Lizzy classic 'The Boys are Back in Town,' St. James pulling off the best Phil Lynott vocal this side of 'Chinatown.'

Keel may not have been the biggest band to emerge from the '80s hard rock scene, but if their first show in twenty years was any indication, they plan on rewriting a little bit of history...

THE LAST RIDE

There's a last time for everything
We never know what tomorrow brings
It's a good day to be alive
It's a lost cause just trying to survive

I been out on the streets all my life
Ready for love and ready to fight
I gotta follow this dream that burns me up inside

With my last breath I'll be screaming loud
On the last ride I'm gonna throttle down
When it's last call I'll take a double shot
When it's time to go I'll go the extra mile
On the last ride – on the last ride

Inside and out I've earned these scars
From the Sunset Strip to the cowboy bars
You never know what's up ahead
But I can't stop – I'll quit when I'm dead

I been under the gun – under your thumb
Outta control and out on the run
I gotta follow this road that burns me up inside

With my last buck – I'm gonna bet it all
On the last ride like a wrecking ball
If it's my bad, I'll take the fall
If I gotta go, I'm going down in flames
On the last ride – on the last ride

Ron Keel: Metal Cowboy - Release Date January 28 2014

1) Long Gone Bad
2) Wild Forever
3) My Bad
4) What Would Skynyrd Do?
5) Just Like Tennessee
6) The Last Ride
7) When Love Goes Down
8) Singers, Hookers & Thieves (duet with Paul Shortino)
9) Evil Wicked Mean & Nasty
10) The Cowboy Road
11) 3 Chord Drinkin' Song (featuring the Sin City Sinners)

bonus tracks:
12) My Bad (radio version)
13) Just Like Tennessee (unplugged)
14) Singers, Hookers & Thieves (solo acoustic version)

www.RonKeel.com

Wild West Media Productions
284C East Lake Mead Parkway #310
Henderson, Nevada 89015

RK – Discography

LUST
COMPILATIONS
HOMEGROWN – NASHVILLE KDF ROCK 106 PRESENTS (HOOKER / SPEED DEMON) KDF 1980
RON KEEL – THE ULTIMATE COLLECTION (HOOKER) RETROSPECT RECORDS 2007

STEELER
ALBUMS
STEELER – SHRAPNEL RECORDS 1983
HOT YOUR HILLS / SERENADE (NOTE INCORRECT SPELLING) DELLA RECORDS 1988
METAL GENERATION "THE ANTHOLOGY" – MAJESTIC ROCK 2005
AMERICAN METAL "THE STEELER ANTHOLOGY" – CLEOPATRA / DEADLINE RECORDS 2006
COMPILATIONS
METAL MASSACRE – (COLD DAY IN HELL) METAL BLADE RECORDS 1981
HOLLYWOOD ROCKS BOXSET (DISC 1) – (COLD DAY IN HELL) CLEOPATRA / DEADLINE RECORDS 2005
REISSUE (COMPACT EDITION) 2008
RON KEEL – THE ULTIMATE COLLECTION (COLD DAY IN HELL / MAKE UP YOUR MIND) RETROSPECT RECORDS 2007
HAIR METAL LIVE (DISC 3) – (YNGWIE IS GOD – GUITAR SOLO FROM HELL) (NOTE RON SPEAKING INTRO) CLEOPATRA / DEADLINE REOCORDS 2008
SINGLES
COLD DAY IN HELL / TAKE HER DOWN – RAVAGE RECORDS 1981
DEMOS
AMERICAN METAL 1982
METAL GENERATION / DYING IN LOVE / LAST CHANCE TO ROCK 1983
BOOTLEGS
EXCITED "LIVE" 1983

THE LEGEND OF STEELER "DEMOS" 1983
AMERICAN METAL LIVE 1983

BLACK SABBATH
DEMOS
RUNNING WILD IN THE STREETS / HUNGER / PIECE OF
THE ROCK 1984

KEEL
ALBUMS
LAY DOWN THE LAW – SHRAPNEL RECORDS 1984 /
REISSUE 2008 / KING RECORDS 2011
THE RIGHT TO ROCK – GOLD MOUNTAIN / A&M
RECORDS 1985 / REISSUE METAL MAYHEM 2000 / 2ND
REISSUE (25TH ANNIVERSARY EDITION) FRONTIERS /
KING RECORDS 2010
THE FINAL FRONTIER – GOLD MOUNTAIN / MCA
RECORDS 1986
TEARS OF FIRE "BEST OF" – JVC / VICTOR RECORDS
1986
KEEL – GOLD MOUNTAIN / MCA RECORDS 1987
LARGER THAN LIVE – GOLD MOUNTAIN / GOLD CASTLE
RECORDS 1989 / REISSUE FRESH FRUIT RECORDS 1995
/ 2ND REISSUE DEROCK RECORDS 1998
BACK IN ACTION – DEROCK RECORDS 1998
STREETS OF ROCK 'N' ROLL – FRONTIERS / KING
RECORDS 2010
COMPILATIONS
U.S. METAL VOLUME IV – (SPEED DEMON) SHRAPNEL
RECORDS 1984
METALSHOP – (THE RIGHT TO ROCK) MJI 1985
KERRANG KOMPILATION – (THE RIGHT TO ROCK) EMI
1985
METAL MADNESS – (SO MANY GIRLS, SO LITTLE TIME)
EMI 1985
ROCK "ALL ORIGINAL ARTISTS" – (THE RIGHT TO
ROCK) VERITGO / PHONOGRAM 1986
METALSHOP – (BECAUSE THE NIGHT) MJI 1986
THE VERY BEST OF METAL HAMMER – (TEARS OF FIRE)
DINO MUSIC 1987

SLOWROCK "GRANDES EXITOS DE ROCK LENTO" –
(TEARS OF FIRE) POLYGRAM RECORDS 1987
THE BEST OF HARD 'N' HEAVY ROCKIN' SONGS –
(TEARS OF FIRE) MERCURY RECORDS 1987
HEAVY METAL MONSTER FESTIVAL – (ROCK AND ROLL
ANIMAL) MERCURY RECORDS 1987
METALSHOP – (SOMEBODY'S WAITING) MJI 1987
FMQB ALBUM REPORT – (SOMEBODY'S WAITING) 1987
ALBUM NETWORK CD TUNE UP – (SOMEBODY'S
WAITING) 1987
HEAVY METAL SHOCK: VOLUME 1 – (ELECTRIC LOVE)
PLAKSAN / POLYGRAM RECORDS 1988
SOFT SIDE OF HARD ROCK – (TEARS OF FIRE)
MERCURY RECORDS 1988
SO HEAVY IT HURTS – (KING OF THE ROCK) DINO
MUSIC 1988
METAL BALLADS VOLUME 2 – (TEARS OF FIRE) ACE
ENTERTAINMENT 1991
PERRIS MUSIC SAMPLER – (BACK IN ACTION) PERRIS
RECORDS 1998
SAINT & SINNER – TOUR 2000 (THE RIGHT TO ROCK)
2000
HOLLYWOOD ROCKS BOXSET (DISC 3) – (NOTE RON ON
COVER) (THE RIGHT TO ROCK "LIVE") CLEOPATRA /
DEADLINE RECORDS 2005 REISSUE (COMPACT
EDITION) 2008
HOLLYWOOD ROCKS 17 SONG SAMPLER – (THE RIGHT
TO ROCK "LIVE") CLEOPATRA / DEADLINE RECORDS
2005
RON KEEL – THE ULTIMATE COLLECTION (ROCK 'N'
ROLL OUTLAW / THE RIGHT TO ROCK / BECAUSE THE
NIGHT / RAISED ON ROCK / TEARS OF FIRE / UNITED
NATIONS / SOMEBODY'S WAITING / I SAID THE
WRONG THING, TO THE RIGHT GIRL / EVIL, WICKED,
MEAN & NASTY / DREAMS ARE NOT ENOUGH / REASON
TO ROCK) RETROSPECT RECORDS 2007
100 HAIR METAL ANTHEMS – (THE RIGHT TO ROCK
"LIVE") CLEOPATRA / DEADLINE RECORDS 2008
HARD N' HEAVY – (THE RIGHT TO ROCK "LIVE")
CLEOPATRA / DEADLINE RECORDS 2009

MASSIVE HAIR METAL – (THE RIGHT TO ROCK "LIVE") CLEOPATRA / DEADLINE RECORDS 2009

HAIR METAL MANIA – (THE RIGHT TO ROCK "LIVE") CLEOPATRA / DEADLINE RECORDS 2009

MUSIC FOR BACHELOR PARTIES – (THE RIGHT TO ROCK "LIVE") CLEOPATRA / GOLDENLANE RECORDS 2009

LONG LIVE ROCK 'N' ROLL – (THE RIGHT TO ROCK "LIVE") SPV GMBH / STEAMHAMMER RECORDS 1997

'80's METAL SOUND & VISION – (RON KEEL / MARC FERRARI / BRYAN JAY INTERVIEW) CLEOPATRA / DEADLINE RECORDS 2011

SINGLES

THE RIGHT TO ROCK – GOLD MOUNTAIN / A&M RECORDS 1985

EASIER SAID THAN DONE (REMIX) – GOLD MOUNTAIN / A&M RECORDS 1985

BECAUSE THE NIGHT / THE FINAL FRONTIER / ROCK AND ROLL ANIMAL – VERITGO RECORDS 1986

BECAUSE THE NIGHT – GOLD MOUNTAIN / MCA RECORDS 1986

RAISED ON ROCK – GOLD MOUNTAIN / MCA RECORDS 1986

TEARS OF FIRE – GOLD MOUNTAIN / MCA RECORDS 1986

TEARS OF FIRE / ARM AND A LEG – JVC VICTOR RECORDS 1986

SOMEBODY'S WAITING – GOLD MOUNTAIN / MCA RECORDS 1987

SOMEBODY'S WAITING / KING OF THE ROCK – JVC VICTOR RECORDS 1987

ROCK 'N' ROLL OUTLAW – MCA RECORDS 1987

LIMITED EDITION COLLECTORS ITEMS

BECAUSE THE NIGHT / ROCK AND ROLL ANIMAL - (SHAPED PICTURE DISC) GOLD MOUNTAIN / MCA RECORDS 1986

BECAUSE THE NIGHT / ROCK AND ROLL ANIMAL - (CLEAR VINYL PITURE DISC) GOLD MOUNTAIN / MCA RECORDS 1986

SOMEBODY'S WAITING – (SQUARE CLEAR FLEXI) GOLD
MOUNTAIN / MCA RECORDS 1987
<u>SOUNDTRACKS</u>
D.A.R.Y.L. – (BACK TO THE CITY) 1985
DUDES – (ROCK 'N' ROLL OUTLAW) MCA RECORDS
1987
MEN IN BLACK II – (SPEED DEMON) 2002
<u>DEMOS</u>
SPEED DEMON / LAY DOWN THE LAW 1984
<u>BOOTLEGS</u>
LIVE AT HARPOS 1985
GENE SIMMONS 80'S HELL 2000
COLD DAY IN HELL 2004
LIVE IN THE CITY 2005
STOCKHOLM 86 2009
<u>VIDEOS</u>
THE RIGHT TO ROCK 1985
BECAUSE THE NIGHT 1986
TEARS OF FIRE 1986
SOMEBODY'S WAITING 1987
ROCK 'N' ROLL OUTLAW 1987
UNITED NATIONS 1987
DREAMS ARE NOT ENOUGH 1989

FAIR GAME

<u>ALBUMS</u>
BEAUTY & THE BEAST – METAL MAYHEM 2000
<u>COMPILATIONS</u>
PERRIS MUSIC SAMPLER – (STREET OF BROKEN
DREAMS) PERRIS RECORDS 2000
PERRIS FREE CD – (BEAUTY & THE BEAST) (NOTE DISC
2 AEROSMITHONIAN – A TRUBTE TO AEROSMITH)
PERRIS RECORDS 2001
RON KEEL – THE ULTIMATE COLLECTION (STREET OF
BROKEN DREAMS / SOMEWHERE IN THE NIGHT)
RETROSPECT RECORDS 2007
<u>SOUNDTRACKS</u>
BAD CHANNELS – (SOMEWHERE IN THE NIGHT / BLIND
FAITH) FULL MOON ENTERTAINMENT 1992 / REISSUE
ANGEL AIR RECORDS 1999 / 2ND REISSUE ZYX / SILVER
STAR RECORDS 2008

VIDEOS
BLIND FAITH 1991
RONNIE LEE KEEL
ALBUMS
WESTERN COUNTRY – WORKING CLASS
ENTERTAINMENT 1995
THE COUNTRY YEARS – A&R ENTERTAINMENT 2003
TED JACOBS – SONGWRITER DEMOS 2005
COUNTRY MUSIC USA – RONNIE LEE PERFORMING AS
RONNIE DUNN 2005
COMPILATIONS
NEW COUNTRY JULY 1995 – (LAST CALL) (NOTE
MISPELLED "LAST CHANCE") CONNELL RECORDS 1995
MASTER SOURCE VOLUME 1 – (MY HORSE IS A HARLEY
/ GIRLS, BARS, STEEL GUITARS / BORN TO BE LONELY)
RED ENGINE MUSIC 1996
MASTER SOURCE VOLUME 2 – (MY BEST WASN'T GOOD
ENOUGH / WE'VE GOT TO STOP MEETING LIKE THIS /
MADE FOR DANCING / EVERYONE'S A COWBOY
TONITE) RED ENGINE MUSIC 1997
MASTER SOURCE VOLUME 3 – (BECAUSE WE LOVE / MY
NEXT EX-WIFE) RED ENGINE MUSIC 1998
MASTER SOURCE VOLUME 9 – (SHE BELIEVES /
REDNECK ROCK 'N' ROLL / MAKING UP FOR LOST TIME
/ IN MY WILDEST DREAMS / I GAVE IT ALL TO YOU /
ALL MY DREAMS ARE COMING TRUE) RED ENGINE
MUSIC 2005
RON KEEL – THE ULTIMATE COLLECTION (I GAVE IT
ALL TO YOU / LONG TIME COMING / MY HORSE IS A
HARLEY / TAKE ME TO THE COUNTRY) RETROSPECT
RECORDS 2007
AS HEARD IN AWARD WINNING FILMS VOLUME 1 – (MY
HORSE IS A HARLEY / GIRLS, BARS, STEEL GUITARS)
MASTERSOURCE 2008
DEMOS
GOODBYE COWBOY 2005
VIDEOS
MY HORSE IS A HARLEY 1995
GIRLS, BARS, & STEEL GUITARS 1995
LAST CALL 1995

WHO'S GONNA LOVE ME TONIGHT 1995

THE RAT'LERS

<u>ALBUMS</u>
THICK AS THIEVES – TWANG TOWN MUSIC 1998
<u>COMPILATIONS</u>
RON KEEL – THE ULTIMATE COLLECTION (SHOW ON THE ROAD) RETROSPECT RECORDS 2007
<u>VIDEOS</u>
THICK AS THIEVES 1998

SABER TIGER

<u>ALBUMS</u>
PROJECT ONE – FANDANGO RECORDS 1997 REISSUE VAP MUSIC 2003
<u>COMPILATIONS</u>
RON KEEL – THE ULTIMATE COLLECTION (RIDE LIKE THE WIND / GIVE ME ALL YOUR LOVE TONIGHT) RETROSPECT RECORDS 2007

IRONHORSE

<u>ALBUMS</u>
IRONHORSE – MELODIC MAYHEM 2001
BRING IT ON – V-TONE / COMPENDIA MUSIC 2004
<u>COMPILATIONS</u>
SAINT & SINNER – TOUR 2000 (IN MY WILDEST DREAMS) 2000
THE TOUR BUS – ROAD TRIP (TEARS OF FIRE) PULSE MUSIC 2001
RON KEEL – THE ULTIMATE COLLECTION (TAKE ANOTHER SHOT / BRING IT ON / FOLLOW YOUR HEART) RETROSPECT RECORDS 2007
<u>SINGLES</u>
AMERICAN THUNDER "LIVE" – A&R ENTERTAINMENT 2003
<u>BOOTLEGS</u>
FREEBIRD CAFÉ "LIVE" 2001
<u>DEMOS</u>
TAKE ANOTHER SHOT / SIN CITY 2001
HEARTS OF STEEL / FOLLOW YOUR HEART / UNDER THE GUN / YOU CAN'T KEEP COUNTRY DOWN 2004
<u>VIDEOS</u>

RUN FOR THE BORDER 2000
SIGNS OF LIFE 2000
DANCING WITH THE DEVIL 2000
AMERICAN THUNDER 2004
THE BEST MOVE 2004
THREE SHEETS TO THE WIND 2004

BORDERLINE
VIDEOS
BROOKS & DUNN TRIBUTE – "LIVE" 2004

KEEL & WAYNE
SINGLES
I GAVE IT ALL TO YOU 2005
VIDEOS
I GAVE IT ALL TO YOU 2005

STEERS AND STRIPES
VIDEOS
A TRIBUTE TO BROOKS AND DUNN 2006

RON KEEL
ALBUMS
ALONE AT LAST – A&R ENTERTAINMENT 2006
 THE ULTIMATE COLLECTION – RETROSPECT RECORDS 2007
METAL COWBOY – WILD FOREVER – WILD WEST MEDIA PRODUCTIONS 2014
SINGLES
WILD FOREVER – 3-SONG CD SINGLE (WILD FOREVER / 3 CHORD DRINKIN' SONG / SINGERS, HOOKERS & THIEVES) WILD WEST MEDIA PRODUCTIONS 2013
COMPILATIONS
AEROSMITHSONIAN – A TRIBUTE TO AEROSMITH (BACK IN THE SADDLE / WALK THIS WAY) PERRIS RECORDS 2001
THE TOUR BUS – RADIO BROADCAST SAMPLER (STRUTTER) (NOTE WITH BRUCE KULICK & MARC FERRARI) 2003
A TRIBUTE TO AEROSMITH (BACK IN THE SADDLE) TRIBUTIZED RECORDS 2004

ROCK 4 XMAS – (THE ROCK 4 X-MAS ANTHEM) RETROSPECT RECORDS 2005
MORLEY SAMPLER CD VOLUME 4 – (THE TIME OF MY LIFE) 2006
RON KEEL – THE ULTIMATE COLLECTION (SERENADE / THE TIME OF MY LIFE / IF YOU CAN ROCK ME / THE HIT SONG) RETROSPECT RECORDS 2007
LICK IT UP – A MILLENIUM TRIBUTE TO KISS (LICK IT UP) VERSAILLES RECORDS 2008
DOUBLE TALKIN' JIVE – A HARD ROCK TRIBUTE TO GUNS 'N' ROSES – (DON'T CRY) VERSAILLES RECORDS 2008
LIBERTY N' JUSTICE – CHASING A CURE E.P. – (SAY UNCLE) LNJ RECORDS 2010 REISSUE (L.P.) ROXX RECORDS 2011
SIN CITY SINNERS – A SINNERS' CHRISTMAS (SILENT NIGHT) SIN CITY SINNERS RECORDS 2011
SIN CITY SINNERS – DIVEBAR DAYS REVISITED (TIE YOUR MOTHER DOWN) SIN CITY RECORDS 2013
LIBERTY N' JUSTICE – THE CIGAR CHRONICLES VOL. 1&2 (CUT ME MICK) LNJ RECORDS 2013
A WORLD WITH HEROES – A KISS TRIBUTE FOR CANCER CARE (ROCK 'N' ROLL HELL) 2013
MELODICROCK.COM – VOLUME II THIS ONE GOES TO ELEVEN (THE COWBOY ROAD) MELODICROCK RECORDS 2013
HOLLYWOOD ROSE – A TRIBUTE TO GUNS 'N' ROSES' GREATEST HITS (DON'T CRY) VERSAILLES RECORDS 2014
DEMOS
A PIECE OF THE ACTION / I NEVER TOLD YOU / COLD LOVE / LIVING TILL MIDNIGHT 1979

LEATHERWOLF
DEMOS
BEHIND THE GUN / GYPSIES & THIEVES 2007

K2
BOOTLEGS
ROCKLAHOMA "LIVE" - 2008

GUEST APPEARANCES

ABLUMS

BLACK 'N' BLUE – NASTY, NASTY (BEST IN THE WEST) GEFFEN RECORDS 1986 REISSUE MAJESTIC ROCK 2005

LEATHERFACE THE TEXAS CHAINSAW MASSACRE III "MOTION PICTURE SOUNDTRACK" – UTTER LUNACY (MONSTER MASH) MEDUSA RECORDS 1989

FASTDRAW – LET OFF THE ALARM (LOVE'S NOT FOR SALE) CAPTAIN RECORDS 1989

HOUSE OF LORDS – SAHARA (CHAINS OF LOVE) SIMMONS / RCA RECORDS 1990 REISSUE AXE KILLER RECORDS 1999

ROX DIAMOND (GET THE LEAD OUT) ACTIVE RECORDS 1992 REISSUE Z RECORDS 2004

BLACK 'N' BLUE – COLLECTED (BEST IN THE WEST) MAJESTIC ROCK 2005

THE BEST OF CHARLIE WAYNE – THE METAL YEARS 1985-2005 (COME HOME WITH ME) 2005

MATT LAPORTE – ONCE MORE...WITH FEELING (UNDER THE GUN) 2006

HOUSE OF LORDS – ANTHOLOGY (CHAINS OF LOVE) CLEOPATRA / DEADLINE RECORDS 2008

KING KOBRA – RONNIE JAMES DIO TRIBUTE / STAND UP AND SHOUT CANCER FOUNDATION (MONSTERS & HEROES) SINGLE/MP3 2010

KING KOBRA – KING KOBRA (ROCK THIS HOUSE / TEAR DOWN THE WALLS) FRONTIERS / RUBICON RECORDS 2011

KING KOBRA – II (HAVE A GOOD TIME) FRONTIERS / RUBICON RECORDS 2013

VIDEOS

BEGGARS & THIEVES – (WE COME UNDONE) 2011

KING KOBRA – (HAVE A GOOD TIME) 2013

PRODUCER

ALBUMS

KEEL – LAY DOWN THE LAW – SHRAPNEL RECORDS 1984 REISSUE 2008

BLITZKRIEG – READY FOR ACTION – TALON RECORDS 1985 REISSUE RETROSPECT RECORDS 2005

KEEL – LARGER THAN LIVE - GOLD MOUNTAIN / GOLD CASTLE RECORDS 1989 / REISSUE FRESH FRUIT RECORDS 1995 / 2ND REISSUE DEROCK RECORDS 1998

RONNIE LEE KEEL – WESTERN COUNTRY – WORKING CLASS ENTERTAINMENT 1995

KEEL – BACK IN ACTION – DEROCK RECORDS 1998

FAIR GAME – BEAUTY & THE BEAST – METAL MAYHEM 2000

RONNIE LEE KEEL – THE COUNTRY YEARS - A&R ENTERTAINMENT 2003

STEELER - METAL GENERATION "THE ANTHOLOGY" – MAJESTIC ROCK 2005

STEELER - AMERICAN METAL "THE STEELER ANTHOLGY" – CLEOPATRA / DEADLINE RECORDS 2006

RON KEEL – ALONE AT LAST – A&R ENTERTAINMENT 2006

RON KEEL – THE ULTIMATE COLLECTION – RETROSPECT RECORDS 2007

COMPILATIONS

METAL MASSACRE – (COLD DAY IN HELL) METAL BLADE RECORDS 1981

JASON BECKER TRIBUTE – WARMTH IN THE WILDERNESS (DISC 1) (ELEVEN BLUE EGYPTIANS) LION MUSIC 2001

HOLLYWOOD ROCKS BOXSET (DISC 1) – (COLD DAY IN HELL) CLEOPATRA / DEADLINE RECORDS 2005 REISSUE (COMPACT EDITION) 2008

HOLLYWOOD ROCKS BOXSET (DISC 3) – (NOTE RON ON COVER) (THE RIGHT TO ROCK "LIVE") CLEOPATRA / DEADLINE RECORDS 2005 REISSUE (COMPACT EDITION) 2008

HOLLYWOOD ROCKS 17 SONG SAMPLER – (THE RIGHT TO ROCK "LIVE") CLEOPATRA / DEADLINE RECORDS 2005

HAIR METAL LIVE (DISC 3) – (YNGWIE IS GOD – GUITAR SOLO FROM HELL) (NOTE RON SPEAKING INTRO) CLEOPATRA / DEADLINE REOCORDS 2008

SINGLES

STEELER (COLD DAY IN HELL / TAKE HER DOWN) RAVAGE RECORDS 1981

SOUNDTRACKS
BAD CHANNELS – (SOMEWHERE IN THE NIGHT / BLIND
FAITH) FULL MOON ENTERTAINMENT 1992 REISSUE
ANGEL AIR RECORDS 1999

WRITER
ALBUMS
VIXEN – REV IT UP – (REV IT UP) EMI 1990
SABER TIGER – THE HISTORY OF THE NEW WORLD –
(RIDE LIKE THE WIND / LAW OF THE LAND / IT'S YOUR
WORLD / GIVE ME ALL YOUR LOVE TONIGHT / I'LL
STILL BE LOVING YOU / THRILLSEEKER / HARD WIRE /
TO HELL AND BACK / RECKLESS AND YOUNG / SEX AT
FIRST SIGHT) VAP MUSIC 2001
JESSE AND NOAH BELLAMY – DRIVIN' NOWHERE (YOU
CAN ALWAYS COUNT ON ME (TO LET YOU DOWN))
BELLEROPHON RECORDS 2005
VIXEN – EXTENDED VERSIONS (REV IT UP) CMG 2006
CHARLIE TATMAN – FREE AND EASY (YOU CAN HAVE
WHAT'S LEFT OF ME) CMG RECORDS 2006
VIXEN – LIVE IN SWEDEN (REV IT UP) CASTLE RECORDS
2009
JESSE AND NOAH BELLAMY – NOWHERE REVISITED
(YOU CAN ALWAYS COUNT ON ME (TO LET YOU
DOWN)) SMITH ENTERTAINMENT 2007 (DELUXE
EDITION) SMITH ENTERTAINMENT 2012

DVD
HOLLYWOOD HAIRSPRAY (IRONHORSE-AMERICAN
THUNDER) PERRIS RECORDS 2004
RON KEEL – THE ULTIMATE VIDEO COLLECTION – A&R
ENTERTAINMENT 2007
HOLLYWOOD ROCKS – THE DOCUMENTARY –
CLEOPATRA / DEADLINE RECORDS 2008

ACTOR
NEVER TOO YOUNG TOO DIE 1986
BAD CHANNELS 1992